1939
1940
1941
1942
1943
1944
1945

STOLEN YEARS

by
Sara Zyskind

A SIGNET BOOK

NEW AMERICAN LIBRARY

A DIVISION OF PENGUIN BOOKS USA INC.

Published in Hebrew by Beit Lohamei Hageta'ot
English translation by Marganit Inbar

This is an authorized reprint of a hardcover edition
published by Lerner Publications Company.

SIGNET, SIGNET CLASSIC, MENTOR, ONYX, PLUME, MERIDIAN
and NAL BOOKS are published by New American Library, a division of
Penguin Books USA Inc., 1633 Broadway, New York, New York 10019

First Signet Printing, January, 1983

5 6 7 8 9 10 11 12 13

PRINTED IN THE UNITED STATES OF AMERICA

*To my daughter Shlomit, now the age I was
when these events took place.
To my two elder children, Miriam and Yossi,
and to their children.*

Prologue

━━━━◆━━━◆━━━◆━━━

Memories of Childhood

The picture of a young girl rises in my mind's eye. She is eleven years old. Her long, blond hair is plaited in two heavy braids, and she wears a beret with a school emblem, tilted at a rakish angle. Her school bag is tucked under her arm, and she is walking along Piotrkovska, one of the most beautiful streets in the Polish city of Lodz. It is spring in the year 1939. So many years have passed and so much has happened since then that I can scarcely believe I was once that young girl. But the days of my childhood are preserved in my memory with the greatest clarity.

On that spring day so long ago, a warm breeze was blowing—the first after the cold months of winter. It was Mother's Day, and I was hurrying home with gifts for my mother. Inside my school bag was a drawing, an embroidered kerchief completed only the day before, a poem composed especially for the occasion, and money for the flowers I wanted to buy. In Platz Wolnoshchi—Liberty Square—the statue of the Polish hero Kosciusko gleamed in the sunlight, and peasant women selling flowers squatted beside buckets full of lilacs. I bought two bunches, one purple, the other all white. Then I crossed the square and entered the courtyard of our house on Novomiska Street. I was afraid that Mother would open the door and all would be lost, for then I'd be unable to surprise her. Luckily, Mother was out and the bell was answered by Father, who welcomed me with his customary good-humored greeting. "Good day! What an honored guest! Come in, come in."

"Daddy," I interrupted impatiently, "it's Mother's Day today! Please help me arrange the flowers quickly."

1

Accomplice to all my secrets, he winked conspiratorially. "What a piece of luck that Mother's not in!"

When the preparations were completed, I asked him not to peep from behind the door as I presented Mother with the gifts and recited my poem. I wanted to feel free and unconstrained on this important occasion. My father understood, as always, and promised to do as I asked.

I remember clearly the happiness I felt on that day and on all the days of my early childhood. An only child, I was proud of my handsome young parents, feeling ashamed only when one of them accompanied me daily to school. Several houses away from the school building, I would insist on walking alone. God forbid that anyone should see me, a sixth grader, still being led to school!

My childhood memories of my father are particularly strong. I remember his beautiful voice and all the wonderful songs that he knew—ditties and lullabies, songs of longing for *Eretz Israel* (the Land of Israel) and merry marching tunes picked up during his service with the Polish army. His fine voice was in demand at both private and public functions. When he was the *chazan* (cantor) during the High Holidays, his chanting would cast a spell over the hushed congregation. He would often sing me to sleep at night, and the sound of his voice enveloped me in a feeling of warmth and security.

Every Sabbath Eve, my father would tell me stories of his own childhood. I could never hear enough of them. Tears would well up in my eyes on hearing about his mother's death in childbirth and about his stepmother's changed attitude toward him with the birth of her own two daughters. Beatings and curses were his lot then, and silent suffering.

"Now listen to the smart trick I thought up," Father would tell me with a twinkle in his eyes. "Every time my stepmother gave me a beating, I'd lash out at my stepsisters afterwards. Faced with such a prospect, she soon gave up."

He also told me about the misfortunes that had afflicted his family following the outbreak of World War I. His father had been drafted into the army and his stepmother came down with cholera. Now the burden of caring for his two small sisters and nursing his stepmother fell upon the shoulders of my father, a ten-year-old boy. Frequently, he would make the long walk from his home in Drochovitz to the city of Lvov, where his uncle lived, to fetch provisions for the upkeep of the family. Then came news of his father's death; several days later, his stepmother followed her husband to the grave. The long trek to Lvov was undertaken again, this time by all three children. After many hardships, they arrived in the city, where the two girls were placed in an orphanage and my father was taken into his uncle's home. It was here that he received his education and grew to manhood.

The uncle in Lvov was a great craftsman in his particular field—the making of ornamental collars for *talits*, the prayer shawls that Jewish men wear during religious observances. He taught Father this delicate art, and thanks to it, my parents first met. My maternal grandfather came to Lvov to order a collar for his *talit*. He took an instant liking to the collarmaker's nephew and invited the young man to his home in Lodz. "Your mother, too, must have taken a liking to him," Father would conclude with a laugh, "for that visit ended in a wedding."

From my father's lips I learned not only the story of his life but also the history of the Jewish people, which he narrated in a vivid manner. I listened intently to the story of Joseph, sold to Egyptian traders by his own brothers, and of the hardships endured by the children of Israel in Egypt. I rejoiced at the happy endings of the stories, with Joseph as the pharaoh's viceroy and the people of Israel crossing the Red Sea on a path of dry land. Father was an avid reader, and he also recounted to me episodes from *Les Misérables* and *The Count of Monte Cristo*. Occasionally he would read stories by the Yiddish writers Sholom Asch and Sholom Aleichem.

Although my father was a part-owner of a knitwear factory, he devoted most of his evenings to the craft he had acquired from his uncle. He had become an accomplished artist, possibly one of the few then left in Poland. While working at his ornamental collars, he would sing and talk, and his pleasant voice would fill our apartment. Sitting nearby, I would watch him stitch the collars with mingled gold and silver thread, or at times with thread of pure gold. He would first draw flowers, leaves, stars, and stardust on a long strip of white paper. Then he would pin the paper to the fabric of the collar, which was spread over a large cushioned stool, and begin covering his drawing with gold and silver thread. The work on such a collar could take days or even weeks, depending on its size. When Father tore off the strip of paper, the *talit* collar gleamed in all its glory.

The customers for Father's collars came from all over Poland—Warsaw, Cracow, Lvov—and even from places outside Poland, such as Germany, Austria, and Latvia. I observed them all with great interest. Some were Jews of considerable means, richly dressed and of stately bearing. They usually purchased the larger *talit* collars brocaded in pure gold. At times thickly bearded Hasidim in their *shtreimlech* (fur hats) came to buy a collar either for themselves or for a revered rabbi. Among them were renowned Talmudic scholars at whom I gazed in awe. There were also customers from the ordinary walks of life, who could scarcely conceal the fact that the purchase of even a small ornamental collar was a considerable financial sacrifice. Yet how could one possibly dispense with such a gift for one's son who was about to marry or for a prospective son-in-law? The cost was high, but it was worth paying for this cherished symbol of faith.

So I watched with childish curiosity as my father's customers came and went. I did not know that in less than five years' time, most of these devout Jews would have vanished from the face of the earth.

1939

The Last Summer

During the spring of 1939, I was looking forward to a
great change in my life. I had graduated from elementary
school and was now ready to enroll in the gymnasium, or
secondary school. I felt grown-up and self-important as I
prepared to take the entrance examination. On the day of
the exam, Mother was unable to accompany me to school
because she was recovering from a gall-bladder ailment
that had kept her bedridden for eight months. I was ner-
vous about the tests, but I did very well. On the way
home, I bought myself a *tartsha*—a blue insignia on which
the number of my new school was embroidered in silver
thread. To wear this insignia on one's sleeve was a coveted
status symbol. I used to envy my boy cousins for having
attained it and to dream of reaching this goal myself. Now
the dream had come true.

I was to spend that summer vacation, as usual, with
Uncle Abraham (Mother's brother) and his family, but
this year we would not go to their country house, a beautiful villa at the edge of a forest. My cousin Moniek, Uncle
Abraham's eldest son, had died recently, and the family
could not bring itself to move to the country for the long
vacation. They would spend the summer in Kalisz, where
they lived throughout the year, and they had asked my
parents if I could come and stay with them.

When Uncle Abraham arrived to take me to Kalisz,
Mother and her sister Hanushka rode to the train station
with us in the *droshki*. I sat in my favorite seat next to the
driver. After my uncle and I were settled in our compartment on the train, I ran to the window to wave a last fare-
well to my mother and aunt. I saw Mother dabbing her

eyes. This separation for a whole summer was hard for her, and even I felt a little saddened by it.

As the train gathered speed, I sat by the window and watched the alternating landscape of forests and checkered fields fly by. My thoughts went back to the previous summer at my uncle's country home. My cousins Moniek and Salek had met me at the bus stop. I was wearing a white dress and my face was tanned from the summer sun. The blood rushed into my cheeks when Moniek whistled and exclaimed, "How tall you've grown! A perfect lady!" Moniek's compliments raised a flutter of pride and happiness. My tall, blue-eyed cousin with his mop of curly black hair was the idol of all the girls he knew. If a flighty ten-year-old like myself could be in love with a boy eight years her senior, then I was deeply in love with Moniek.

That summer, Moniek taught me many new things. We danced tangos and waltzes while Salek turned the handle of the record player, and we played table tennis, chess, and cards. Monick seemed to be in a hurry, as if sensing that this was to be his last summer on earth. The following winter, he died at the age of eighteen, his life cut short by a malignant disease. During Moniek's illness, the whole family took turns looking after him, and not a night passed without one of us sitting by his bed. I myself spent hours reading to him from his favorite books.

Suddenly I was roused from my memories by the sound of a shrill whistle. We had arrived in Kalisz, and the train was coming to a halt in the station. I looked guiltily at Uncle Abraham, for I had hardly exchanged a word with him the whole trip. My uncle seemed preoccupied. Perhaps, like me, he was haunted by memories.

Salek and his mother, Aunt Faiga, were at the station to welcome us. Salek had changed. He seemed to have grown up, and his face had a sad look, perhaps because of the glasses he now wore. There was nothing about him to remind me of his handsome older brother. His round face was covered with freckles, and his mousy-colored crew cut made me think of a porcupine. Only the large black eyes behind the new glasses were still beautiful. In the past, my cousin and I had constantly been at one another's throats, vying for the upper hand. My senior by a year and a half, Salek had stung me to fury by his scornful taunts that I was a terrible swimmer, a poor runner, and a failure at climbing trees. Now, as we eyed each other shyly, both of us knew that all this childish competition was irrevocably past.

My uncle's apartment in Kalisz was located near the river, which could be glimpsed through the poplar trees lining the avenue alongside it. For hours, Salek and I used to stand by the window watching the passing steamers, sailing boats, and racing canoes, and the people crossing the bridges or sauntering along the avenue. That summer, however, Salek was too busy to spend much time at the window. He read a great deal, and most of his mornings were taken up by the private tutoring he received in Hebrew and English.

Left to myself, I struck up a friendship with a girl of my own age named Wanda. She, too, had just enrolled in secondary school. Wearing our new school insignias on our shirt sleeves—slightly smudged to lend them a worn look—the two of us took long walks or read each other poems from a volume Father had given me. Tears would fill our eyes as we read and re-read a poem called "The Sun," about an orphan accusing the brightly shining sun of complete indifference to human suffering. The sun replied that she had nothing to do with human suffering—that was the concern of heaven. Her own duty was to preserve a cheerful exterior by continuing to shine brightly.

One day, Wanda and I were sitting on a bench in the park, reading our favorite poem. A little distance from us, several small Jewish children were playing at knucklebones when, all of a sudden, three teenaged youths began hurling stones at them and shouting "Dirty kikes! Go to Palestine!" The youngsters scattered in all directions, leaving behind a little boy of about three who had been hit on the head with a rock. A girl, perhaps his sister, returned, took the bleeding child in her arms, and ran off. I was horrified by the scene I had just witnessed, unable to comprehend such unprovoked violence. My first impulse was to run after the attackers and give them a piece of my mind. But I didn't. Instead, I looked at Wanda and noticed her absolute indifference to what had happened. It made me furious.

"Didn't you see that, Wanda? Those hooligans mustn't get away with it!"

But Wanda only shrugged her shoulders. "What are you getting so worked up about? They're only Jews."

I felt the blood rush to my head. Scarcely five minutes earlier, this girl had been moved to tears by a sad poem, but now she looked on unruffled at the pain of an injured toddler because he was only a Jew!

"Aren't Jews human beings? Besides, those kids weren't hurting anybody!"

Wanda shrugged again.

"Do you know that I happen to be Jewish?" I asked.

Wanda turned and looked me full in the face. "Stop talking nonsense!" she said scornfully.

"You heard me!" I repeated. "I'm Jewish!"

My flushed face and agitated speech finally convinced her, and she began to hem and haw about my being altogether different. I didn't respond. We sat uneasily for a while longer, sensing a high wall rising between us. Then we stood up and parted politely. Whether by design or by accident, we never met again.

This incident left me with a painful impression that was over-shadowed only by a series of events that seemed to happen with breathtaking speed. All during July, rumors had persisted of the possibility of war with Germany. The newspapers and radio were full of speculation as to when war would break out. Hitler's appetite, it appeared, had only been whetted by swallowing Austria and Czechoslovakia. Now he was bullying Poland, demanding the cession of Gdansk and the surrounding territory, claiming these as original German lands. The Poles, imbued with fighting spirit, talked contemptuously of how the Czechs had given up their country without firing a single shot. We had heard a great deal at school about the dauntless courage exhibited by the Poles during World War I and were convinced that Poland would inflict a crushing defeat on any invader. There was talk of general mobilization. The radio kept broadcasting military tunes, and air-raid shelters were being dug everywhere. Salek and I, allowed to help with the digging, felt proud to be doing our bit for the war effort. On our way home, we bought a toy: four little cardboard piglets that, when joined, formed the features of Adolf Hitler.

By August, general mobilization was under way, and trains were being commandeered by the army. Uncle

Abraham decided to send me home, thinking it safer for
me to be with my parents at such a time. I, too, wanted to
be home. I was frightened by the thought that Father
might be drafted into the army and haunted by the recol-
lection that my grandfather had been killed in a war when
Father was just my age.

When Uncle Abraham took me to the railroad station,
we found it crowded with soldiers carrying dufflebags.
Uncle Abraham put me into the care of a woman who
was also going to Lodz. In return for her willingness to
look after me, he carried her suitcases along with mine on
his shoulders, pushing his way into the packed train. So
great was the throng trying to get on that Uncle Abraham
scarcely managed to make his way out before the train began to move.

On this train trip, I didn't watch the scenery or dream
about the happy days of the past. I was filled with apprehension about what the future might bring.

The War Begins

The railway station in Lodz, too, was jammed with soldiers and civilians. Before boarding the streetcar for home,
I managed to say a few words of gratitude to the woman
who had taken care of me. On reaching our apartment, I
found the place locked up and was told that Father had
gone to fetch Mother from Czehoszynek, where she had
been spending the summer months recuperating from her
recent illness. I left my luggage with neighbors and went
to Mother's other sister, Tsesia, but she, her husband,
Shimshon, and their five children were still away in the
countryside. Only Aunt Hanushka and Uncle Hersh were
at home. They were overjoyed at seeing me back safe and
sound. By the end of the week, all my relatives had returned, each excitedly describing his or her own experiences.

By now August was drawing to a close, and we were all wondering whether the school year would begin at the scheduled time. We were not left in the dark for long. On September 1—the very day the school term was to begin—the German army crossed the Polish frontier, and war broke out.

Panic seized everyone in Lodz, especially us Jews. We had heard rumors of atrocities committed against Jews in Germany and had read about the bloody events that had taken place in Berlin on *Kristallnacht* (Crystal Night), but it had all seemed far removed from us. In fact, we didn't believe most of those rumors and considered them at best grossly exaggerated. How was it conceivable, we argued, for a cultured nation like Germany, and in the twentieth century, to persecute people simply because of their ethnic origins? Nevertheless, echos of Hitler's anti-Semitic ravings had not failed to reach us. With the entry of the German army into Poland, all our hidden fears sprang to life.

Father proposed moving to Lvov to stay with his sisters for a while and then trying to cross into Russia. But Mother would not consider it. She couldn't bear the thought of living so far away from her sisters and her only brother at a time like this. Father explained that it would be so much easier for the three of us to get away than it would be for Aunt Tsesia's family of seven, or even for Aunt Hanushka and Uncle Hersh, who were no longer so young. But Mother was determined. The fate of her relatives would be her own! Besides, she argued, how long could this war last? Hitler himself kept talking about a blitzkrieg—a lightning attack—and England and France were bound to come to Poland's assistance at any moment.

Barely a week after the outbreak of hostilities, the German army entered Lodz. I was sitting on the curb in Liberty Square, in the same spot I had occupied scarcely ten months earlier when I had watched the parade on November 11, Poland's Independence Day. I had been thrilled by the pageantry of the Polish soldiers dressed in their ceremonial regalia, marching in step to their own full-throated singing; by the sight of the military bands led by bandmasters swinging their batons in white-gloved hands; above all, by the handsome Uhlan cavalry in their distinctive uniforms, proudly riding their thoroughbreds. On that day, both sides of the street had been packed with cheering crowds that showered the passing soldiers with bouquets of flowers.

How utterly different was the parade of the German soldiers, who symbolized a power that struck terror into our hearts. The crowd in the square watched in silence. These were steel-helmeted troopers in unfamiliar uniforms and highly polished jackboots, their faces frozen into masks, striding with the self-confidence of conquerors. The forest of swastika banners accompanying the goose-stepping soldiers deepened the impression of military might and made me tremble with fear. Armored columns of tanks and rolling artillery, roaring past in the wake of the soldiers, shook the ground beneath us. I couldn't help recalling the recent Polish proclamation about not yielding an inch of Polish soil. Now, only a few days later, the country lay prostrate at the feet of the conqueror, with only its capital city still keeping up some sort of resistance.

Soon after the German army occupied Lodz, posters in Polish and German appeared on the walls of houses calling on the citizens to resume the normal course of their lives, to return to their jobs, to reopen the schools. School did begin, and people went back to work. But nothing was the same.

One day when I was walking down Kosciusko Avenue on my way to school, I was brought up short by a horrifying sight. Lodz's largest synagogue, with its splendid high dome and huge stained-glass windows, was on fire! German soldiers with grins on their faces stood idly by, while policemen and members of the fire brigade watched the flames engulf the entire building. Rooted to the spot, I, too, watched, unable to understand why no one was lifting a finger to put out the fire.

When policemen dispersed the crowds of onlookers, I made a dash for school, filled with the terrifying news. There I learned that the burning of this synagogue was no isolated case; all the synagogues of Lodz—the pride of its Jewish inhabitants—were going up in flames at the instigation of the Germans. Stories were circulating of German soldiers urinating on the Holy Scrolls or tearing them to shreds. In dismay I asked myself how God could allow such things to happen. Why didn't he punish the culprits? Raised on precepts of mutual respect among religions, I recalled the sense of awe I had experienced when visiting the great cathedral of Vavel in Cracow. It seemed incredible to me that someone would deliberately destroy a place of worship. From that day on, a great many things were to elude my understanding.

The streets of Lodz now swarmed with German soldiers going about in small groups, jarring our ears with the noise of their raucous laughter. One day, I was walking to school with a classmate, and we met two soldiers who pointed at the *tartshas* on our coat sleeves and demanded to know what they represented. Proudly showing off our knowledge of the German language, we explained that this was the insignia of our secondary school. Before we realized what was happening, the soldiers whipped out their knives and slashed the *tartshas* off, together with a patch of the sleeves. Speechless with fright, we reached school and discovered that there had been other victims that morning.

Every day as I walked to school, I read the new posters plastered on the walls of the houses:

All radio sets owned by Jews are to be handed over to the Gestapo.
Furs of any kind owned by Jews are to be handed over to the Gestapo.
All cinemas and theaters are out-of-bounds to Jews.
Jews are prohibited from using the public conveyances.
Jews are prohibited from walking along Piotrkovska Street.

"Good Lord!" Father cried in alarm. "What about all the businesses owned by Jews on that street? This will deprive them of their livelihood."

This decree was not the only thing that prevented Jews from earning a living. Trading of any kind had come to a standstill in the city. Father himself hadn't sold one ornamental *talit* collar since the outbreak of war, and his knitwear business had fallen off completely as soon as the stock ran out and wool imports were discontinued. Consequently, Father and his partner no longer went to work. The German appointed as supervisor prevented them from taking anything out of the factory.

With the closing of Piotrkovska Street to Jews, I was forced to make my way to school by a circuitous route winding through obscure lanes and alleys. Mother now worried about me more than ever and would stand by the window every day anxiously awaiting my return.

One night we were aroused from our sleep by explosive charges following one another in close succession. Panic-striken, we grabbed the first thing that came to hand and rushed downstairs with all our neighbors. No one knew the cause of the explosions, but one old man was convinced that deliverance was at hand. He launched into a prayer of thanksgiving, believing that the French and English had finally entered the war and had sent their planes out on a bombing mission. The next morning, we learned that the Germans had blown up the Kosciusko statue in Liberty Square. Now when I passed the square on my way to school, my heart contracted on seeing this splendid monument reduced to rubble.

As the German occupation continued, I became aware of what seemed to me to be the strange behavior of the Polish people. After the fall of their country and the Germans' systematic elimination of Polish leaders and intellectuals, the Poles had begun collaborating with their enemy! I was startled by this, knowing how deep-rooted Polish hatred of the Germans had always been. What had become of their defiance and their determination to wipe out every German daring to violate Poland's sovereignty? Instead of resisting the Germans, the Poles seemed to have turned the full force of their hatred on their Jewish fellow citizens. Notices forbidding Jews to enter Polish shops began to appear in display windows. There were even shop owners especially eager to curry favor with their German overlords who extended this prohibition to "Jews and Dogs." Newspapers started publishing insulting verses ridiculing Jews as parasites who had sucked the blood of Poles for far too long. These verses were accompanied by cruel caricatures depicting wild-bearded, hooked-nosed, hunchbacked creatures trampling the poor Poles underfoot.

My family suffered deeply because of this persecution. Father had always spoken with pride of us Jews as being better citizens of Poland than the Poles themselves and of the Jews' contribution to the economic growth of the country. Poles, he explained, preferred working for Jewish employers because working conditions were better and salaries higher. I myself loved Poland deeply and felt an inseparable part of the country. I used to sing its national anthem with fervor at parades and always felt a patriotic thrill when I was permitted to carry the red-and-white Polish flag.

Now even the attitude of our Polish maid, Maria, began changing. She would often grumble under her breath, as if to herself but loud enough for us to hear, that "those dirty and contemptible Jews are to blame for the outbreak of the war." This was the same Maria who had been in charge of our household for many years, who had come to us straight from her backward village underfed and in tatters. Mother had fitted her out with clothes from head to toe, had given her gifts of silk stockings, gloves, and perfume every Christmas, and had taught her to read and write. Never before had Maria spoken to anyone in the family disrespectfully but had addressed even me, a little girl, as "Madame"!

At first I wanted to upbraid Maria for the change in her attitude, to remind her who had invaded her country and blown up Kosciusko's monument. But I soon gave up the idea, doubting whether she had any comprehension of what was going on. My parents forbade me to talk to her altogether, afraid of the disaster I might unwittingly bring down on our heads if she were to go and report our conversations to the Gestapo. So we suffered her insulting comments in silence and when she finally ceased coming to our home, we all breathed a deep sigh of relief.

By this time, food had become very scarce, and people had to wait in long lines each day to buy bread. One morning my father returned from the breadline in a state of great alarm. He told us that German soldiers had appeared suddenly, pounced upon all those whose beards gave them away as Jews, dragged them out of the line, and prevented them from buying bread. Hardly less alarming was his account of seeing Poles who pointed out to the Germans beardless men whom they recognized as Jews. These too were deprived of their rations.

"Luckily no one pointed at me," Father said, "but this has taught me a lesson. When the war is over, we won't stay in this country even one day longer. We'll all go to *Eretz Israel*." He ruefully recalled the mistake made by my uncles Abraham and Shimshon, who had migrated to

Palestine with their families but had returned after having suffered financial setbacks there. They should have stayed, Father said, and begun everything anew. They should never have come back to Poland. "We will not make the same mistake," he declared. "We will go and never return."

1940

Decrees

After my father's experience in the breadline, Mother went every day to receive our daily ration of bread. With her thick honey-colored hair, greenish-blue eyes, and snub nose, it was virtually impossible to detect her Jewish origin. Standing in line one morning, Mother witnessed a sight so unnerving that she was still trembling when she described it at home. This time the Germans dragged a bearded Jew out of the breadline and, with leering smiles, began to pluck wisps of hair from his beard. The soldiers were unmoved by the blood-spattered face of their victim, who was on the verge of fainting. This ghastly spectacle affected even the Poles in the line.

Although beard-plucking became a favorite pastime of the German soldiers, religious Jews couldn't bring themselves to shave off their beards. Attempting to hide them, they wound shawls and wrappings around their head and face, as if they were suffering from toothache. It was a ruse quickly discovered and as quickly abandoned. Well-known and respected Jews, whose bearded faces had never failed to arouse veneration, now slunk like shadows along the walls of houses, desperately trying to elude detection.

As a further indignity, all Jews were now required to step off the sidewalk as soon as a German soldier came in sight. I myself was able to evade this humiliating decree because of my non-Jewish appearance. It always gave me a sense of satisfaction as I walked past those crude, red-faced German soldiers holding my head proudly erect. My satisfaction, however, would be short-lived.

Winter was now approaching. The Germans had been in Lodz for three months, and they had made many changes.

16

The city had been annexed to the Third Reich and re-named Litzmannstadt. All public buildings, including my high school, had been confiscated by the army. The students at my school had been transferred to another gymnasium, where we attended class in two shifts: one week in the morning, the next week in the afternoon. There were signs that even greater changes were to come. Rumors kept circulating about German intentions to isolate the Jewish population of Lodz within a ghetto to be set up in the suburb of Baluti. Famous for its huge market, Baluti was also full of factories and workshops, and its crowded tenements housed the poorest members of the Polish and Jewish working class. Many Jews from other areas of the city were already looking for living quarters in Baluti, and others lost no time transferring their possessions to places within this suburb. My family had begun moving some things to the home of Aunt Hanushka and Uncle Hersh, who lived in Baluti.

My aunt and uncle's apartment was located close to a metal plant owned by Genia, the widow of Uncle Hersh's brother. After his brother's death, Uncle Hersh had taken over the management of the factory, which produced spare parts for bicycles and stoves. He had continued handling its affairs even after Genia remarried some time later.

One evening my father and I were returning from Baluti after transferring some reels of valuable gold and silver thread to Uncle Hersh's apartment when we were startled by a commotion in one of the streets. Squads of German soldiers were rounding up Jews for forced labor. The street had been cordoned off, and trucks already packed with bewildered Jews stood in the middle of the road. Horrified, I gripped Father's hand. Two soldiers rushed past without seizing him, and I relaxed my grip. Suddenly, a Polish child of seven or eight raced after the Germans and, pointing at my father, shouted, *"Jude! Jude!"* The two Germans ran back, tore my father away from me, and shoved him toward a waiting truck.

I ran home, weeping loudly all the way. When I told Mother what had happened, she almost fainted. Father did not return until late that night; he was bruised, frozen to the marrow, and hardly able to give a coherent account of what he had been through. He and the other men had been forced to carry pails of water up to the fourth floor of a building, past a gauntlet of soldiers who struck the workers with truncheons as they passed. Water spilled from the pails had frozen, causing the men to skid and fall on the thin coating of ice that formed on the stairs. Then the blows hailed down even faster on those who were unable to rise again and get on with the job.

That very night, Mother decided to move to Warsaw, which had not been annexed to the German Reich. We would join Genia, who had already left behind her factory and the apartment house she owned and gone to Warsaw with her husband and two older children, leaving only the youngest in the care of Aunt Hanushka until she found suitable accommodations.

While we were making plans for our move to Warsaw, a new humiliation was forced upon us. A decree was issued making it compulsory for all Jews to wear yellow tags for instant identification. I shall never forget the day I went to school for the first time with the identification tag on my sleeve. In the same place where I had proudly worn the blue *tartsha* symbolizing my status as a high school student, I now bore a yellow badge that singled me out as a Jew. When I went through Liberty Square, people whom I had passed daily without arousing the slightest interest now turned their heads to look and pointed me out to others.

I had never been ashamed or particularly conscious of being Jewish. Now, however, it was driven home to me how different I was—so different that a mark was required so that everyone would know "There goes a Jew!" I grew accustomed to wearing the hated yellow tag, which was soon replaced by patches in the shape of the Star of David that had to be sewed onto the back and front of our garments.

Another decree issued by the Germans prohibited any Jew from being out of doors after 5 P.M. All gates in the city were locked at that hour, and those violating the curfew did so at the risk of their lives. School hours were drastically curtailed to enable us all to reach home in time.

On my way home from afternoon classes one day, I ran into Slavka, a girl friend from my elementary school days.

Since we still had an hour before curfew time, I accepted her invitation to go to her house for half an hour. After telling her mother of her arrival, Slavka took me into a little garden bordering on the courtyard. There, as in former times, we lost ourselves in playing games, forgetting the world around us. When we finally became aware of the late hour, we rushed back into Slavka's home. Her mother, on seeing me, burst out in alarm, "Good heavens! What are you doing here at such an hour? It's already past six, and your parents must be frantic with worry. What's to be done now?"

She quickly removed the yellow patches from my coat and advised me to walk home with an air of unconcern, trying not to arouse suspicion in passersby. I stepped outside with a heavy heart, deeply upset by the thought of the anxiety I was causing my parents, and walked home without daring to turn my head. The courtyard gate was opened by our Polish concierge, who was waiting there with my father. Father asked no questions; he only murmured with a sigh of relief, "Thank the Lord you're home. Now if only Mother would come back soon."

Mother, I learned, had gone out in search of me, and now I was trembling with anxiety for her. She eventually returned after her fruitless search at both my aunts' homes. It was the only time in my life that Mother raised her hand against me. I took the punishment submissively, knowing how thoroughly I deserved it.

It was now February of a new year—1940. We were in the grip of winter when the rumors about the ghetto became reality. To keep the city *Judenrein* (cleansed of Jews), the Germans were forcing all Jews into the suburb of Baluti. A deadline was established after which no Jews would be permitted to live outside the boundaries of the area. In freezing weather and amid occasional snow storms, long columns of Jews—men and women, children and the aged, people from all walks of life—could be seen trudging toward the ghetto. These were people who only a short while ago had lived unsuspectingly in the seeming security of their homes. Now they moved in an unending stream, carrying their belongings in huge packs on their backs or heaped on pushcarts, pulling sledges loaded with tables, chairs, kitchen utensils, and bedding. All heavy fur-

niture such as wardrobes, dressers, and sofas had to be left
behind for lack of space in the single rooms that were all
most families had managed to obtain, and even those only
with great difficulty.

Since my parents and I intended to join Genia in Warsaw, we had already dispatched to her lodgings our
bedding, crockery, and most of our clothing. The remain-
der we now heaped on a huge sledge and transferred to
Aunt Hanushka's apartment in the ghetto, where we would
stay until we went to Warsaw. Uncle Abraham, Aunt
Faiga, and their son Salek had locked up their apartment
in Kalisz and moved in with the rest of us. Aunt
Hanushka's apartment now housed three families, including Genia's eighteen-month-old baby girl, Rishia. Living
conditions were acutely crowded, with each of us having
to take turns using the one lavatory and washbasin.
Mother and I spent the nights with Aunt Hanushka, and
Father stayed with Aunt Tsesia, who had moved her
family of seven into the single room and kitchen formerly
occupied by the Polish concierge of the apartment house.

The overcrowded living conditions in the ghetto soon
began to make themselves felt, particularly affecting those
who had always lived in spacious apartments and were
now forced to squeeze into cramped quarters. My parents
and I took comfort in the thought that this state of affairs
was only temporary as far as we were concerned. The
peasant who was to transport us to Warsaw with Genia's
baby and our belongings had been hired, and the date of
removal set for May 2. On April 30, Father exchanged all
the deutsche marks in his possession for Polish zlotys,
which could still be used in Warsaw. I was thrilled at the
prospect of our imminent departure.

But our plans to leave Lodz were thwarted by the news
on the morning of May 1. The ghetto had been entirely
sealed off the night before, preventing anyone from entering or leaving. German patrols guarded all exits and en-
trances, and any attempt to break through could cost one's
life. Utterly at a loss, my parents and I surveyed our situation. All our essential goods had by now been forwarded
to Warsaw, leaving us virtually destitute, for the Polish
currency Father was left with was worthless within the
ghetto. We were therefore compelled to live off whatever

valuables we still had on us or to draw on those my parents had kept hidden away.

Father now spent his days hunting for lodgings. He walked the length and breadth of the ghetto for three weeks before he was able to come up with a room. In order to pay the rent, he had to part with his precious gold watch, a wedding gift, and to borrow a lot of money from the family. The room was located in a building on Marinarski Street, which bordered on the open fields of Marisin. It was fairly large but devoid of any sunlight and very chilly. We consoled ourselves with the thought that summer was coming. As for the winter after that—who could tell? The war might be over by then. Right now we had to make a home for ourselves. We borrowed the necessary household furnishings from our relatives and settled down in the ghetto.

The lives of all the ghetto inhabitants were beginning to assume a kind of routine. The Germans appointed a man named Haim Rumkovski as *Judenältester* (Eldest of the Jews), in charge of general ghetto affairs. A Jewish police force, the *Sonderkommando*, was set up. Ration cards for bread were issued, as well as special coupons called *ratzia*, which we used to buy the monthly allotment of other food supplies and coal. We now became familiar with new types of so-called edibles—a murky oil of repulsive taste, indigestible barley, and bread made of imitation coffee and rotten potatoes that resembled lumps of clay.

Slowly order was introduced into our daily lives. Even the schools reopened. All former gymnasium students assembled in a large building on Dvorska Street, and the small teaching staff was put under the directorship of Mrs. Rein, former principal of the school where I had been enrolled. Young boys and girls who belonged to the various Zionist youth movements in Lodz also reorganized and set up *Hachshara* (agricultural training) units on the fields of Marisin. I would occasionally join in their activities and would look with admiration at those young people who, poverty-stricken and on the verge of starvation, never gave up their dreams of *aliya* (immigration) to *Eretz Israel*.

Young people in the ghetto were kept busy by school and other activities, but most adults had no occupation. There was always work for bakers, and some enterprising persons found jobs in grocery stores, coal distribution centers, and public utilities. Others, however, were without employment. My father had been offered a position in the *Sonderkommando*, but he turned it down, unwilling to become a lackey of the Germans and impose their decrees on his fellow Jews. Mother supported Father in this decision, but I was secretly disappointed at his refusal to join the police force. I was swayed by the impressive uniform, which would have suited him so well, and by the prospect of the extra food ration allotted *Sonderkommando* members. I also didn't see anything wrong in Jewish policemen preserving law and order within the ghetto. Only some time later did I understand how right Father had been in rejecting this kind of employment.

My father was unable to find another job, but there was plenty of work available on a voluntary, unpaid basis. Therefore Father, who knew German well, would fill in forms for unemployed neighbors who were unable to pay for their monthly allotment of foodstuffs and coal and had to apply for aid. Another voluntary task he took on was the distribution of the food rations to all the families on our block. Occasionally we ourselves came off second-best because Father gave every other family a full measure and left us with less than our share. But Mother didn't complain. She was happy to see Father busy at any kind of job.

A Woman I Admired

After the Lodz ghetto was closed, many people attempted to get past the German patrols guarding the area. Those who hadn't managed to join their families in time tried to break in; others tried to get out. Most of these attempts were foiled by the German guards, but some succeeded.

One day when my family was visiting Aunt Hanushka, we were astonished to see Genia entering the room. She had gotten into the ghetto by crawling through the barbed wire enclosure extending along the cemetery. After hiding for three hours in the undergrowth, she had seized an opportune moment during a change of guards and had been able to slip through undetected.

I had always admired the dynamic nature of this young woman who, though extremely wealthy and always surrounded by servants, was never known to be idle. In her factory, she could often be seen supervising the employees who worked on the large machines; inspecting supplies in the storeroom; sitting in the office receiving incoming orders or checking accounts. At home, one would find her in the large garden, conferring with the gardener about the placement of the flower beds. Her many occupations never prevented her from spending time with her children, from looking after her elegant home, or from acting as hostess at the numerous social gatherings held there.

Now Genia had risked her life coming from Warsaw in order to take her baby girl, Rishia, back with her. She told us that the conditions in the Warsaw ghetto were far better than in the ghetto of Lodz. Although all Jews were forced to live in a special area and to wear the yellow patch, the ghetto was open, with its inmates coming and going at will. The Polish population even came there to carry on a lively trade with the Jews.

Genia didn't conceal the fact that her husband and his family had objected strongly to her coming to Lodz, but they had given in to her indomitable will. She had obtained a forged identity card bearing a Polish name, put on a bulky peasant skirt, and tied a flowered kerchief around her head. She wrapped her money in a piece of cloth and tucked it inside her bosom, in the manner of all peasant women. "So here I am," Genia concluded, "and just as I got in, so I'll get out again."

Genia's resolve sent us all into a panic, for it was virtual suicide to try to break out of the ghetto, let alone with a baby. But nothing could budge her. She was determined to get back to her husband and family in Warsaw and to take little Rishia with her. Genia planned to drug the child with sedatives so that she would make no noise during the escape. Avramek, Tsesia's eldest son, would hold Rishia in his arms, and as soon as Genia managed to crawl through the barbed wire fence, he was to push the child out after her.

Genia made several attempts to carry out her scheme, but the vigilance of the patrols was impenetrable, and searchlights kept the entire fence area brightly lit. Nevertheless, Genia actually managed to cross over the fence twice by herself. The first time, Avramek was about to push the child over to her when they heard the sounds of dogs barking close by and soldiers running toward them. Genia barely made it back to our side again. The second time, shots were fired in their direction, waking little Rishia from her sedation. She began to scream at the top of her voice, and, scared out of their wits, Genia and Avramek fled back into the ghetto compound. The next morning, we heard that two escapees had been killed during the night.

The failure of her escape had a sobering effect on Genia, but it didn't break the spirit of this courageous woman. She accepted the inevitable, finding comfort in the thought that the war was bound to come to a speedy end and she and her family would soon be reunited. She solved the problem of finding living quarters by moving into the attic of her own house, all the rooms of which were, of course, occupied by new inmates of the ghetto. Fitting it out with the furniture she managed to salvage, she turned the attic into a cozy home for herself and Rishia.

One day on my way to Genia's, I saw a long line of huge horse-drawn wagons extending from the Baluti Market to Ceglana Street, right up to No. 15—Genia's factory and house. The courtyard was swarming with German soldiers. My cousin Temcha came running to tell me that the Germans had confiscated Genia's factory and were now seizing all its heavy equipment. Using the labor of Jews caught at random in the street, they were loading the wagons with dismantled parts of machinery, heavy iron pipes, and pieces of sheet metal. Holding Rishia in her arms, Genia stood by, watching the upheaval. It took six days to dismantle the plant and 120 heavily loaded wagons to haul away all the equipment, the raw materials, and the finished products from the supply depot. At the end, Genia was handed a receipt itemizing every single article removed.

This was only the beginning of Genia's tribulations. Soon afterwards she and Uncle Hersh were taken to the KRIPO (Criminal Police Department)—infamous for the terrible tortures used in its investigations. We feared for their lives and prayed for them. More than a week later, a truck drew up in front of 15 Ceglana Street, and Genia, escorted by officers of the KRIPO, climbed down from it. Our hearts contracted at the sight of her—hollow-cheeked and disheveled, her once bright blue eyes now red and swollen, with black rings around them. Genia led the KRIPO men straight to the courtyard of the plant and indicated the spot where the safe containing our most precious possessions was buried.

Immediately after the fall of Poland, the whole family had decided to conceal its valuables—gold and silver articles, strings of pearls and other jewelry handed down from one generation to another. A special stainless-steel container had been built in Genia's plant, and the adult members of the family had buried it in the courtyard, planting grass over the spot to conceal it. Someone, probably the concierge, must have suspected something and tipped off the authorities, which had led to the questioning of Genia and Uncle Hersh.

With the discovery and removal of our valuables, Genia and Uncle Hersh were released from custody. Genia avoided talking of what she had been through during the investigation. She even began to minimize the importance of the lost jewelry, which, she consoled us, could always be replaced. She knew her money could not be touched, for as soon as the rumors about an impending war began, she had deposited most of it in a Swiss bank.

Before long Genia was her old self again, but not Uncle Hersh. The period of detention had made an incredible change in him. His hair had turned white, and a dour expression had settled on his face. He now flew into a rage at the least trifle, was irritable with everyone, and scared of everything. Uncle Hersh had been through a horrifying ordeal: his toe nails had been ripped off; a blinding light had been directed at his eyes for days and nights on end to prevent him from falling asleep; water had been dripped onto his head until he was almost driven out of his mind; he had been starved and then forced to eat very salty herring but denied water to quench his maddening thirst. After this experience, Uncle Hersh was never himself again.

Winter Funeral

Hunger was now stalking the ghetto. It could be seen in the pale, hollow-cheeked faces, in the frequent cases of utter exhaustion, and in the way that clothes dangled loosely from emaciated bodies. Mother and I didn't feel the shortage of food so much, for even in good times we had eaten sparingly, but Father, with his healthy appetite, suffered badly from hunger pangs. Mother tried hard to supplement his diet, salvaging every grain of barley or crumb of bread to make an additional meal. To disguise the terrible taste of the rotten potatoes we were now receiving, she grated them finely and made fritters out of them. When Father discovered her hidden culinary talents, he responded with good-humored praise.

I, too, did what I could to supplement Father's ration of food. During the long summer vacation, our school scheduled daily activities during which we received two slices of bread for breakfast and another two with soup for lunch. In spite of the strict injunctions against smuggling the bread outside, I often managed to slip away with two slices of my own and two more given me by my girl friend Lilka, whose father worked in a food supply store and brought extra food home.

This summer vacation spent playing volleyball, basketball, and other games was a very happy time. No less happy were the hours I spent with Mother, who, despite our difficult circumstances, did all in her power to make our home a cheerful place. Only later was I able to appreciate how precious these moments had been for me.

The vacation came to an end all too soon, and the new

school year began. It was October 1940, and there was still no sign of the war ending. Then the winter arrived with its fierce winds and heavy snowfalls. The three measures of coal allotted to us were nowhere near enough to keep our room warm for even a little while. Father was still out of work, and his chances of finding a job were very slight. I so longed to do something for him that, overcoming my natural reticence, I turned for assistance to my friend Lilka, whose father was employed in the central store in the Baluti Market. Maybe she could ask him about finding my father some kind of a job there. Expecting nothing but a positive response, I daydreamed about how I would tell my parents the happy news. But several days passed and Lilka made no mention of the subject. Though reluctant to be the first to say something, I eventually asked her point-blank if her father could help. Her reply—that all vacancies had long since been snatched up and that there was nothing whatsoever available—was a painful surprise.

That winter, food supplies became even scarcer. The potatoes we received were so frozen they seemed like lumps of ice. Though Mother wore thick woolen mittens while peeling them, her small delicate fingers were always red and swollen. I once overheard her mumbling to herself, "It can't go on like this much longer!"

One morning before leaving for school, I saw Mother drawing something on a large piece of cardboard. Amused, I asked her if she were about to take up a new hobby here in the ghetto, of all places. Though usually frank, this morning she did not answer. Instead she quickly rolled the sheet up and put it away without saying any more about it. But returning from school that day, I found the cardboard nailed to our door with the words HOT COFFEE SOLD HERE printed in large block letters on it. When Father came home after another futile day of job hunting, he laughed on seeing the sign, but he didn't laugh for long. Mother's idea turned out to have been an excellent one. People rushing to work in the early mornings usually had no time to get the fire going and wait for the kettle to boil. They therefore seized the chance of warming up over a cup of steaming coffee for the price of only five pfennigs.

The sense of shame that Mother's "business" at first induced in me soon turned into admiration as I watched her coping bravely with the circumstances of our life. It never occurred to this gentle and intelligent woman to turn up her nose at the lowest of tasks, so long as she was able to help her family. Though selling coffee wasn't a profitable enterprise, it did make it possible for us to buy an additional ration of bread for Father, acquired on the black market, and an adequate supply of coal. Now our room was well-heated, greatly lessening the fear of the winter.

My weak and ailing mother was never once heard to complain about the deplorable conditions of our lives. Used to eating a strict diet, she marveled at how she was now able to survive on barley and potato fritters fried in black oil and still feel well. "The Almighty must be watching over me," she used to say.

But her good fortune did not last. One day, I came home to find my mother lying in bed, with her sisters, Tsesia and Hanushka, sitting beside her. The doctor diagnosed a severe inflammation of the gall bladder. Father and Mother's two sisters watched over her anxiously as the daylight faded and night came on. The last thing I heard before I fell asleep was Mother's voice calling me by an affectionate nickname. "Salusia, cover yourself well. It's cold in here!"

The sounds of screams roused me from my sleep. I leaped up and rushed to Mother's bedside. Her body was still warm, but she was no longer breathing. I called out to her, I wept and begged her not to leave me, reminding her of how she had always pitied Father for having been an orphan.

"I don't want to be an orphan, Mother!" I cried. "I'm still so young!"

I recalled having read somewhere that if one kept massaging a person's feet, the blood would start circulating again. So I bent down and began rubbing Mother's feet frantically. But the doctor, called in hastily, could do nothing but certify Mother's death at the age of thirty-six.

When I followed the black carriage carrying Mother's coffin to the cemetery, I prayed as I had at my cousin Moniek's funeral that the door of the carriage would fly open and my loved one would step out alive. But the sad journey continued uninterrupted. When the coffin was lowered into the grave, my father—usually so strong and restrained—wept like a child. Shocked at the sight, I resolved to pull myself together to do all in my power to stand by him and live solely for him. I didn't keep my resolve. The very first night after Mother's burial, awakened by the storm raging outside, I sobbed and screamed that Mother was lying out there in the snow and cold. Father took me into his arms and told me that Mother's soul did not feel the cold; it was in heaven, united with the souls of her parents and of Moniek. Lulled by his soothing voice, I fell asleep once more.

During the seven days of mourning, Uncle Abraham, my aunts Tsesia and Hanushka, Father, and myself received the condolences of many people. Some of my classmates came to call, and among them was my friend Lilka, who brought the news that finally there was a job available for Father. Thinking she was acting out of pity, I was about to decline when Father, who had overheard, accepted the offer at once.

With Father at work all day long, the problem arose as to who was going to look after me. Aunt Tsesia insisted on taking me into her home. I heard her say, "What do you mean, overcrowded? I've got five children and now I'll have six!" I personally preferred living with Aunt Hanushka, who, in normal times, would have been overjoyed to have me. In view of Uncle Hersh's unpredictable behavior, that was now out of the question. Instead I begged to be allowed to remain home with my father, but he refused to let me stay since our room would be inadequately heated without Mother's coal ration and the extra fuel we had been able to buy with her coffee money. Father reminded me how important it was that I continue my studies as Mother would have wished. The war was bound to end sooner or later, and I would be able to graduate from high school. The very thought of Mother not attending my graduation brought on another burst of tears. A glance at Father standing depressed and helpless, however, had a sobering effect on me. I calmed down and submitted to whatever was decided, but I made Father promise to come and see me every single day and to spend all his spare time with me.

Aunt Tsesia and Uncle Shimshon treated me with the same loving care they gave their other children. I shared a bed with my cousin Temcha, and every morning before school, Aunt Tsesia would tenderly brush and braid my hair the way Mother would have. Aunt Hanushka and Uncle Hersh dropped in daily to see how I was doing. I was surrounded by my family's love.

My school had been relocated several times, and we were now occupying a number of small huts in the fields of Marisin formerly used by the Zionist agricultural units. I was delighted at the transfer of the school from a closed-in building to the open spaces of Marisin. More-over, the area was near the cemetery where Mother was buried; I could now visit her grave daily after school. I would talk to her as I used to in the past, telling her of Father's work compressing coal dust into briquets, of life at Aunt Tsesia's and at school. I kept those daily visits a secret, not sharing it even with Father. On my way to school in the mornings and again on my way back, I would also make a detour in order to pass by the house on Marinarski Street and peep through the window into the room that had once been my home. Though I knew there would be nobody there, I was irresistibly drawn to the cold, dark room.

When Father came to see me after work, Aunt Tsesia, salvaging whatever food she could, always had something ready for him to eat. I awaited his arrival with great agita-tion and was upset whenever it was time for us to part. I would accompany him part way home, and then he would walk me back again. Setting off together once more, we'd retrace our steps several times. There was so much we had to tell each other. And when we talked of Mother, a deep longing for her overcame both of us.

Once, in a fit of anger, I accused him of intending to re-marry after the war and forcing me to live with a stepmother. As soon as I said it, I could have bitten my tongue off. Father, halting abruptly, turned to me and said softly, "You're all I have left, my darling. So long as I live I won't allow anything to harm you. I won't get married again unless you want me to."

At each parting, my heart grew heavy at the thought of him entering that empty, cold room whose very walls were sheeted with ice. Father had lost weight alarmingly, and his cheeks were sunken. His walk, formerly so light and energetic, was now heavy and slack. The suffering of the last weeks had taken its toll on his health and his spirit.

1941

Deportation

As the snows of that winter turned slowly to sleet and mud, new sources of income began to appear in the ghetto. Taking advantage of the cheap, captive labor supply, the Germans were setting up workshops to manufacture all kinds of goods. Although the salaries were barely adequate to pay for the meager monthly *ratzia*, employees in the workshops were entitled to an extra slice of bread each day.

At first, most of the workshops made uniforms for the soldiers of the Third Reich, but others were soon established to manufacture luxury goods like carpets, brassieres, and corsets. Uncle Abraham was able to obtain a job in the supply store of a corset factory. Genia, experienced in the management of a large concern, was put in charge of a workshop making metal products. Her position immediately entitled her to a greatly increased food ration like the other privileged managers and high-ranking police officers. She had been elevated into the sphere of the ghetto elite—the "millionaires" who were able to acquire whatever they needed by trading their surplus food. The principal of our school, Mrs. Rein, was also entitled to extra rations, but she refused them, maintaining that so long as her pupils went hungry, she could not accept such favored treatment for herself.

I did not have a job like my relatives, but schoolwork kept me busy during the day and studying took up most of my spare time. In addition to the compulsory German and Latin, I was also taking classes in Yiddish and Hebrew this year. One day, the pupils at our school received an important visitor: Haim Rumkovski, the *Judenältester*. Rumkovski was an elderly man, close to seventy but of tall and upright bearing, with gray hair and bronzed features that gave him a look of eminence. Because of the authority given him by the Germans, he had become the virtual "king" of the ghetto, even issuing his own currency for internal circulation.

When he visited our school, Rumkovski gave a speech expressing his great admiration for us high school students—we were the future of our people, he said. He would see to it that our schooling would not be discontinued and that nobody went hungry. In the near future, Rumkovski informed us, a field kitchen would be set up within the school compound so that we could receive some soup and a little meat.

Rumkovski kept his promise, and a few days later the ghetto's high school students could be seen coming to school in the mornings with tin bowls and spoons dangling from their schoolbags. When we discovered that we were eating patties made of horsemeat, our stomachs turned with nausea. We quickly overcame our revulsion, however, and were glad to fill our bellies.

The list of the monthly *ratzia* for ghetto residents, pasted periodically on grocery windows, kept shrinking visibly. The barley and the murky oil that used to disgust us so had disappeared long ago and now almost seemed like delicacies. The rations of pickled cabbage and kohlrabi were being cut down drastically. The only commodity in ample supply was soap—a green substance smelling of fish oil, with the letters R.J.F. on each bar. If only we had known the meaning of those initials!

Under these conditions, people changed so much in appearance that many of them were unrecognizable. Faces were bloated, with puffy bags beneath the eyes. Legs became so swollen that walking was virtually impossible. We called people suffering from such symptoms of starvation *musulmen* and knew that their days were numbered.

It was at about this time that the Germans put into operation their plan of deporting Jews from the ghetto. Hundreds of people received official notice that they would be taken from Lodz and transferred to special labor camps in the countryside. The notices were accompanied by detailed lists of the possessions that could be taken along. At the assembly point in the courtyard of the prison on Czarniecki Street, every deportee would be given a loaf of bread for the journey. Many of those served with orders of deportation were already employed within the ghetto, but they easily found "volunteers" to take their places. These volunteers were usually the half-starved, who jumped at the chance of getting a whole loaf of bread on the spot. For many of them, the prospect of working in a village held out the hope of escape from a lingering death in the ghetto.

News of the imminent deportation of Aunt Tsesia, her husband, and their five children came upon us like a thunderclap. Father, so weakened that he could barely hold on to his own job, would gladly have joined them. That was what I, too, wanted more than anything else. The thought of parting from those who had given me such a loving home was unbearable. Like everyone else, I was longing for the chance to get out of the ghetto. The prospect of living and working in the countryside excited our imaginations. Aunt Tsesia and Uncle Shimshon weren't unduly worried about the deportation order, and the children looked forward to the change most of all.

In preparation for their departure, Aunt Tsesia and her family exchanged all their household goods and kitchen utensils for strong boots and warm clothing. Aunt Hanushka, Uncle Abraham, Salek, and I accompanied them to the assembly point in the prison courtyard. But as soon as they passed through the gate, Aunt Hanushka burst into uncontrollable sobbing, unnerved by the thought of having to part with her second sister. Uncle Abraham reproached her, insisting that they'd all be together again as soon as the war was over. But Aunt Hanushka was inconsolable. She couldn't rid herself of the terrible feeling that she might never see any of her relatives again.

We watched Aunt Tsesia and her family as they walked away from us, each carrying a heavy knapsack. My eyes followed Temcha, whose auburn hair, parted into two thick braids, stood out in the crowd. Only now did I become aware of how tall Temcha had grown. Though a year younger than I, my twelve-year-old cousin had outgrown me by a head. Looking at Temcha reminded me of something amusing that had occurred while we were both in elementary school, and I burst out laughing. When Uncle Abraham turned on me with a reproachful look, I realized that this was hardly an appropriate moment for laughter. But on our way back home, I told Uncle what had made me giggle earlier.

When Temcha was in the third grade and I was in the fourth grade, our classrooms were on the same floor. Our mothers loved dressing us up in the same clothes, and one day Temcha and I came to school wearing identical green coats with collars of gray rabbit fur. We hung our coats in the hall, along with all the others. After school, we were in a hurry to get to Sienkiewicz Park and stake out our hopscotch squares. I hurriedly put on my coat and was astonished to find out that the buttons didn't reach the buttonholes and the sleeves were too short. Was it possible, I wondered, that I had grown so much in half a day that the coat that had fitted me perfectly in the morning was now too small on me?

My classmates were calling me, and I had no time to think about it. But when I got home, my mother burst into hysterical laughter. With the tears streaming down her face, she tried to tell me that I was wearing Temcha's coat. Temcha had put on my coat, and she couldn't understand why it was so roomy, with sleeves so long that her hands got lost inside them. Our mothers met halfway between our two houses with the coats in their hands, still laughing so much that passersby stopped and stared at them.

I had hoped that my tale would cheer my listeners a little, but only Salek smiled faintly, while Aunt Hanushka broke into tears again and Uncle Abraham busied himself polishing his eyeglasses.

The days that followed were particularly trying for me. I moved in with Aunt Hanushka, where I had my own bed and plenty of living space but had to cope with the erratic moods of Uncle Hersh. His nature was so changed that I could hardly remember the elegant, kindly, and good-humored gentleman he had been, the jolly uncle who never came to visit without some surprise hidden in one of his pockets. Now he was extremely jealous of me, grumbling whenever he saw Aunt Hanushka doing up my hair, begrudging every bit of bread she put into my lunchbox, and complaining about whatever I happened to be doing. Sick of it all, I begged to be allowed to move out and live with my father. But time and again, Aunt Hanushka and Uncle

Abraham pleaded with me to ignore Uncle Hersh's behavior and to concentrate on my studies instead. I realized that they meant well and that there was nothing I could do about the situation except to suffer it in silence, which I did with great difficulty.

I didn't tell Father about my troubles, not wanting to worry him more than was necessary. Instead, I hurried to the cemetery as soon as school was over and poured out my heart over Mother's grave. I told her of the deportation of Aunt Tsesia and her family, reminded her of the episode with the two coats, and complained about Uncle Hersh's erratic conduct. Unburdening my heart at Mother's graveside brought great relief. Those moments were the only bright spots in my life now, but I was not permitted to enjoy them for long.

Father's Illness

My father's health continued to deteriorate, and he eventually came down with a severe case of dysentery. Because of his condition, he lost his job and, with it, his extra bread ration. Aunt Hanushka tried to compensate for this by occasionally sneaking a slice of bread for Father into my lunchbox.

Father's illness put me in a spot. I couldn't leave school to look after him for then I, too, would forfeit my additional food ration, which I shared with him. I had to continue receiving this ration and also figure out how to get more food for Father. Racking my brain, I finally hit upon an idea. Since my girl friend Lilka could easily do without the extra ration we received at school, I offered to buy it from her for the sum of five pfennigs. She agreed to the deal. I now set out to Father's place each morning before school started, left him half of my bread ration, and rushed back right after school with the soup and meat patty bought from Lilka. In the evenings, I returned with his own daily bread ration and the coffee prepared for him by Aunt Hanushka. All this kept me so busy that I had no time left to visit Mother's grave.

In order to prevent the smuggling of food outside the school precincts, a guard was always on duty at the gate. One day when I was passing the sentinel's box, my way was barred by a policeman. Looking up, I recognized Mietek, an old acquaintance. I was overjoyed and on the point of calling out to him, but seeing the scowl on his face, I realized that he was determined to draw the line between us.

Mietek was the son-in-law of the Shor family, our former neighbors and my parents' closest friends. For years their place had been like a second home to me, and I had looked upon their daughter Sabcia—Mietek's wife—almost like an older sister. Mother and I had been to see the Shors several times during our first days in the ghetto. They had obtained a two-room cottage with a plot of land next to it. Mrs. Shor raised vegetables there and proudly showed them off to us whenever we called. During our last visit to them, I was struck by the change in Mrs. Shor's appearance. After a whispered talk with Mother, she emerged from the room with eyes swollen from weeping. I had caught snatches of her conversation and heard her say that it would have been far better for herself and her husband were Sabcia and Mietek to live somewhere else. Telling Father about it later on, Mother said, "Mietek has sold his soul to the devil."

Not long after Mother died, I ran into Sabcia and accompanied her to her parents' home, where I found Mrs. Shor sick in bed. She burst into tears on hearing of Mother's death and kept repeating. "Ach, so young, so young." She told me then that Sabcia and Mietek had separated. Their daughter, she said, had become her parents' sole means of support. Several weeks later, Mrs. Shor herself died.

And now, here was Mietek, treating me like a complete stranger. He curtly demanded to know what I was carrying, and on seeing the soup and meat patty, he told me sharply that it was forbidden to take food away from the school. I managed to stammer something about an upset stomach and intending to save the food for later. The scowl on his face warned me against blurting out my true intentions. Mietek let me off—miraculously—but not without a warning about what would happen if he caught me at it again. He never had to carry out his threat for I discovered another exit where I could slip out unobserved, though it took me considerably longer to reach Father's place.

Despite the extra food, Father's condition deteriorated alarmingly. His face assumed a pallor that frightened me. Dr. Kshepitzki, our family doctor in better times, came to see Father and prescribed a strict diet to stop the diarrhea. He told us that only hospitalization could give Father a fair chance of recovery and added that he could count himself lucky because of his strong constitution; a weaker person would have succumbed long ago.

Dr. Kshepitzki's opinion put us all in a quandary, for there was no chance of Father being admitted into the already overcrowded hospital. We knew of many sick people who had died long before their names reached the top of the long waiting list. Unable to help us himself, Dr. Kshepitzki said to me, "Maybe *you* could do something about it. The pleading of a girl your age might arouse someone's pity and speed up the process." After leaving a letter recommending hospitalization, Dr. Kshepitzki went away.

After that, I stood in line at the hospital reception desk every day. But my sad story didn't impress anyone, least of all the stern-faced reception clerk, who kept turning me away with the invariable refrain: "No beds available. Your father's turn hasn't come up yet."

Though I attended school as usual, my heart wasn't in my studies. The dread of going to see Father and not finding him alive haunted me, and all I could think of was how to bring him the extra food from school. Running from the field of Marisin right up to Father's door, I'd stop short in front of it with a pounding heart, not daring to enter. An unspeakable terror would take hold of me. Was he still alive? I'd first peep in fearfully through the window until I could see him lying with eyes closed and face so white that it almost blended with the pillow case. Then I would rap softly on the pane, wait a moment, and give a much louder rap. Panic-stricken at the lack of response, I'd shout at the top of my voice, "Daddy, Daddy!" Only after seeing him open his eyes and smile weakly would I dare to enter his room.

Finally the school year ended. It was the summer of 1941, and I now had two years of high school behind me due to the determination of our teachers to keep the school going despite almost overwhelming odds. For the first time in my life, I had received two low marks on my report card—in Hebrew and in Latin. The time needed for language study was now taken up standing in line every day at the hospital reception desk or waiting to receive our food rations and our allotment of coal. All I could do was to prepare my lessons hastily between one break and another at school.

On the last day of the school year, I went to visit Mother's grave. I told her about the low marks I had received and begged her to intercede in heaven for Father's sake. When I told Father about my bad grades, he had only praise for me.

With the beginning of summer vacation, I was faced with a new worry that nearly drove me crazy: I could no longer bring Father my ration of food from school. Every day I hoped that a miracle would happen and he would be admitted to the hospital. But every day I was turned away with the same laconic refrain: No beds available. His turn hasn't come yet.

The first day of vacation brought all my problems to a head. When I went to Father's place to prepare his food, I had trouble getting the fire started. I had never learned to perform this simple household chore, and I wasted countless matches in the process. Finally Father had to get out of bed and light the fire for me. I hadn't seen him standing up for some time, and the sight of his frail body and legs thin as sticks shocked me deeply. It took all the strength I could muster not to burst into tears. After the fire was lit, I quickly peeled the turnips—the only food distributed lately—and put them into the boiling water. But the fire went out after an hour, and all I could offer Father was a soup consisting of salted water and half-cooked turnips, when he needed a strict diet!

That day was marked by many more mishaps. After preparing Father's food, I went to get our monthly coal ration. There weren't many people in line that day, and I was soon on my way home doubled up under a load of thirty kilograms of coal. The way wasn't short at the best of times, but now it seemed endless. Halfway there, my sack ripped open and small pieces of coal began tumbling off in all directions. Somehow I managed to gather them all up and lug the load to Father's place.

I was in a downcast mood when I reached Aunt Hanushka's in the evening. I found Uncle Abraham there, waiting impatiently to tell me of an idea that had occurred to him. He wanted me to appeal to our neighbor Dr. Leider, who lived across the landing, to use his influence on Father's behalf. He had meant to take the matter up himself but thought that a young girl pleading for her own father might be more effective.

Dr. Leider was a veterinary surgeon whom the Germans frequently called outside the ghetto to treat their horses and dogs. With the exception of Haim Rumkovski, he was the only person who had the use of his own carriage and a personal driver to take him in and out of the ghetto as he pleased. My acquaintance with Dr. Leider, his wife, and son was most casual and never went beyond the exchange of polite greetings on the staircase.

My fervent wish to save Father's life made me forget my shyness, and that very evening I stood outside the Leiders' door with a thumping heart. My knock was answered by Mrs. Leider, who listened to my stammered request to see her husband, led me to the dining room, and invited me to share their evening meal. For a second I halted on the threshold, dazzled by what I saw. In front of me there was a white-clothed table heaped with food—a whole loaf of bread, chunks of various cheeses, sliced sausage, butter, jam, a bowl of sugar, and a pot of coffee!

Before I had time to collect myself, I was seated at the table. A plate with several slices of bread was put before me. "Go on," I heard voices urging, "butter it and help yourself to the rest." I buttered the bread with a trembling hand but didn't dare to reach out for anything else. Mrs. Leider helped me to some slices of sausage, whose spicy aroma set my head spinning. But the food stuck in my throat as I remembered Father and what I had come here for. I felt my chin quiver incontrollably and was on the verge of tears when Dr. Leider came to my aid by inquiring how things were going at home. He encouraged me to talk about myself and my reason for coming to see him.

I repeated word for word what Dr. Kshepitzki had said about Father's state of health. Then for some reason, I started talking about my life before the war, something I hadn't done since Mother's death. When coffee was served, the spoonful of powdered milk added to my cup brought back a smell and taste I had forgotten. Then the sugar bowl was pushed toward me. Hoping that no one was looking at me, I put two sugar cubes into my cup and kept a third for Father. When I took my leave, Dr. Leider assured me that he would arrange for Father to be admitted to the hospital at once. Completely overcome, I burst into tears, which prevented me from expressing my gratitude.

I raced home to Father with the wonderful news. I told him over and over about all that had passed that evening and described in minutest detail the room, the meal, the people around the table. Sucking on the sugar cube, Father smiled wearily. "And to think that it was less than two years ago," he said, "that your mother had to force you to eat an apple or a buttered roll."

An apple! A buttered roll! Only two years ago—two summers, two winters. It seemed like centuries.

Dr. Leider kept his promise. The following morning, I was walking toward Father's place, thinking with a heavy heart of all the chores to be done and trembling with fear that I wouldn't find him alive. Then a horse-drawn Red Cross ambulance overtook me, heading in the direction of Father's house. My heart missed a beat. Was it possible? I broke into a run and managed to get there first. Bursting into the room, I shouted, "Daddy, Daddy! They're coming to take you to the hospital!" I had scarcely finished my sentence when two men entered with a stretcher. Father's face was radiant with happiness.

"God hasn't forsaken us yet," he murmured. "I'd given up all hope of ever leaving this bed alive."

Too happy for words, I hugged Father and followed the men who were carrying him outside. As soon as the ambulance was out of sight, I ran to the cemetery to tell Mother about what had happened. There was no doubt in my mind that the miracle had taken place thanks to Mother's intervention with the Divine Powers. For days afterwards, I was aware of a sense of relief, as if I had been released from a heavy burden. My mind was at ease now, knowing that Father was receiving the proper medical care. Recalling what Dr. Kshepitzki had said about his strong constitution, I was convinced he'd get well again.

The Bread of Life

My joy over Father's getting into the hospital was so great that it made me forget my own unhappy situation, but not for long. With the absence of the school ration, hunger was beginning to torment me again, especially since I now had too much time on my hands. Released from anxiety about my father and from the burdensome household chores, my days were empty. Reading had always been a favorite pastime, and I still loved it, but the gnawing and rumbling of my stomach wouldn't let me concentrate on my books. This was also the case with my cousin Salek, who, like myself, had been dependent upon the rations we received at school.

Salek and I looked forward eagerly to the beginning of the new school year, when we would again have enough to eat. But when summer was over, classes did not start. Haim Rumkovski's solemn promise to the high school students had been broken. Our school would never open again.

Of course, we young people were not the only ones suffering from lack of food. The number of ghetto residents dragging themselves about on legs swollen with malnutrition was increasing daily. Particularly affected were the unemployed, who had only their weekly loaf of bread to depend on. Many of these people couldn't make the bread last more than three or four days and were compelled to live out the rest of the week without any kind of nourishment whatever. They became so weak that they died of tuberculosis and other diseases that attack malnourished bodies. So numerous were the ghetto dead that, instead of taking them for burial one by one, the funeral wagons now passed by heaped with corpses. Very soon there were not enough wagons to cart all the dead away.

At the same time as the death rate rose, the ghetto was

being repopulated with Jews transported from Czechoslovakia and Germany. We were mystified by this development: not long ago, thousands had been deported from the ghetto, and now thousands of others were being brought into it. But the Germans seemed to know what they were doing. Their goal was to replace "those who were too weak to turn out the production quotas with others, still healthy and strong and unaffected by the diseases of malnutrition."

We gazed in awe at the newcomers in their well-tailored suits and well-padded coats. They looked down on us at first and shrugged off our advice to divide their weekly loaf of bread into equal daily portions. Instead, they went through their rations within a few days. Before long, however, they began selling off their clothes and valuables to the ghetto "millionaires" in return for more bread to fill their hungry bellies. Even this extra food did not prevent them from becoming victims of starvation. Unlike the original ghetto inhabitants, who had been exposed to malnutrition over a period of several years, these newcomers had no time to develop a defense against the disease. The death toll among them soon reached inordinate proportions.

Bread had now become so coveted a commodity to the famished ghetto population that, in order to obtain it, brother stole from brother and children from parents in the dead of night. There were, however, exceptions: my Uncle Abraham couldn't bear to see his son Salek and me go hungry, and he always divided his daily ration from work equally between the two of us. Though greatly tempted, I didn't want to accept the food at first, arguing that, unlike Salek—his own son—I had no right to deprive him of his share and also that since he was working and I wasn't, he needed the bread much more than I. I had barely finished saying this when, quite out of the blue, my good-humored and kindly uncle flew into a towering rage and yelled at me, "You little upstart! Who's asking your opinion! It's still mine that counts around here!"

Intimidated, I took the bread with a trembling hand and a murmur of thanks. Aunt Hanushka watched this exchange, dabbing tears from her eyes.

One chilly fall day, Salek and I were sent to the butcher's to get the 100 grams of horsemeat that was occa-

sionally allotted to each individual. On the way a closed
wagon passed us, and we got a whiff of freshly baked
bread! So intoxicated were we that we changed direction
and followed the bread van with our mouths watering. In
a flight of fantasy, I imagined a loaf falling from the van,
saw Salek and me racing to pick it up and taking it to
some dark corner, where we devoured chunks of the still-
warm and crunchy bread, experiencing for once, just for
once, the gratifying sense of being full.

The apparition dissolved and was replaced by the
memory of a long-forgotten scene from childhood. During
the summer months spent at Uncle Abraham's estate in
the country, Salek and I were sent out early in the morning—he carrying a small can and I, a basket—to fetch
milk and bread from the peasants in the village. On those
mornings, the dew was still pearly on the grass, and shafts
of sun rays filtered through the fragrant pine trees. Holding hands, Salek and I walked along the road, past hazel
trees and berry bushes, listening to the chirping of birds
and the echo of our own voices in the morning stillness.
The aroma of bread being baked down in the village
mingled with that of the ripe apples in the orchard we
were passing. As we got closer, the fragrance of fresh
bread surrounded us.

On reaching the village, we bought our loaves of warm
bread and then went to the home of the peasant who supplied us with milk. He led us into his cowshed, seated himself on a low stool, and began milking the cow. We stood
near him and watched in fascination as the jets of milk
spurted from the udder into the pail. Soon, with the milk
can filled and bread in the basket, Salek and I were on our
way back to our house at the edge of the forest.

And now, years later, we were walking together again,
lured on by the aroma of fresh bread. We came to a sudden halt only when the bread van drove into a courtyard
and the gate clanged shut behind it. My cousin and I exchanged a look of profound sadness.

Other than errands like the one that had led us to the
bread van, I had little to occupy my time. I was not able
to see my father due to the strict prohibition against visiting patients in the hospital. Instead I received progress reports from the receptionist, who told me that his condition
was steadily improving. Although I longed to see him, my

mind was at ease knowing that he was on the road to recovery. I resumed my visits to Mother's grave, but time hung heavy on my hands and each day seemed to crawl by more slowly than the one before.

Salek, in a similar limbo, suggested that he and I should use the time to further our studies. Since he was one class ahead of me, he would teach me the subjects he had studied the previous year, while he himself would get hold of the textbooks needed for his fourth and final year and try to keep up with his own requirements. If nothing else, Salek argued, the work would take our minds off the gnawing hunger.

Salek had always been the studious type, but somehow I lacked the enthusiasm for such pursuits at a time like this. In the midst of hunger, poverty, and death, the study of Latin, physics, algebra, or the sayings of Socrates and Aristotle seemed utterly absurd to me. What would these great thinkers say if they could see us starving inside a ghetto for no other reason than having been born Jews? But Salek applied himself stubbornly to the task he had set himself, spurred on by the conviction that when the war was over he'd be able to take up his studies again. My cousin's fervor finally infected me, and we both became absorbed in our new occupations. Salek worked hard tutoring me in the morning and devoted the rest of his time to catching up with his own studies.

In my eyes Salek was a genius. He excelled in both the sciences and the humanities and was a gifted linguist as well. He also wrote poems, some of which became well known in the ghetto. One of Salek's poems made a great impact on me. Though I never knew it by heart, its theme remains in my memory even now. It was about a small boy lying awake beside his mother, father, and little sister, the pain of hunger gnawing in his belly. In the corner of the room stood the breadbox and what was left of the loaf that was to last the family for the rest of the week. The boy couldn't take his mind off the bread, and he fought hard against the temptation to sneak over and cut off a slice so thin that no one could tell the difference. Why not? an inner voice kept prompting. Hadn't the bread already been whittled down to less than what it should be? It wouldn't last the week in any case. So why not? Why not? His conscience told him to think of all the others who were as hungry as he, but that didn't help. Overcome by hunger, he stole past his sleeping family to the breadbox. With the slice of bread in his hand, he got back into bed and pulled the blanket over his head. The boy nibbled at the bread, now seasoned with the salt of his tears.

Salek's own hunger was eased when Genia got him a job in a machine-repair shop that carried with it a ration supplement. Now Uncle Abraham had to share his work ration only with me. My greatest need at this time was a new winter coat. Luckily, we had a length of woolen material that Father had bought before the war for a new suit. The manager of a tailoring workshop made it into a coat for me, complete with a fur collar taken from one of Mother's winter garments.

My life during this period seemed tolerable enough compared to the ordeals I had faced during Father's illness. I still had to put up with Uncle Hersh's bad temper, but he was away from home much of the time, working at a job that Genia had gotten for him. I lived from day to day, not thinking about the past or the future.

1942

In the Workshop

It was not long before I joined Salek in the ghetto work force. Uncle Abraham got me a job in his workshop, which manufactured brassieres and corsets for German women. His eyes shone with happiness as he described to me how he had managed it. He had simply gone up to the supervisor and told her about his eighteen-year-old niece who had worked in a bra and corset factory before the war.

"But Uncle, I'm only fourteen!"

"Don't interrupt!" he said sharply. "I know exactly how old you are! Guess what happened then," he continued. "She hired you on the spot and was even annoyed because I hadn't mentioned you before!"

"But I haven't the slightest idea how to make such things," I protested, shaking all over. "I've never even touched a sewing machine before! They're sure to find me out!"

"Take it easy," Uncle Abraham said. "You think I haven't thought of that myself? You don't have to know much. I've been watching the sewing machine operators for a long time. All you do is put your feet on the treadle, turn the wheel with your hand, and the machine goes by itself. The rest is done mechanically. Besides, no one makes the bras from start to finish. You're part of an assembly line. All you need to know is how to sew a straight seam. Tomorrow you come to work with me."

"Oh no, I'm not. I won't tell a lie. It's hard enough to convince people of my real age."

"You have to lie, my child," Aunt Hanushka interceded quietly. "And you'll do it convincingly. After all, it won't

47

harm anybody. Having a job is the only thing that's likely
to save you and perhaps enable you to see the war
through. You need the extra ration of food. And you
know that the jobless are constantly being deported. Look
at Tsesia and her family. No one has a clue where they've
gone to."

They were right, of course. I had no other choice except
to fib my way into the workshop. I consoled myself with
the thought that if I succeeded, at least Uncle Abraham
would no longer have to share his daily ration with me.

Early the next morning, Aunt Hanushka worked hard at
changing my hair style to make me look older. Undoing
my long braids, she cut my hair shorter and, with the aid
of numerous hairpins, built it into something resembling a
tower. On our way to work, Uncle Abraham explained
once again how easy it was to operate a sewing machine,
but the more he talked, the more scared I became.

When we arrived at the workshop, he introduced me to
the supervisor, who sized me up from top to bottom.
Standing stiffly erect and on tiptoe to add to my height, I
stammered out my uncle's story about my age and the
trade I had supposedly acquired before the war. Without
further ado, the supervisor led me to a place between two
women who kept on working away at their machines without so much as giving me a glance. She showed me how to
stitch two pieces of satiny material together in a straight
line and told me to repeat the process until the batch before me was finished. Then she went away to accompany
Uncle Abraham to the door.

I began to work, pairing the two pieces as I'd been instructed, setting the wheel in motion, and pushing the
treadle up and down. Wonder of wonders! The machine
started turning. It purred pleasantly, and the pieces of
material moved forward. I reached out for the next pair
and the next. A thrill of happiness ran through me. Uncle
Abraham was right. I could handle a sewing machine
without a hitch. If only Father could see me now! He
didn't even know about this new turn of events.

But what was this? No sooner had I moved the completed batch aside than all the pieces fell apart as though
they'd never been stitched together. I was baffled, for the
machine had been running without a snag. I threw furtive
glances at my neighbors, both of whom were doing exactly

the same work. Maybe I hadn't pushed the treadle down as hard or as fast as I should have. I started all over again but even after repeated attempts, the result was the same.

Just then, the door to the workroom opened, and Uncle Abraham peeped inside. I sighed in relief. I'd show him what was wrong, and he'd get me out of this fix. But seeing me bent over my machine, Uncle Abraham assumed that everything was all right, and with a wave of his hand, he disappeared again. After several more attempts, I gave up. It was useless. My happiness had been premature. I found out later that while Uncle Abraham had told me about the wheel and the treadle, he had neglected to mention that the sewing machine also needed to be threaded!

Just then the supervisor passed by. She came to a sudden halt on seeing the mess I'd made of my assignment. I stood up.

"Listen," I said, feeling the hot blood rush into my face, "I can't do it. I don't know anything about this work. I've never touched a sewing machine in my life!"

I was trying hard to keep my composure, but despite desperate efforts, I burst into tears. "I told you a lie," I sobbed, "but I'm not a liar, and I didn't mean to cheat you. It's work and bread I want."

Most of the machines had stopped running by now, and the heads of the women were turned in my direction. Overcome with shame, I tearfully continued my confession. "I'm not eighteen at all! I'm only fourteen."

I bowed my head, expecting the supervisor's wrath, but instead I felt a hand softly stroking my hair. "Stop crying, child," she said. "I could tell at once that you weren't eighteen. Never mind about that. You can stay on. We need youngsters your age, and we'll find something you can do. In time you'll also learn how to work a sewing machine."

I smiled through my tears, unable to believe my good fortune. A few minutes later, I was seated at a table where I learned how to fasten buckles on corsets. But I did that work for only a few weeks. The supervisor kept her word, and she herself taught me to operate a sewing machine. I again took my place between the two women, but this time I knew how to handle my machine. I had found a job and a skill I could use.

Although winter was again upon us—the third winter since the beginning of the war—I felt contented and warm. Father was still in the hospital, receiving the care that he needed to get well. I had a job and a daily ration of bread, which meant that Uncle Abraham could keep his own ration for himself. (I had a hunch that he wasn't keeping it, though, but was now sharing it with his sister Hanushka.) I was happy at work. The supervisor treated me with affection, despite my earlier deception of her, and my fellow workers were kind. I eventually got to know most of these women well, but two in particular stand out in my memory.

Mrs. Frankel, who sat opposite me, was about twenty-six years old. Despite her pallor and her hollow cheeks, the remarkable beauty of her face was still quite evident. Her chestnut-colored hair fell down her back in rippling waves, and her eyes were large and green. But the most beautiful thing about her was her voice. As she worked at her machine, she sang Polish and Yiddish songs about longing for love, about trees and birds, about hills and forests. We forgot our hunger and our suffering for a while as the sewing machines purred and Mrs. Frankel sang.

I listened with fascination to the story of Mrs. Frankel's life, recorded in the many snapshots she showed us. The only child of well-to-do parents, she had been married to the son of a wealthy industrialist soon after her graduation from high school. She had lived a happy life with her husband; her photographs showed the young couple skiing in the mountains on winter holidays or bathing and sailing at the seashore. There were many snapshots of their chubby baby boy, who had inherited his mother's radiant coloring.

Their son was three when Mrs. Frankel, her husband, and her mother moved into the ghetto. She had been the first to get a job, and thanks to her iron will, she never once touched the bread she received at work but took it home to share with the rest of her family. In time her husband also obtained work, but, she told us sadly, he could never refrain from finishing off his entire ration as soon as he got it.

As time went on, Mrs. Frankel's songs were heard less often in the workshop. She began to tell her fellow workers about the terrible problems caused by her husband's behavior. Her family had always shared the weekly allot-

ment of four loaves of bread equally, finishing the first
loaf before breaking into the second, and so on. But her
husband, in total disregard of the others, kept sneaking
pieces of bread whenever he felt hungry. Things got so
bad that two days before the next rations were due, the
family was often without a crumb of bread. Finally Mrs.
Frankel and her mother decided that the husband had to
take care of his own loaf and make ends meet by himself.
But far from solving the problem, this only made matters
worse, since he went through his loaf within four days and
then took a share of his son's ration, arguing that, because
he was a child, he didn't need an entire loaf for himself.
Now the boy was constantly hungry, having nothing to eat
but what was left of the bread, which his grandmother fed
him soaked in his soup.

These ordeals left their mark on Mrs. Frankel, and before long her appearance changed beyond recognition. Her
singing ceased altogether and, along with it, the stories of
her glamorous past. She even stopped talking about the
troubles at home and instead maintained an embittered
silence, withdrawing completely into herself.

My neighbor on the right was Rachelka, a girl of about
eighteen. Rachelka's large black eyes shone with a peculiar
gleam, and she gave off a smell that grew more repellent
from day to day. I asked her if she were ill, but she answered evasively, and from hints dropped by Mrs.
Frankel, I understood that I shouldn't say anything more.
Rachelka, she told me, was suffering from galloping consumption (a severe case of tuberculosis).

Overcoming my strong aversion, I befriended Rachelka
and thus learned more about her life. Born into a very
wealthy family, she had been in high school when the war
broke out. Her father was drafted into the army and was
never heard of again. Rachelka, her mother, and her little
brother, Haimke, moved to the ghetto, where her mother
suffered a breakdown. Sunk in a deep depression, she
would sit by the window for hours with a glassy stare in
her eyes, responding to nothing, not even to her own children. Finally, she even refused to eat. The entire burden
for the upkeep of the family now fell upon Rachelka, who
had to look after both her little brother and her sick
mother. One day she found her mother dead in her chair
by the window. Rachelka and her brother were all alone.

Whenever we received our daily bread rations at work, I couldn't help noticing Rachelka's inner struggle not to eat all of hers. She'd place the bread beside her and take tiny bites from it every now and again. She so wanted to leave some of it for her little brother, but, overcome by her own hunger, she rarely succeeded. When there was nothing left of the bread, I often saw her weeping softly to herself.

Rachelka was full of praise for her brother, who kept the house clean and stood for hours in the long lines. She kept inviting me to her house, and one day I came to see her. As soon as I reached the floor where she lived, I was aware of the familiar offensive odor. It positively hit me in the face when Haimke opened the door. I stepped back involuntarily on seeing the monstrous shape of the child, with his large head and tiny, feeble trunk. Haimke was seven but he looked no more than four or five. His round black eyes shone with the same peculiar luster I had observed in his sister's eyes. Only much later did I learn that this sheen was characteristic of all consumptives.

Rachelka brought me a chair, and I sat down to talk with Haimke, whose thick voice made him sound like a much older person. The boy told me about a rumor going around that the next monthly ration would include 100 grams of marmalade. He was very excited about the prospect of receiving this sweet. It was with a feeling of great relief that I left their place soon afterwards.

For several days after my visit, Rachelka failed to show up at work, and finally, I went to her home to find out why. She opened the door, and the stench coming from within the room all but overwhelmed me. I noticed a small heap on the floor covered with a blanket. Seeing me looking at it, Rachelka informed me dryly, "My little brother died yesterday afternoon."

Staring in fear at the small form under the blanket, I shouted, "Why didn't you tell them to take him away? Why are you keeping him here like that?"

"Look here, Salusia," she said in a hoarse tone of voice. "He's dead, and there's nothing I can do about it. But tomorrow the weekly ration is due. If I had reported his death yesterday, they'd also have taken away his coupons. This way, at least, I'll get an extra loaf of bread."

"And you're going to keep the corpse here until tomorrow?" I asked in horror.

"What else should I do? Forfeit the bread?"

Her questions gave me the answer I sought. I broke into a mad scramble to get away as fast as I could.

Another Ordeal

With Father in the hospital and me working, I naively assumed that I'd reached the end of my own troubles. But of course I was mistaken. The road before me was very long and the end not yet in sight.

The next crisis in my life began to unfold when I stopped by Father's place one day and found two envelopes shoved beneath the door. I wondered who they could possibly be from. Perhaps a sign of life from Aunt Tsesia? But that was unlikely since our contact with the outside world was completely cut off. I opened the envelopes with trembling hands and was frozen to the spot. They contained orders of deportation from the ghetto for Father and myself! In two days he and I were to report at the prison on Czarniecki Street.

I was shaking all over, but not because I feared leaving the ghetto. Far from it! I was only too eager to get out into the countryside; perhaps we'd see Aunt Tsesia, Uncle Shimshon, and my cousins again. But we couldn't leave now. When Father was well enough to undertake the journey, then we would be glad to go. Only yesterday I heard from the gatekeeper at the hospital that Father had got out of bed for the first time and was now learning to use his legs again, just like a baby.

With the deportation orders in my hand, I rushed to the hospital. The receptionist set my mind at ease by assuring me that Father would get a letter from the doctor recommending a temporary exemption and that I would be exempted as well. It was inconceivable, he said, that they would send a child away all on her own.

The next day I reported at the office at the *Sonderkom-*

mando with the doctor's letter. Father's deportation was put off on the spot. Mine was not. In tears I tried to explain that I wasn't asking for a cancellation but for a temporary delay. I assured them that Father's health was improving and that he'd be fit by the time the next transport was due. Then we could go together. Surely the policemen could understand that I was my father's only child and if I weren't there when he returned from the hospital, it would be the end of him. But nothing could make them change their minds. I could fill in a form requesting a delay, they said, but if the reply did not come in time, I had to report for deportation as ordered. There was nothing they could do. Now would I move aside to make way for the next applicant in line?

My knees were buckling under me as I made my way to Aunt Hanushka's. I won't go, I said to myself. I won't leave Father behind! I'll skip this transport, and then they'd have to let me take the next one. Father would be quite well by then, and we'd leave together. I knew that by doing this, I'd forfeit my ration coupons, since all prospective deportees were immediately struck off the list. But I wouldn't let that stop me; I was resolved not to budge without Father.

When I told Aunt Hanushka and Uncle Abraham of my plan, they agreed. "As long as we're around, you won't starve," Uncle Abraham said.

I knew that searches were conducted for all those deportees who didn't show up as ordered, but I wasn't scared. They wouldn't be able to trace me so easily, I reasoned, since I was hardly ever at Father's place. The next morning, the day I was to report for deportation, I passed by the house but found the entrance sealed by two red blotches of sealing wax affixed to both ends of a strip of white paper. I went on to the police station to inquire about my application for a delay. The answer was negative. Perhaps it would come the next day, but meanwhile, they reminded me, I was to report at the assembly point without delay. Of course, I had no intention of doing that.

The next day I went to the workshop and found that a policeman had been there looking for me after I failed to report for deportation. My fellow workers had tried to explain that I was only a child and that my father was sick in the hospital, but the policeman was under strict orders to track me down and bring me to the assembly point. Then they tried to put him off the scent by pretending ignorance of where I went after work. All the time, they had been in constant dread that I would turn up suddenly, as I had done now. My friends urged me to hide somewhere, and they promised to take my daily soup ration to Aunt Hanushka. (Lately we had been given soup instead of bread, a welcome change.)

Following their advice, I left quickly. I felt like a hunted animal: Father's place was out of bounds for me, the workshop forbidden territory, and I didn't dare to approach the hospital. There was danger everywhere. I finally went to Genia's attic, where I spent most of my time playing with little Rishia, who was now already four years old. Uncle Abraham asked at the police station for news about my application, which was not forthcoming.

A few days later, I stopped at Aunt Hanushka's, and the door was opened—by a policeman. I was so stunned that I didn't immediately connect his presence with a search for me, nor did I heed Aunt Hanushka's desperate signals warning me of the danger. When the policeman asked for my name, I unsuspectingly gave it. Only on seeing his eyes widen did the truth dawn on me, but by then, it was too late. The policeman could barely hide his own confusion. It had never entered his mind that it might be a child he'd been sent to find.

Aunt Hanushka sank on her knees before the man, telling him in a tear-choked voice that I was an orphan whose father was mortally ill in the hospital and that she was responsible to her dead sister for my well-being. The policeman was obviously flustered, but he said that he had no other choice but to take me along with him. He was deaf to my aunt's appeal as well as to my own plea that he tell his superiors he hadn't been able to trace me. The policeman simply repeated his story that he'd been commanded to track me down at all cost, even if it meant lying in wait for me throughout the night. These last words sent a shudder through me. They brought to mind criminals whom the police were determined to trap by any means necessary. But what had all that to do with me? What was I guilty of? Suddenly I felt a horrible fear.

The policeman told my aunt to gather my belongings together but to take her time, lest she forget something.

He would sit down and wait. When he saw my fellow workers bringing me the soup from the workshop, he was genuinely moved. But it was beyond his power to help me, he repeated. Weeping silently, Aunt Hanushka shoved into a knapsack whatever came into her hand, even the bread that happened to be in the house—her own and Uncle Hersh's. She didn't care what he'd do when he found out about it. With trembling hands, she braided my hair for the last time and helped me into my new coat. She wanted to tie a woolen kerchief about my head as a protection against the cold winds, but I refused it. Instead, I put on my beret from which the old high school emblem had been removed long ago. Aunt Hanushka was crying bitterly as she took leave of me.

In the street, people were startled to see a child carrying a knapsack and being escorted by a policeman. They all knew what it meant. They were used to seeing people being led away, often entire families, but a child alone was a rare sight. When we came near the hospital, I begged the policeman to let me ask the receptionist about Father's health and to leave word that I was about to be deported. The policeman didn't object. When we went inside, the receptionist stared at us as if unable to believe his eyes. He recognized me and understood now why I hadn't called lately. Turning to the policeman, he said he hadn't the heart to send me away without letting me take leave of my father. He would permit us to enter the ward although it was against the rules and might even endanger his own job.

The policeman and I entered a large hall filled with beds occupied solely by men. All eyes focused on us. Father's bed was vacant; he'd just gone out to the lavatory, someone informed us. The other patients knew at once who I was, for Father had often talked about me, his only child. I saw fear and sympathy in their eyes.

Then Father entered supported by a nurse; he was still unable to walk by himself. When he saw me standing in the middle of the hall with my knapsack on my back and a policeman at my side, he understood instantly. His face went white. He began to sway and would have fallen to the floor if the nurse had not been holding him up.

I ran forward and hugged him tightly. "Daddy! They're going to send me off all by myself. I don't want to go without you. Help me, Daddy! Don't let them send me away!"

Groans and weeping could be heard from all sides of the room. Father ordered the nurse to bring him his clothes at once. He was going away with me. Instead the nurse dragged him to his bed and forced him to sit down. She explained the obvious to him: he was incapable of taking even a single step by himself. But my father wouldn't listen. If his clothes weren't brought to him immediately, he said that he'd leave in his pajamas. No one would be allowed to take his only child away from him.

A doctor was called in quickly, and he told Father that if he tried to leave now, the diarrhea was bound to return and death could result. The doctor attempted to console Father by pointing out that his daughter was only being sent to a labor camp. She was healthy, and they were sure to meet again at the end of the war.

By this time, I had stopped weeping. I could see how weak Father was, and I tried to calm him down. "They're right, Daddy. You can't walk as yet. I'm healthy and can look after myself. We'll meet . . . after the war. Try to get well quickly for my sake. Go and see Aunt Hanushka often and talk with her about me."

But Father refused to listen. He struggled with the nurse and the doctor until they finally forced him down on his bed and gave him an injection. I left the hospital with shaking knees, the tears drying on my face.

When we arrived at the gate of the prison courtyard, the policeman handed in the search warrant together with his "delivery." We entered, and the gate closed behind us. The courtyard was teeming with men, women, and children huddled together in family groups and sitting on their baggage. I stood apart, watching the scene. Soon I saw several policemen entering the courtyard. One of them stood out because of his smart uniform and his epaulets studded with stars. Moving about energetically, he barked out orders that were obeyed with abrupt salutes. Suddenly the policeman's eyes came to rest on me out of the more than 5,000 people there at the time. His gaze swept the entire courtyard and then once again settled on me. Finally, pushing aside the people around him, he walked up to me.

"What's your name?"

"Sara Plager."

"How old are you?"

"Fourteen."

"Who are you with?"

"No one," I said. I told him about my situation, and the policeman who had brought me confirmed the fact that my father had been unable to accompany us. The officer gave his subordinate a tongue lashing for not having informed him and then led me from the courtyard. He took me into a large room, where he sat down behind a desk littered with paperwork. After scribbling something on a sheet of paper, he stamped and signed the document with determined movements. He handed it to me with the words "You're released. Produce this form at the exit. There you'll get bread coupons and a two month's *ratzia*. Remember me to your father and may God restore his health."

In a daze, I thanked the policeman. I should have gone down on my knees and kissed his feet, for through his intervention, I had been born again. I learned later that he was the head of the *Sonderkommando*.

With the precious piece of paper in my hand, I walked toward the courtyard gate. Its bolts were withdrawn, and I stepped into freedom—freedom within the ghetto! So elated was I that, oblivious of the weight of my knapsack, I ran straight to the hospital. Again the receptionist could scarcely believe what he saw. His eyes filled with tears.

"Go on! Run to the ward but don't burst into it. Enter it quietly," he instructed me. I ignored his warning and burst into the ward like a whirlwind.

"Daddy! They released me! Daddy, I'm free!"

Father sat up in bed, as did most of his fellow patients, and cried out, "Salusia, my child!" He rose and ran toward me unassisted. We hugged and kissed and wept tears of happiness.

From the hospital I ran to Aunt Hanushka's. I found my aunt lying in bed pale-faced, with closed eyes. She had caught a glimpse of me from the window but had feared that it was an hallucination. Only when she saw me before her in the flesh did she believe. Aunt Hanushka began to laugh and cry alternately and, in her excitement and confusion, kept calling me by my mother's name—"Mini'le, my little sister Mini'le." Uncle Abraham and his wife, Faiga, shared in the joy of my escape, and my reappearance at the workshop was greeted with shouts of delight and affectionate hugs. It was as if I had returned from another world.

Return to Life

After my miraculous escape, my life and the lives of my loved ones seemed brighter, at least for a while. It was around this time that Aunt Hanushka was finally able to get a job. At first I was delighted by this, for my dear aunt was wasting away before our eyes and desperately needed the extra food ration to help restore her failing strength. Aunt Hanushka's weakness and her physical appearance had put off most prospective employers, and it was with great difficulty that Genia had managed to find her a job at a metal plant. When I found out what kind of work it was, I trembled for her sake.

Aunt Hanushka would be employed in the ghetto transportation system. As I have mentioned, there were very few horsedrawn vehicles in the ghetto. In addition to the two used by Haim Rumkovski and Doctor Leider, there were only three others: the van that delivered the precious bread, the white ambulance that took sick people to the hospital, and the black hearse that carted the dead away. Horses were too valuable to be wasted on Jews; even horse meat for human consumption had become far too expensive.

The inmates of the ghetto were therefore compelled to supply their own horsepower by harnessing human beings to wagons. In this fashion, raw materials were delivered to the workshops, and vegetables and coal were taken to the supply depot and the distribution centers. People pulling wagons also disposed of our garbage and waste since the sewage system of the ghetto had ceased to function long ago.

The work that Aunt Hanushka had obtained was pulling

a wagon and delivering metal parts to various workshops. I saw her at work one day and was appalled at the sight. It reminded me of the time not long ago when I had seen Mrs. Rein, my former high school principal. I had remembered her as the elegant First Lady of our school, sprightly and energetic on her clacking high heels, but now she was dragging her feet along in squat wooden clogs. I caught a glimpse of her bloated face with the puffy bags beneath the eyes before I ducked into a doorway. I didn't want Mrs. Rein to notice me. Her appearance shamed me deeply, though to this day I don't know why I should have felt such shame on her account when my heart was weeping for her.

Now, on seeing Aunt Hanushka at her degrading work, I felt the same shame and looked around for a hiding place. At the same time, I thanked God that Mother was not alive to see what was happening to her favorite sister. This was the same Hanushka who had had all her costumes tailored in the big city of Lodz rather than in her small hometown, who spent a great deal of time and energy looking for a handbag to match her lizard-skin shoes. This was the same woman who advised her sisters in all matters of fashion and whose own elegant figure and perfect taste always drew the attention of other women.

Now at the sight of her, I prayed for the ground to open and swallow me up! She was wearing large flat shoes, much too big for her feet, and a long coat, both belonging to her husband. A wide woolen shawl was wrapped about her head, and her hands, once so beautiful and delicate, were muffled in rags to protect them against the frost. But worst of all—good God, how had it ever escaped my notice?—was her bloated face and swollen legs, the signs of a *musulman*! After she passed by, I remained as if rooted to the spot.

Aunt Hanushka's failing health worried me greatly, but I was cheered by Father's recovery. After many long months of fear for his life, he had returned home in a fairly good state of health. Though still pale, his cheeks were no longer sunken and even his gait was lighter than before. The doctors had wanted him to stay on at the hospital for at least another week to regain his strength by eating the hospital's nourishing food, but he had turned down their kind offer. So great was his longing to be with me that every minute spent in the hospital seemed like an eternity. When he came home, I moved in with him, deaf to Aunt Hanushka's pleas that it was too cold there and too far away from my workshop. I felt sorry for Aunt Hanushka and knew that she'd miss having me around. I solemnly promised that I would visit her every single day, but I had made up my mind to live at home with Father. We needed each other.

It was wonderful to be with Father. Once, when he asked me if I didn't regret living with him in the cold room, I almost laughed out loud. He still didn't know about Uncle Hersh's crazy fits and how much trouble they had caused me. Now all that—all the fears and hardships—were like a long nightmare finally over. I cherished every moment spent in Father's company, and my happiness was complete.

Two days after Father's return from the hospital, I was on my way to work when I saw people standing in little groups shouting and gesticulating excitedly. Some were weeping and wringing their hands. I approached to ask what had happened, and what I heard numbed me as if I had been struck by a heavy blow.

The previous night, several trucks had careened through the ghetto and had come to a halt in front of the hospital. A squad of German soldiers with fixed bayonets had leaped down and rushed through the hospital, dragging the patients out of bed, regardless of their conditions. Clad in nothing but pajamas or nightgowns, the men and women were pushed and prodded downstairs at the point of the bayonets and hustled into the waiting trucks, which then vanished into the night.

A few patients had retained enough presence of mind to jump out of the windows and escape the soldiers' clutches. But those leaping from the upper stories were either killed by the fall or finished off by bullets. In the confusion of the swift raid, several doctors and nurses were also caught and whisked away with their patients.

I ran back home as fast as I could and threw my arms around Father's neck. On hearing the terrible news, he turned pale and stood motionless, as if he couldn't take in what I had just told him. Finally he said, "And to think that I might have been one of them if I had let the doctors persuade me to stay another week!" Father sank down heavily on the bed, covered his face with both hands, and spoke as if to himself. "All those who were with me for the last two months—taken away to who knows where! What will become of them? Many were already on the road to recovery. We dreamed together about the end of the war—we were like one family—they wept with me when you were taken away and shared my joy when you were restored to me. Where are they all now?" Father cried as he named his friends one by one.

He had planned to look for work that day, but now he didn't have the strength to go out. I went to my workshop, where the "hospital deportation" was the sole topic that day, as it was all over the ghetto. Everyone was dazed and in anguish over the fate of the deported patients. Those whose relatives and friends had died leaping from the windows could do nothing but weep and bury their dead. People were numbed by the cruelty of the action and its suddenness. The unexpectedness of it! Such things had never happened before.

In the past we had all but resigned ourselves to the deportations from the ghetto, not doubting for a moment that those people were all being sent to labor camps. We were lulled into believing it because of the twelve kilograms of luggage that each deportee was allowed to take along. Those people were generally healthy, strong enough to work. But this particular deportation smacked of something altogether different: the people were invalids and they had been snatched away half-naked in the dead of night. Our suspicions were aroused. Where were they being sent to? What was being done to them? Such questions were on everyone's lips, but so far no one could answer them. The answer, when it eventually reached us, was that the Germans made no distinction between the invalids and the healthy. All, without exception, were destined to end up in exactly the same way.

It took some time before the ghetto recovered from the blow of the hospital deportation and a while before Father regained his own bearings. But life had to go on. The days and weeks dragged, but they passed. Father was working again, loading coal, potatoes, and vegetables onto wagons pulled by others. He was contented and thanked God for being well and having me with him again, but he hadn't regained his strength yet and greatly overrated his physical fitness.

At home Father tried to make up to me for all I'd had to endure in his absence. He coddled me and wouldn't let me do a thing. He always lit the stove and dragged home the coal ration all by himself, reminding me with a smile of that time when the sack had ripped and all the coal had scattered along the way. He even washed my hair and braided it for me. I was his little girl once again. Every now and then he'd bring home a few carrots or potatoes to augment our meager monthly ration. From these he'd make a vegetable broth, which we then had as a third meal. Since we worked different shifts, we usually didn't meet during the day, but there would often be a saucepan of soup kept hot for me beneath the feather quilt on the bed. This hiding place served a double purpose: the soup stayed hot and the bed warmed up a little.

By now the spring of 1942 had come and gone, and the war was still going strong. Hitler's much-vaunted blitzkrieg had turned into a protracted affair. In the ghetto, our lives were much the same, except that now nobody dared to be hospitalized. People preferred to die at home in their own beds rather than risk another hospital deportation.

Due to our two miraculous escapes, Father and I began to believe that we were destined to stay alive and to survive the evil days that the future was sure to bring.

The Children's Hall

Haim Rumkovski, the "king" of the ghetto, loved children with all his heart. Childless himself, he had been known as a patron of orphans before the war. Even here in the ghetto, their welfare was one of his major concerns. Rumkovski set up orphanages and saw to it that their inhabitants had an adequate supply of food.

Of course, our king had broken his promise to the high

school students, most probably for lack of any other
choice. Though absolute king of the Jews in the ghetto, he
was nothing but a pawn in the hands of the Germans. He
was successful, however, in his efforts to help the young
working people of the ghetto. In one of his speeches,
Rumkovski expressed his sense of obligation to us working
youngsters and announced that he had succeeded in reduc-
ing our workday to only five hours. He had also arranged
for special juvenile halls to be set up in the various workshops, where young people would work together and spend
their spare time in social activities.

A hall was soon set up in my workshop, and the new
plan instituted. It was a welcome change for me to spend
at least a part of the day in a lighthearted and pleasant atmosphere with girls of my own age. The long hours I
spent sitting between Mrs. Frankel and Rachelka had become an insufferable burden for me. Both women were
immersed in themselves, working the whole day without
uttering a word. The work itself had become tedious, and
time dragged by at a snail's pace, each day seeming longer
than the previous one. It had a depressing effect on me,
and I could barely wait for the workday to end.

All that changed, however, with the opening of our hall;
here everything was cheerful and carefree since most of us
were still full of zest for life. Although hunger, disease,
and bereavement had struck every home, most of the
young people in the workshop still had their parents, sisters, and brothers around them. Above all, we were young
and able to take the hardships in our stride and still look
hopefully toward the future. Laughter and singing could
now be heard coming from our hall, mingling with the
constant humming of the sewing machines in the back-
ground. The happiest hours of our lives during that period
were spent at the workshop where we could, at least tem-
porarily, put the misery and squalor of the ghetto out of
our minds. There was, however, one snag to this arrange-
ment. Our daily soup portion was considerably reduced—
less hours of work, less food. Instead of three-quarters of a
liter a day, we now received only half a liter.

The change in our working day meant that Salek and I
now had more time for our studies. My ambitious cousin
hadn't given up his plan of catching up on what he had
missed during the past semesters of a normal school year.

I also dropped in on Aunt Hanushka more often, taking care to do so only when Uncle Hersh was away at work. The days passed pleasantly because I was surrounded by those I loved and who loved me.

Before long, the youngsters of our workshop became a close-knit group, and our hall, named after its manager, Gonik, made quite a name for itself. It became a showcase for all other workshops, and delegates from the Red Cross, as well as German employers from other workshops, were brought to observe us at our recreation.

There was a marked difference between our workroom and that in which many married women and mothers of small children worked. There, constant anxiety for hungry families or aged and ailing parents had silenced both song and laughter. Our spirits were higher and our productive capacity far greater than theirs, though we were working only five hours a day. When we youngsters ran down to get our daily soup rations, the stairs shook beneath our feet. Our exuberance could be seen even while we stood in line before the hatched window. There the first one to receive her portion of soup would pass along word of how many pieces of potatoes she had been "blessed with" that day. The announcement was hailed with shouts of delight, and the news of good fortune passed from mouth to mouth all along the line, like a game of "broken telephone."

My closest friends in the workshop at this time were two girls of my own age, Rosie and Tola. The three of us had very similiar backgrounds as the only children of well-to-do parents, but the gap between them and me was wide indeed. They were still the pampered darlings of their parents, while I had lost my mother and had gone through a great deal of suffering during Father's illness. I felt as if I were much more mature than my two friends. True, Tola had lost her father, but her mother was still young and healthy and did her best to shield her daughter from the wretchedness of ghetto life. Similarly, Rosie's parents, who had arrived here from Berlin less than a year ago, still coddled her like a baby. In Germany the Jews had been separated from the "pure Aryan race" several years previously, but not until their transfer to the ghetto had they known what hunger was. Rosie's parents, like all other new arrivals, were forced to trade their surplus clothes and valuables for extra food.

Rosie had a vivacious personality that affected all those around her. She loved to dance and sing, and she knew many German songs. When I heard Rosie's music, I couldn't help wondering how the people we saw swaggering about us could have created such sensitive and gentle love songs. Rosie still sang the old songs as they were sung in the past. The Nazis had now revised many of them and had composed others that vaunted their own superiority and strength and put "Deutschland Über Alles."

Rosie and I became close friends. I was charmed by her singing and her attempts to speak Polish, which sounded like childish babble. In fact, all her actions were childlike, and she often turned to me for advice and assistance. She would not sing or dance for anyone unless she first sought my approval.

But the poisonous spirit of ghetto life didn't spare anyone, and soon Rosie and her family were infected by it. Like most other refugees from Germany who had never been exposed to hunger and privation, Rosie's father was unable to make his loaf of bread last for more than four days of the week and was therefore forced to go hungry until the next ration. Unable to see him suffer, his wife and daughter would share their loaves with him though they themselves were left without any bread for several days. Consequently, their home life was torn by bitter and humiliating quarrels. Rosie often spoke of the change in her father, who had formerly been a jolly and good-natured man but had now become surly and even violent. She was greatly disturbed by it all, and I could often see tear stains on the shiny pink material that passed through her sewing machine.

The Big Hunt

In the ghetto we had no need of a calendar. Our lives
were divided into periods based on the distribution of
food: bread every eighth day, the *ratzia* once a month.
Each day fell into two parts: before and after we received
our soup. In this way the time passed. But there were in-
terruptions in the dull routine of our existence. Every now
and again the Germans electrified us with some new
shock, jolting us out of our lethargy and plunging us into
a state of utter consternation. Such an event occurred in
September 1942. It began with the *Shpera* (curfew) and
lasted nine terrible days. Even now a tremor runs through
me when I recall that time—nine days that seemed more
like nine years, like ninety years!

In ancient times, the Jewish people held captive in
Egypt saw their first-born male children slaughtered.
Thousands of years later, the Jews of the ghetto were ordered to deliver into the hands of the Germans all their
small children—their most treasured possessions. The sick
and the aged were to be taken as well, all to an unknown
destination. Everyone was told to remain indoors and
await the call of a policeman who would come with a list
of those who were to be handed over. A strict curfew was
instituted, and violators would be shot on sight.

The suddenness of the action caught us all off guard
and gave us no time to collect our thoughts or to defend
ourselves. Trucks full of armed troops were already
speeding through the streets of the ghetto, sealing off an
entire quarter at a time. The areas in which the searches
had not begun were guarded by armed patrols. Not a soul
was allowed to enter or leave. In spite of the severe curfew restrictions, however, hair-raising rumors about the
savagery of the action spread through the ghetto.

A policeman with his list would enter a home to take a

child into custody. Intimidated and confused, the mother
would hand over her son or daughter, often no older than
two, three, or four. The moment the deed was done, the
woman would suddenly realize what was happening. She
would dash after the policeman and try to wrench her
child out of his grasp. But by then it was too late, for the
policeman was already out in the street. There one German trooper would hold the mother back at bayonet point,
while another would snatch her child and shove it onto the
waiting wagon. The wagon would move off and soon disappear from sight. Then the crazed mother would claw at
her face, clutch at her hair, scream, wail, but all in vain.
Her child was irretrievably lost to her.

In some homes, parents managed to conceal a child before the policeman came, hiding it in a wardrobe, under a
bed, or beneath the feather bedding. Even the smallest
toddlers, sensing the danger, understood that they mustn't
cry. Many infants died of suffocation in their airless hiding
places.

The Jewish policemen conducting the search were in a
terrible predicament. Failing to produce a child on his list
might mean instant death for a man. But the very moment
that he was ferreting a child out of its hiding place, another policeman was conducting a search for his own children! There were several policemen whose minds became
unhinged in the course of their grisly task. Others, encoun-
tering the terrified eyes of their little victims hiding in
some dark corner, pretended not to have seen a thing, re-
porting back that the children simply couldn't be found.
But this effort didn't succeed, for it failed to produce the
stipulated number of children.

Changing their tactics, the Germans eventually sent
their own soldiers to carry out the task. The German
troops cordoned off house after house, burst into every
room, searched in every corner, stuck their bayonets into
featherbeds and pillows. They dragged the screaming and
struggling tenants out into the courtyards where other soldiers with fixed bayonets kept them at bay. Inside the
houses the search went on. The children were tracked
down in their hiding places and flung outside, where many
stood looking around in dry-eyed terror. Only when they
were herded past their mothers would they start screaming
and shrieking, calling for help, for someone to save them.

A mother running toward her child would be hurled aside or finished off with a bullet. In some instances, a soldier "took pity" on a mother and pushed her onto the wagon together with her child. As soon as the wagon full of children had moved off, the soldiers began the next weeding-out operation. All the sick, the emaciated, and the aged were picked out of the group one by one and forced, with kicks and blows of rifle butts, onto other wagons already waiting for them.

When we heard what was happening, Father and I looked at one another in silence. I was no longer an innocent little girl who believed that all sinners would be punished or that the earth would open and swallow them up. The earth had opened up beneath us. We were the sinners for having been born Jews! I had stopped asking questions long ago for there was no one to answer them. I did not try to comprehend what was going on. It was all totally beyond reason. Father, too, was uncomprehending and stricken with terror. No longer could he tell me stories that ended happily.

On the third day of the *Shpera*, rumors reached us that the operation was now centered in the area surrounding the Baluti Market. My heart missed a beat. I looked at Father and knew that the same terrifying thought had flashed simultaneously through both our minds. Aunt Hanushka! She was so sick, so frail . . . "Daddy," I said, "I've got to go to Aunt Hanushka's."

His eyes opened wide in terror. "Have you gone out of your mind? The curfew—there are German patrols at every corner!"

"I know, but I can't stand it any longer! I've got to see if . . . if . . . everything's all right over there."

"Don't be stupid!" Father said in a high-pitched voice. "You'll get caught instantly. Besides, there's nothing you can do."

"Daddy, I can't help myself. I've got to go. Don't worry," I said to calm his fears. "I won't get caught. I know many secret passages and shortcuts that I used to take when school was in the field of Marisin. I'll be back right away. There's really no need for you to worry."

Ignoring Father's pleading, I ran out of the house. The streets were deserted. Fast as a cat, I scurried from court-yard to courtyard, peering out in both directions at each gate and then dashing across the street. In a few minutes time, I was knocking at Aunt Hanushka's door. It was opened by Uncle Abraham. There was no need for him to speak—his pale face and red eyes told me everything.

Uncle Abraham nodded his head, and then the words poured from his mouth. "There was nowhere for her to hide . . . they appeared so suddenly. We did everything we could. She had dressed up in her best clothes and put on several blouses to make herself look heavier. She rouged her cheeks with beet juice, and we all stood like a wall around her. Nothing helped. The soldiers pushed past us. They dragged her out." I could see Uncle Hersh sitting on the bed, staring into space with glazed, unseeing eyes.

With slow, heavy steps I left the house. In a daze, I found myself walking down the middle of Dvorska Street. An echo like the dull roar of a wave rose within me, increasing in intensity until it burst forth in a long wail. "Mummy, Mummy!" Then the sound of excited shouts and the thudding of horses' hooves wrenched me back to reality. A Jewish policeman appeared out of nowhere and shoved me through an open gate into a courtyard. "What do you think you're doing," he bawled at me. "Run quick! Hide somewhere!"

I had barely managed to duck into a urinal in the courtyard when I saw two wagons full of little children drive past the open gate. It was a scene that I shall never be able to erase from my memory. Many of the children were dressed in their holiday best, the little girls with colored ribbons in their hair. One might almost have thought they were being taken to some holiday celebration, but it wasn't a party or picnic they were headed for. That was obvious from the appearance of the soldiers with fixed bayonets sitting among them. In spite of the soldiers in their midst, the children were shrieking at the top of their lungs. They were calling out for their mothers.

Then the wagons were gone, and a stillness settled on the street. I stood a while longer, trembling all over, but dry-eyed, unable to weep. I, who used to weep at the most trifling thing, now held back my tears at the sight of such a terrible scene and at the knowledge that my beloved Aunt Hanushka had been taken away!

I didn't have to tell Father what had happened. The moment I entered, he looked at my face and took it all in at a glance. When I fell into his arms, he sat down and wept. I didn't. Only very late that night did my tears begin to flow freely. Father did his best to soothe me, talking about the end of the war when we'd surely see Aunt Hanushka again; about better times to come when we'd all be together and would forget these awful days. His words were unconvincing. I no longer believed them.

I did not sleep at all that night. Just before dawn, I got out of bed and looked down at Father, studying his sleeping features carefully. After he had returned from the hospital, he seemed to be strong and healthy again. Now, however, I saw that he was all skin and bone. He had weighed himself at work several days ago; the eighty kilograms he had weighed before the war had shrunk to a mere forty-five. And the Germans were taking away the sick and the starving.

Father awoke and opened his eyes.

"Daddy," I said, "I just had an idea. You know that house buried in wild grass at the end of our street? The one with broken doors and windows? It's completely abandoned. Nobody would ever look for us in such a hole. Let's go there, Daddy, and hide from the Germans, at least until the curfew is over."

Father's eyes lit up. "How odd," he said. "The same idea occurred to me at this very moment. I know the place. I don't think anyone will search for us in that tumbled-down shack."

Father hastily lit the fire. We still had a loaf of bread, some flour, and one head of kohlrabi left. I cut up half the kohlrabi and put it into a pot of water. Not waiting for it to cook completely, Father added half the flour. By then the sun was rising. We had to make haste—the hunt would begin again any minute. Taking the pot of soup and a quarter of the loaf of bread with us, we slipped out of the house. In the dim light of the dawn, we saw other shadows flitting past and disappearing in the gray mist.

When we reached the house, we found that all its staircases had been destroyed. Father constructed a makeshift ladder from a chair and a few boards, and we used it to climb up to the attic of the house, pulling the ladder up after us at each floor. Half the soup got spilled in the process. After reaching the attic, we sat down and huddled close to each other. The wind whistled and howled about us, carrying echoes of isolated machine gun fire and shrieking voices. Thus began our long spell of waiting.

The Hideout

The first day in our hideout dragged interminably. We ate our bread and what was left of the soup, but the hunger gnawed inside us. At nightfall we slipped back into our house. The following morning at the crack of dawn, we were back in the hideout with more bread and a pot of soup consisting of the other half of the kohlrabi and the remaining flour. Father had brought a hammer and nails along and put together a firm ladder. It was the fifth day of the *Shpera*, and we were still in hiding, hungry, frightened, and shivering with the cold. On the sixth day, no more soup was left. Of the remaining half loaf of bread, we took only a quarter with us and left the last quarter at home. Had we taken it along, we'd have finished it off there and then and would have had nothing at all to eat.

The hours stretched endlessly. By now the thudding of horses' hooves was clearly audible, as were the barked exchanges of the Germans, the screaming of people, and the crackling of rifle shots. That night, while slipping back home, we saw a horrible sight. Our neighbor had been shot dead. He lay open-eyed, sprawled across the footpath in a pool of black blood. Father pushed the body back against the wall of the house, pressed its eyelids shut, and covered it with a coat.

The next morning we took the last quarter-loaf of bread with us. Father also brought his prayer shawl, his phylacteries, and his book of Psalms. From the moment we entered the attic until we left it in the evening, he sat wrapped in his shawl, keeping up a continuous murmur of the Psalms.

It was seven days now since the big hunt had begun, and its end was not yet in sight. How much longer could it go on? I began to eat the last morsel of my bread, nibbling at it crumb by crumb to make it last another minute and yet another. If only I could scream out loud! But I mustn't do that. If I had been here all alone, I'd have jumped onto one of those wagons. Let them take me away! So long as they gave me something to eat, I wouldn't care what happened. But I wasn't alone—I was with Father. I had to hold out for his sake. After all, Father, too, was hungry but he suffered it in silence, without a complaint. In fact, he was ready to give me his last piece of bread, claiming to be better off without it since eating only aggravated his hunger.

That night at home, my sleep was troubled by nightmares. All the terrifying impressions of the last few days returned to haunt my dreams in a confused series of images: My Aunt Hanushka, harnessed to a cart, is dragged away by soldiers. A wagon full of children passes by and they push her toward it. I want to run and help her, but I am rooted to the spot—something keeps me tied down. I want to scream but can't make a sound. An old neighbor runs outside and struggles with the soldiers, who shoot him . . .

"Salusia! Salusia! Wake up! Stop shouting!"

I opened my eyes and saw Father bending over me, shaking me awake. "You were screaming in your sleep. Come on, get up quickly," he said. "It'll soon be light."

Again Father took his prayer shawl and phylacteries, and again we hurried back to our hiding place. That day there was no food left, and a maddening hunger kept tearing at me. I cast about me desperately for something to eat and found it—plaster. I scratched and peeled dirty flakes of plaster from the wall and ate them.

Then I glanced at Father, who stood near me wrapped in his *talit*. Sun rays coming through an opening in the roof fell upon its ornate collar, which he had embroidered himself a long time ago. The gold and silver threads shone with multicolored light, a strangely exotic sight in this dark, cold place. It struck me that there was something very strange about Father's praying form, as if it were an apparition from another world.

Another world? What am I thinking? I mustn't think of

such things. Father was still part of this world, and he was all that I had left here. I gazed at him again. There was nothing about him that recalled the image of my once young and exuberant father, always laughing and joking and singing songs. I suddenly remembered his wonderful voice. When had I last heard him singing? And what about me? Could I be that same happy girl who had run home with two bunches of lilacs for Mother's Day?

"Daddy," I whispered, "will you sing me your songs again when the war is over?"

"Of course, my darling," he said in a weak voice. "Of course I'll sing them all again."

"But I'll be too big for you to sing me to sleep with lullabies."

"To me you'll always be my little girl."

That evening back in our house, Father sat down on the bed and started singing to me. His voice, though much weakened, was still beautiful. Overcome with pity for him, I wanted to tell him to stop singing and save his strength. But I couldn't say the words. Instead, I buried my head in the pillow and wept softly.

That night I couldn't fall asleep. The prospect of spending another hungry day in our hideout almost drove me out of my mind. Noticing that Father was also awake, I told him what had just occurred to me. I recalled that a *Hachshara* group had once raised vegetables in the fields of Marisin. Maybe I could go there and dig up something for us to eat.

"Don't be silly," Father said. "You wouldn't find anything there now. The place is nothing but a wasteland."

I wasn't convinced. I simply couldn't bear the thought of spending another hungry day up in the attic. Anything, even death, was preferable to that. I began to cry.

"Let me try, Daddy," I begged. "Even if I find nothing at all, at least I'll know that I've done something."

Never able to resist my tears, Father said that he would go there himself, though he thought it was sheer madness.

"No, Daddy," I objected. "You'll never get back before daylight. Let me go. I can run much faster than you."

I dressed in feverish haste and hurried outside. It was still dark. Groping my way along, I reached the desolate fields of Marisin just as the day was dawning in dull grayness. I walked onto the hard and barren earth. As I stood there, scanning the field for some sign of growth and ready to give up all thought of finding something to eat, I saw some figures ahead of me. They were stooping very close to the ground and seemed to be digging. I bent down and began digging with the spoon and knife I had brought along. The earth was very hard, but I scratched away with all my might. As I dug, I glanced about me. What did this scene remind me of? Poor people stooping low to the ground, scavenging for something to eat? Then the story of Ruth and Naomi from the Bible sprang to my mind. But they had come to a field full of the gleanings left behind for them by the reapers, whereas we had come to a barren field, land on which there was nothing left at all.

By now the hole I was digging was quite deep, but I still hadn't struck anything worthwhile. Since the bent forms around me were still burrowing away stubbornly, I took it as a sign that there must surely be something there and redoubled my efforts. The grayness of the dawn was beginning to brighten when suddenly I struck something. It was a root. I dug frantically around it. My hunch had not let me down after all! I pulled hard and finally held in my hands a root with several potatoes clinging to it—very small ones, but potatoes nevertheless. Now the grayness had dispersed completely and, along with it, the dark forms around me. Another day was coming—another day of treacherous brightness. But at least we would have food.

Elated with my find, I ran home. Father lit the stove while I washed the root and the potatoes and chopped them up finely. After boiling them for a while, we had a wholesome and nourishing soup. When we ate it in our hideout, it affected us like an invigorating tonic. The day did not seem to drag as usual, and that evening we learned that the curfew had been lifted. The nine days of terror were over.

After the *Shpera* ended, people began to emerge from their houses. At first they avoided looking at one another, too stunned as yet to take it all in. It was as if a huge tidal wave had washed over them, or a typhoon had been raging all around. Not yet daring to walk the streets freely, people scuttled past furtively, keeping close to the walls of the houses, their heads bent, their eyes downcast.

Hardly a family remained unscathed by the storm that

had passed over us. In our workshop, there were many vacant places and machines standing idle, orphaned, it seemed, by the women who had operated them. None of the younger workers was missing, but many of their dear ones had been taken away. When I went into the workroom of the older women, I saw that the machines of Mrs. Frankel and Rachelka stood idle. A fellow worker and neighbor of Mrs. Frankel had seen what had happened to her and told me about it.

Mrs. Frankel had concealed her little boy beneath the feather bedding around which she had sewn the linen bed casing. She had piled some more bedding and a pillow on top of it. In the course of his search, a soldier poked his bayonet through the pile, flinging the pieces about the room. The child was injured in the process but didn't let out a sound. Giving up his search, the soldier was about to leave the room when his eyes fell on a pool of blood on the floor and more blood dripping from the bed. He returned, ripped the casing apart, and pulled out the bleeding boy, who was too terrified to cry. When Mrs. Frankel saw her child being dragged outside, she leaped forward and began to struggle with the soldier, undeterred by the pistol aimed at her breast. The frenzied woman would not loosen her grip on him, and he finally flung her like a sack onto a wagon. Mrs. Frankel's mother, too, was taken away. Now her husband remained all alone in the ghetto.

No one knew what had happened to Rachelka, so after work I went to her place. There was no response to my knock, but the door was unlocked. The familiar, unpleasant stench still lingered in the dark room. Everything there was topsy-turvy, but Rachelka was gone. I went to a neighbor, who told me that when Rachelka had been driven outside and lined up with all the other tenants of the building, she stepped out of her row and climbed voluntarily into the wagon. Before it set off, she stood up, turned around and, with a smile spreading over her face, waved good-bye to all her neighbors in the courtyard. She was happy to be taken away.

Immediately after the *Shpera*, the food ration in the ghetto was increased dramatically. I saw posters plastered on the walls announcing that the next distribution of potatoes would be thirty-nine kilograms a person! Such a large quantity had never been handed out before. At our work-shop the soup ration, too, was greatly increased because there were fewer people to share it. Never before had we eaten so well as during the days following the *Shpera*. We no longer counted the pieces of potatoes in our soup, and even at home the broth was thick and wholesome.

All of this made me think of an incident in the novel *All Quiet on the Western Front* in which, having lost half of their comrades on the battlefields, the surviving soldiers fall joyously upon the double portion of food left to each man. When I first read the book, such behavior had been incomprehensible to me. Now I understood it.

The weeks that followed the *Shpera* were dreary and oppressive. Now even Salek gave up his studies. He saw no point in returning to his books after what we had all gone through. In our workroom silence reigned; nobody laughed, nobody sang. The only sound heard was the purr and hum of the machines, and many of the girls could be seen weeping silently over their work. It was I who started singing again, at first softly to myself and then louder. Astonished looks were turned on me, but gradually other voices joined, a few at a time, until in the end everyone was singing *Der Veg Forois* (The Road Ahead), a song we had learned at our workshop "club." We sang with tears streaming down our faces.

> *The road ahead is our destination,*
> *And hope is our brother.*
> *The whole world is like a boat*
> *That we must row ashore.*
>
> *Although today is dark,*
> *Our goal hidden in clouds,*
> *The sun will rise tomorrow*
> *And life will be renewed.*

As the days passed, people began to notice that it had been quite a while since Haim Rumkovski was last seen walking about the streets of the ghetto. This was out of keeping with his habit of appearing in public each time our food ration was increased or augmented by something new. At those times he used to be everywhere, making speeches promising further improvements, spreading encouragement about him. Now, it was as if the earth had swallowed him up.

There were rumors that Rumkovski had fallen ill or that the *Shpera* had caught him unaware. Perhaps he had been duped by his German masters, who had kept him in the dark about their plans. When the blow fell, its suddenness and savagery must have struck him like a bolt of lightning. He had been so proud of his role as protector of all the children in the ghetto.

1943

My Illness

After the *Shpera*, life in the ghetto returned to its usual
routine, although those terrible events remained vivid in
our memories. Several months later, on one of the last,
beautiful days before winter finally set in, I decided that
our room needed a thorough housecleaning. While at work,
I went over in my mind what I had to do, and when my
shift was over, I set out on my way home along Dvorska
Street. But something seemed to be wrong. A route that
never took me more than twenty minutes to travel now
stretched endlessly ahead of me, and I regretted not having taken the shortcut through the courtyards. By the time
I reached home, I felt unusually tired. I began to air out
the bedding but had no strength to open the window. So I
started sweeping the room—it seemed to have grown to a
gigantic size. Finally I stopped sweeping and lay down on
the bed.

When Father returned from work in the evening, he
found me lying in bed, unconscious, my face a flaming
red. When he took my temperature, the thermometer registered 106° F. Dr. Kshepitzki was called in and, after
one glance, diagnosed typhoid fever. Father was deeply
alarmed. He stayed away from work for the next couple
of days and tried to give me the care I needed, but he had
no idea of how to handle this new situation. Father was
afraid to leave me alone at home, but he had to return to
work or he would forfeit the additional bread ration.
Besides looking after me, he also had to stand in line for
the *ratzia* and the bread, and then do all the cooking and
cleaning at home.

As for myself, I lay in a coma most of the time. I was

racked by a maddening thirst, and I suffered from hallucinations, one of which I remember to this day. It began with me lying in bed reading, waiting for Father to finish cooking some soup. When it was ready, he propped me up and began to feed me the soup, which was very tasty. Suddenly it wasn't my father I saw in front of me, but Hitler. Hitler was sitting on my bed feeding me soup! I was filled with rage.

"You!" I shouted. "You dare to come here and sit on my bed! You think you can buy me off with your soup? I'll kill you first! There! Take that!"

And the plateful of hot soup flew straight into Father's face.

Several days after this terrible dream, I was lying in bed, only half-conscious. I heard voices but couldn't seem to open my eyes. It was Dr. Kshepitzki talking to Father.

"Mr. Plager," I heard him say, "you've got no other choice but to take her to the hospital. It may be her only chance for survival."

"I can't do it, Doctor," Father replied. "What if they deport all the patients again? What if they come in the dead of the night like that other time? Isn't there another way?"

"There's nothing more I can do, Mr. Plager," Dr. Kshepitzki said in a calm but determined voice. "Nor can I assure you that another deportation won't happen. That would be too great a responsibility. Though I quite understand your fears, I feel it my duty to warn you. If she were my child, I'd take her to the hospital without delay. She'll never get well in this freezing room with its ice-covered walls. She's in need of proper medical care, hot fluids, and she mustn't be left alone for even a moment."

I heard Father weeping as he followed Dr. Kshepitzki outside. The next sound I heard was that of the key being turned in the lock. I opened my eyes. I could see water dripping from the icicles on the walls of the room. My thirst became unbearable, as if a fire were burning inside me. A drink! I had to have a drink!

My thoughts focused on one thing: how to get water, how to quench the fire within me. I knew that there were two buckets of water standing on a low bench in the corner of the room. I had to get to them somehow. But hard as I tried, I couldn't get down from the bed, which seemed extremely high. I eventually managed to roll out of bed and stand up, but I immediately collapsed on the floor. Crawling on all fours, I reached the bench. After repeated efforts to get up, I finally succeeded in propping my elbows on the bench and lifting myself sufficiently to reach the rim of the bucket. I was then able to dip my face into it. Breaking the thin sheet of ice covering the surface of the water, I drank and I drank. It was so good! It put out the fire consuming me. I crawled back to the bed but lacked the strength to climb into it.

When Father came home some time later, he found me still lying on the floor. One glance at the broken pieces of ice floating in the bucket was enough to tell him what had happened. At his wit's end, Father decided at that point to have me hospitalized, realizing that all his efforts to help me had been in vain.

I was brought back to consciousness by a strong breeze sweeping over my face. I felt a gentle swaying motion and, on opening my eyes, saw Father walking alongside a stretcher that was carrying me away. When he noticed that I was awake, he stretched out his arms in a helpless way and said in a tear-choked voice, "Salusia, forgive me. I had no other choice. You're being taken to the hospital."

I wanted to soothe him, to tell him that I had heard him talking to the doctor and that I understood. I tried to smile at him and wave my hand, but instead I sank back into darkness. When I came to again, I was sitting up in bed leaning against a nurse and gazing at a curious-looking, hairless creature opposite me whose face was the color of chalk.

I spoke, forming the words with difficulty. "Who are you, little boy? What are you doing here?"

A gentle voice that seemed to come from far away said, "That's not a boy. That's you—you're looking at yourself in a mirror on the wall. We had to shave off all your hair. Look, here are your braids. Don't worry. Your hair will grow back again as soon as you get well."

From that time on, I lapsed in and out of consciousness while the doctor and nurses struggled to save my life. A rubber tube was attached to my arm and connected to a flask filled with a white fluid, hanging above my bed. Whenever I came to, I always found someone sitting at my bedside. Eventually, I became very familiar with my surroundings. My bed stood by a window through which I could see the high barbed-wire fence separating the hospital from the buildings beyond it, which were outside the boundaries of the ghetto. Many times on awakening, I'd see a small, pigtailed girl standing by the window of the house opposite. Sometimes her mother stood beside her feeding her some bread, an egg, or an apple. In the confusion of my mind, I would see myself standing at that window, with my mother feeding me. Then darkness descended on me again.

My hallucinations obscured the dividing line between fantasy and reality. Even during moments of lucidity, I was sure that a suitcase stuffed with food was lying beneath my bed. I would stretch out my hand and grope for it, and then, sinking back into delirium, I would go through the motions of opening the suitcase, taking out some bread and an egg, peeling the egg, and feeding myself with a spoon. Some of my ward mates were amused at my behavior, but others looked on sadly. So vivid was this image that for some time afterwards I couldn't get used to the thought that the suitcase was nothing but a figment of my sick imagination. Long afterwards I'd still stretch out my hand to grope for it beneath my bed.

For twenty-one days my life hung in balance. Every evening my temperature rose to 106° F. and on the twenty-first day I was still unconscious. In the evening of that day the thermometer registered over 107°F, and even the doctors abandoned all hope of saving my life. A doctor and two nurses were in attendance at my bedside that night when, all of a sudden, I sat up and looked smilingly about me. The doctor drew a sigh of relief. The crisis had passed. The joyful exclamation of the nurses—"She made it! She'll live!"—woke many of the other patients, who sat up in alarm.

I had survived my illness. The next morning I was told that Father had stood and prayed outside the hospital throughout the night. As soon as he heard of my turn for the better, he begged the doctors to let him take me home. They would discharge me in a couple of days, he was told, but I still needed more injections and nutritious food to help me get over my exhaustion.

But the joy at my recovery was short-lived. In the evening my temperature shot up again. Incredulous, the nurse thought that something must be wrong with the thermometer. But it soon became clear that I was suffering a relapse, for I lost consciousness and became delirious again.

This time I couldn't recall any of my hallucinations. From the others in the ward, I later learned that I kept begging Father to sing to me and that I sang a great deal myself. I carried on long chats with my mother, with my aunts Hanushka and Tsesia, and with my cousin Temcha. I quarreled with my cousins Moniek and Salek, who had become military officers while I, a lowly private, was compelled to salute them because I was a girl. Judging from my roommates' reports, my delirious ravings made no reference to the ordeals I had suffered in the course of the past three years. That most horrible, fear-haunted period of my life seemed to have been altogether erased from my fantasies.

This second bout of typhoid fever lasted another three weeks, and once again I recovered. Yet it was not the end of my hospitalization. One day during a routine checkup, the doctor noticed that my skin had turned yellow as a lemon. I had come down with jaundice. The doctor prescribed large quantities of sugar, a commodity hard to come by within the ghetto. Since the hospital was unable to provide me with the sugar, Father was asked to procure it for me. This he did by trading his daily bread ration for a small quantity of the precious sweet, which he would send me wrapped in a piece of paper. It didn't always reach its destination.

When I had gotten over the jaundice, I was suddenly assailed by unbearable pains that failed to respond to sedatives and injections. Then I broke out in boils the size of eggs, caused by the innumerable shots I had received. There was hardly a place left on my arms or legs for another injection. The doctors decided to lance all the boils. Just before I went under the anaesthetic, I overheard someone saying, "She's certainly lucky to have such a strong constitution. Otherwise she'd never have survived."

Finally, after three months in the hospital, I was on the road to recovery. Fed and pampered by the nurses, my health improved from day to day. As my appetite grew, my food ration was increased steadily and requests for more were never turned down. When I got out of bed for the first time, the sight of my legs shocked me thoroughly. They resembled two spindly sticks and reminded me of Rachelka's poor little brother. The nurses who had looked after me with such selfless devotion now began teaching me how to walk again.

When I left the hospital, I took a grateful leave of everyone there. The Red Cross carriage brought me home, and I got down unassisted and knocked on the door. Father was there waiting for me. We fell into each other's arms.

There was a gift waiting for me at home. At no other time in my life—neither before nor after the war—did a present delight me as much as the one I now received from my father. It was a new pair of shoes made of shiny brown leather. After looking at them lying on the bed, I rubbed my eyes in disbelief. Was this another one of those hallucinations?

"No, my child, you're not imagining things. Those shoes are real ones."

"But, Daddy, where on earth did you get them?"

Ever since the day we moved into the ghetto, I had owned only one pair of shoes. All my others had been forwarded to Warsaw along with our other belongings. Because I had grown a lot during the past three years, my shoes, down at the heel and battered by now, had become too small. They pinched my toes painfully, and in winter my feet froze inside them, but it was virtually impossible to acquire new shoes inside the ghetto. And now, a completely new pair, in my size, lay on the bed in front of me.

"Don't keep me in suspense, Daddy. Tell me how you got them."

This was the story Father told me. On the twenty-first day of my illness, the doctors had said that Father should expect the worst. They had lost all hope of saving my life. Throughout that night Father prayed for me, standing outside the gate of the hospital in the freezing cold. After a while he sat down on a stone and dozed off. Then Mother appeared to him in a dream, looking gay and beautiful, and she urged him to get me a new pair of shoes. She knew that there was no money in the house, but she pointed at my schoolbag and told Father to exchange it for a new pair of shoes.

Father awoke with the deep conviction that I would

live. He had already offered up a prayer of thanksgiving hours before the gatekeeper told him about my recovery. But the dream kept haunting him. Where could he buy shoes? How could he sell a schoolbag that was of no use to anyone in the ghetto? Then one day at his workshop, a fellow worker mentioned that he had been a cobbler before the war. Father suddenly understood the meaning of the dream. He offered the man a whole day's food ration if he could turn my schoolbag into a pair of new shoes. The man agreed.

"So here they are—new shoes made from the leather of your schoolbag, as suggested by Mother in my dream. I'll buy you a new bag after the war," he added, "and a nicer pair of shoes than these."

"No, Daddy. There aren't any nicer ones. I'll keep them to the end of my days."

Father sighed. "Those shoes are very precious. They stood there waiting for you throughout the days of your illness. When you had the relapse and the doctors doubted whether you'd pull through, the sight of those shoes gave me the courage to believe that you'd walk in them some day. Whenever your condition worsened, I'd pick them up, caress them, and talk to them."

"But Daddy, you traded your food ration for the shoes. What did you eat that day?"

"I forgot my hunger when I thought about the joy of giving them to you," he said.

It occurred to me then that there had been other times when Father had had to forego his bread ration. I recalled the small packages of sugar he used to send to me, each one of which was paid for with his much-needed daily bread. In my initial joy at being back home, I hadn't noticed how sick Father really looked. Now it came to me as a shock. His cheeks, which had filled out somewhat with the increased food rations after the *Shpera*, had sunken alarmingly. His beautiful brown eyes now seemed even larger, and they gleamed with a strange and unfamiliar light.

During the three months that I had been in the hospital, Father had gone through hell, fearing for my life both on account of my illness and because of his constant dread that I would be deported during one of those terrible nighttime raids. I had regained my health, but now Father

... A sudden fear took hold of me as I recalled a saying common in the ghetto:

Whoever saves another from illness must pay for it with his own life.

A New Home

During the time that I had been in the hospital, poor Uncle Hersh had died. After Aunt Hanushka's deportation, he had sunk into a deep depression, refusing to leave his bed or to eat. Uncle Abraham and Genia looked after him, but they succeeded only occasionally in making him take nourishment. In a short time, he lost his hold on life.

After talking the matter over with Uncle Abraham, Father decided that he and I should move into the room formerly occupied by Aunt Hanushka and Uncle Hersh. It was in a warm and comfortable apartment on the first floor, incomparably better than our damp and chilly room in Marisin. Uncle Abraham, Aunt Faiga, and Salek lived in one room of the apartment, and the third room was occupied by another family. Whenever a fire was lit in any one of the rooms, it warmed up the entire place.

At first, I was very pleased about Father's decision, not only because of the apartment's proximity to my workshop but also because the room in Marisin had been the scene of so much suffering. I was not happy, however, when I realized that Aunt Hanushka's apartment was a great distance from Father's workshop, which was in Marisin. But Father was determined.

"My mind's made up and that's that," he said decisively. "You're still very weak, and every additional day spent in this damp, cold room could cause irreparable harm. I prefer walking the extra distance to staying here. No," Father concluded, "we won't stay here another day. Tomorrow we're moving."

The following day we piled our belongings onto a huge

wheelbarrow and pushed it all the way to the new apartment. Yet even after the door had closed on the room on Marinarski Street, I could not forget our lives there; in my mind I saw Mother's poster, HOT COFFEE SOLD HERE, or the image of myself standing outside the window, trembling with fear that I would find Father lying in bed never to rise again. But these sorrowful memories faded once we were settled in our new room, which was as comfortable as we had hoped. There was no longer any need for us to keep warm by stomping to and fro for hours, fully dressed in coats and gloves. I had only a few minutes' walk to my workshop, but Father's work place was several kilometers away, and he had to rise very early each morning in order to get to work in time. Already greatly weakened by the sacrifices he had made for my sake, his strength diminished visibly with each day that passed.

The third room of our apartment was occupied by a family named Milewski, who had lived there since the ghetto had been closed in 1940. I was acquainted with two members of the family—Lola, a girl two years my senior, and Avramek, a boy my own age. Their mother, a widow, had died several months earlier, leaving the two children to shift for themselves. Now I found out that there was a third Milewski, a girl named Gucia, who was nine but looked no more than five or six. She was the youngest child of the family and had been living in an orphanage in Marisin until the time of the *Shpera*. Gucia had seen the German soldiers burst into the orphanage and had managed to lock herself inside the lavatory. Before the Germans succeeded in forcing the door, she had climbed up and wriggled outside through an opening at the top. She had been injured in dropping to the ground but had nevertheless dug a pit with her bare hands, lay down in it, and covered herself with dirt. When the wagons drove off, the terrified child ran to the nearby cemetery, where she hid for forty-eight hours, listening to the shrieking and rifle shots coming from the houses in the vicinity. On the third evening of the *Shpera*, she managed to drag herself to her family's apartment, reaching it only a short while after the soldiers had taken Aunt Hanushka away. Now she was living with her sister and brother in the room next to ours.

When I met Gucia and renewed my acquaintance with

Lola and Avramek, I saw the shock on their faces when they first set eyes on me. Although I had recovered from my illness, there had been a tremendous change in my appearance. I had always been considered a pretty girl, with thick, blond hair and a blooming complexion. Not even the hungry years in the ghetto had destroyed my looks. But my illness seemed to have changed me into something monstrous. My neck, legs, and arms were so thin that they looked like sticks attached to my body. Particularly repelling was the sight of my shaven skull, emphasizing the pallor of my gaunt face with its hollow cheeks. Though my hair had begun to grow again, it was short and bristly and stood on end like the spikes of a scared porcupine.

In the hospital where no one had known me before, my appearance had not aroused comment. The doctors and nurses had showered affection on me, partly because of the successful struggle they had waged to save my life. And Father, overjoyed at having me back with him, didn't seem to be aware of the immense physical change in me. I became acutely conscious of it myself, however, when I noted the looks of astonishment, pity, and even revulsion that I aroused in almost everyone else around me. Even Uncle Abraham, who gathered me into his arms affectionately, couldn't hide his shock when he saw me for the first time. Little Rishia, who had miraculously survived the *Shpera*, failed to recognize me altogether and denied ever having played with this person called Salusia in the past. At work the girls hastened forward in welcome but halted instinctively on seeing me. Only Rosie embraced and kissed me, and I saw tears in the eyes of several other fellow workers.

When my cousin Salek saw me, he squeezed my hand violently but was stunned into utter silence. Salek, too, had been changed by all that had happened in the past months. After the *Shpera*, he had tried to take up his studies again, but his heart was not in them after the cruel outrages we had witnessed. In fact, both my cousin and I felt it somehow shameful to be studying as if we were unconcerned with what had been going on around us.

Instead, Salek and I now held lengthy discussions about the rosy future he foresaw with the end of the war. The Germans, he argued, were suffering defeats on all fronts, and fortune had begun turning against them. With the news that German armies had been defeated by the Russian winter and forced to retreat like Napoleon's army in its own time, Salek's hopes soared high. He even indulged in dreams of a new and better world emerging as a direct result of the war: a world where no Jew would ever again be discriminated against; a world of absolute equality in which neither abject poverty nor fabulous wealth would exist. Salek's theories were incomprehensible to me. I had ceased to believe in the possibility of a world in which we Jews could ever be treated as equals.

Salek's attempts to convert me to his point of view had in them the zeal of a fanatic. He vowed to devote his entire life to the furthering of his lofty ideals. I, too, had a desire to reform this world, but how could it be done? When I thought of the Poles and their blind hatred for Jews, I was unable to believe in their essential humanity. And the Germans? There I stopped theorizing altogether.

Salek read voraciously on this new subject and made me read some of his books as well: books by Upton Sinclair and Ilya Ehrenburg, as well as political tracts written by Karl Marx and other socialist utopians. Salek found in these writers his most powerful allies. Each one of them, he tried to prove to me, had aimed at changing the existing order of the world and introducing total equality into it. According to them, it was so simple and easy. Salek believed in their words with all his heart.

"You can see for yourself," he would say, "that there are people who are still ready to lay down their lives for a future world of equality. And let me tell you that this great goal has already been achieved in the Soviet Union. You won't find anyone there who is suffering from hunger."

I envied Salek his deep conviction, but I could not share it.

Potato Peels

Once again there was widespread hunger in the ghetto, and once again we youngsters at the workshop were counting the pieces of potato in our soup. Immediately after the *Shpera*, no more musulmen had been seen in the streets; they had either died or had been deported. Now they began to appear again, with their puffy faces and enormously swollen legs.

At this time, we learned to prepare two new kinds of food, which we dubbed *babka* (ghetto cake). The first kind consisted of something resembling coffee grounds and was the only foodstuff in plentiful supply. The grounds were boiled in a small quantity of water until they solidified. The resulting substance had such a pungent smell and was so bitter in taste that one could scarcely bring oneself to swallow it. This *babka*, sweetened with some sugar or marmalade, was our standard food at the beginning of each month.

The second kind of *babka* consisted of the peels of rotten or frozen potatoes. After being washed thoroughly, the peels were brought to a boil in salted water, which was then strained off to reduce the rank taste. After a second boiling, they were mashed or minced into a kind of mush. This, too, had a pungency to it that left a smarting sensation in the throat and a musty taste in the mouth. But it stilled our hunger for a while.

Potato peels soon became a most coveted commodity in the ghetto. Hunger-crazed people could be seen rummaging for them in the garbage cans outside the big workshop kitchens, where the daily soup rations were cooked for the employees. When the demand for the potato peels increased, the kitchen workers no longer threw them out but gave them to anyone asking for them. This resulted in the formation of long lines outside the many workshop kitchens.

Father, too, would line up in the early mornings for a share of the peels, but he rarely managed to get any, for he usually had to give up his place to reach work on time. He always objected to my taking his place in the line, but one morning after he had left for work I decided to surprise Father with a dish of *babka*. On that morning and on several consecutive mornings, I stood in line until my feet turned into blocks of ice, but I always returned empty-handed. As soon as the kitchen door opened up, people pushed and pressed forward from all sides, and by the time I reached the head of the line, there wasn't anything left over.

Soon there were no more lines outside the workshop kitchens because the workers decided to keep the peels for their own families and their friends. Unfortunately we didn't have any friends among those working in the kitchens. A short time after that, the kitchen staffs were forbidden to take away potato peels. The ghetto doctors, aware of the peels' nutritional qualities, hoped that their vitamin content might reduce the swellings caused by malnutrition. Henceforth, those rotten, rank-smelling potato peels could be obtained only by prescription.

My father was soon in need of this repulsive medicine, for his health had taken an alarming turn for the worse. Every day, he'd get up earlier in order to reach work on time, and he would return home later every evening. His walk had become sluggish, and his strength was waning visibly. There was nothing I could do to help him. As I regained my own health, my appetite increased and I was always hungry. It was with great difficulty that we made our bread ration last for eight days. Only the dread of remaining without a crumb before the eight days were up prevented us from taking more than the exact amount each day. I would eat my portion just as it was; Father, on the other hand, broke his bread into tiny morsels and soaked them in a lot of water. This way, he said, it seemed more filling, while eating it plain only aggravated his hunger.

About this time, Father began complaining of a constant pain in his back. In addition, his legs had begun to swell badly. Dr. Kshepitzki found that his body contained

too much water; he drained several hypodermic needles
full from Father's back. Water in the back, the doctor explained, was a result of malnutrition and a common occurrence in the ghetto. The only cure for it was more food.
That was obvious even to us. Dr. Kshepitzki forbade Father to soak his bread in water and told him to avoid other
fluids. He also prescribed a kilogram of potato peels. As
the doctor was about to leave, he came back into the room
and added another kilogram of peels to the prescription.

Armed with the prescription, I took my place in line at
the kitchen the following morning but failed to obtain any
potato peels. They ran out long before my turn came. The
next morning I got up at dawn, even before Father left for
work, and this time I succeeded in procuring two kilograms of peels. Their nutritional value had become a
much-talked-of topic, and I put a great deal of faith in
their ability to cure Father's disease. The *babka* I prepared
from them had so repulsive a taste that I couldn't get it
down my throat, but Father ate it uncomplainingly. The
"medicine" didn't help him. The swelling in his legs increased, and walking became even more difficult for him.
In the mornings when he set out on the long walk to work,
I was full of apprehension for him.

Father struggled bravely against his weakness and refused to give in to it. He tried to carry on as best he
could, often remarking humorously that, instead of his legs
dragging him along, now it was he who dragged them
along. If he sat down, he couldn't get up again without my
help, so he avoided sitting unnecessarily. He seemed to be
fading away like a flickering candle. One day his legs
failed him altogether. The look in his eyes that day was
one of sorrow and deep despair; I shall never, ever forget
it. He was only thirty-nine years old.

Since Father was now bedridden, he forfeited the soup
ration he always received at work. I was desperate for, unlike the time of Father's first illness, I now had no extra
food to give him. I could only bring him half of my own
soup ration from work.

At lunch hour I was so hungry that the flavor of the
soup would set my head spinning. Before starting to eat, I
would count the potato cubes in the soup and divide them
into two equal portions. I'd eat very slowly to prolong the

relish, but before I knew it, I had finished my share. I'd take another spoonful, just a last drop, and was shocked to see how little was left. Good God! I had hardly tasted the soup and now the pan was nearly empty. Scarcely anything was left to take home to Father. Of course, Father never said a word in complaint. He knew how hard I struggled with myself. He understood and even reproached himself for depriving me of my share.

I recalled Rachelka and her daily contest with hunger. Now that I was in the same plight, I no longer thought ill of her. I, too, wept because I couldn't resist the temptation to take another drop of soup . . . and yet another. This daily war with myself nearly drove me crazy. Each morning I vowed anew not to exceed my share. The days on which I managed to keep my vow were happy ones, but whenever I failed, I would invariably burst into tears.

A Medicine Called "Wigantol"

It was not long before Father was completely unable to walk. Dr. Kshepitzki diagnosed "lack of calcium in the bones," another disease common in the ghetto. But there was a cure for it, a tonic called "Wigantol," which was purported to contain a lot of vitamins. The doctor assured us that one bottle of it would put Father back on his feet again. The trouble was that this medicine could be obtained only at the dispensary of the *Sonderkommando* station. The dispensary opened daily at 8:30 A.M., and despite the long lines, no more than twenty-five bottles were handed out each day. Dr. Kshepitzki prescribed this miraculous tonic for Father, with an additional prescription for two kilograms of potato peels. "Who knows if you'll manage to get it," he sighed. "People line up from five in the morning."

I looked at Father. His voice full of despair, he spoke of his sense of helplessness, of not being able to do the least thing for himself any more.

"If you could get the tonic for yourself, Daddy," I tried to console him, "you wouldn't need it."

With tears in his eyes, Father tried to persuade me not to attempt to get the medicine. "You heard what the doctor said about the long lines for only twenty-five bottles. What chance have you got? You're too small and still so weak from your own illness."

I didn't reply, for I had already made up my mind to obtain the Wigantol. The following day I was up before dawn, ignoring Father's protests and the snowstorm raging outside in the darkness.

"Don't try to stop me, Daddy. I'll be among the first there and I'll get that medicine. You'll see."

Still determined to dissuade me, Father reminded me that the gate on Sigorski Street, through which I had to pass, was locked at that hour. He was right, of course. The houses on Sigorski Street were considered to be within the ghetto, but the road itself lay outside it. Both sides of this road were fenced off by barbed wire, and in order to cross from one side to the other, one had to pass through gates, each of which was guarded by a Jewish policeman. The road itself was constantly patrolled by a German soldier. There was a bridge spanning the road that could be crossed unhindered, but it was too far away from where I lived. This left me no other choice but to try to get through the gates, which were opened to traffic only in the mornings.

Before I left, Father tried to make me take his portion of bread. Since he'd be sleeping most of the time, he said, he wouldn't feel hungry, whereas I would be standing in line for many hours and would need the extra bread. I turned down his offer and even left my own portion at home, afraid that if I took it along, I would eat it immediately and then have no solid food for the rest of the day.

I put on my coat and Father's fur cap with the earflaps, which completely covered my head. Outside, the stormy wind almost swept me off my feet. I groped my way along the dark streets until I reached the gate on Sigorski Street. A lamp was burning there, but the gate itself was still locked. The freezing wind kept roaring about me, and in order to remain on my feet, I had to hold on firmly to the grille of the gate. The police guard and the German soldier on patrol cast wondering glances at me through the driving snow. I explained to the policeman that I had to get to the *Sonderkommando* dispensary; he told me to go back home and return when they opened the gate. The German, who was pacing back and forth, came to a halt now and then in front of the gate to take a look at me. At length he asked the policeman what "that boy" was doing there in the middle of the night, but he resumed his beat after the policeman repeated what I had told him. Finally he returned to the gate and ordered it opened to let me pass through.

When I reached the dispensary, I discovered that I wasn't the only one there. Through the darkness I saw several forms huddled together on the top landing of the stairs. Those people lived across the road and could reach the place merely by crossing the bridge. There were only five of them, and I sighed with relief, knowing that I would be the sixth in line to receive one of the twenty-five bottles of Wigantol.

It was now 4:30 A.M. The snowstorm roared relentlessly. My teeth were chattering, and the frost bit at my fingers and my toes. I nevertheless considered myself lucky because my new shoes had kept my feet dry despite the deep snow I had waded through. Time crawled by at a snail's pace. Every now and then, a new snow-covered form popped up out of the darkness. One newcomer pushed himself into the line in front of me, claiming to have been there before I was. His claim was backed up by another man standing immediately ahead of me. He also said that he was keeping another place for a woman who had been there earlier as well. I didn't take it too hard, since I would still be only eighth in line. The line behind me grew longer. Then the woman arrived and, pushing herself in front of me, forced me two steps further down. Two more people claiming to have been here earlier pressed in ahead of me. Though I objected vehemently, they shoved me down. Again I stood two steps lower. Never mind, I consoled myself, I'm still tenth in line.

The man in front of me took out a piece of bread and

began to eat. I was tormented with hunger at the sight. It was only 6 A.M. now: two and a half hours to go before the dispensary opened. My feet were frozen, and I was shivering all over. What could I do to make the time pass faster? Perhaps I could entertain myself with thoughts about the past. A memory floated up in my mind of a time when my feet had been as cold as they were today. Now what was it? Of course! . . .

One winter day, a hundred years ago, Uncle Hersh presented me with a pair of skates manufactured at Genia's metal plant. I also received a skating outfit that included a sweat suit and special leather boots to which the skates could be attached. Father took me to the skating rink in Poniatovski Park for my first lesson. He sat in a sled with runners, which could be pushed over the ice, and I held onto the sled for support.

Skating was a great deal more difficult than I had thought. The blades of my skates were extremely sharp, and I had the feeling that I was walking on knives. The moment I entered the rink, both feet skidded in opposite directions, and I fell down. I had scarcely managed to stand up when I was down again. I was insulted when Father laughed at my predicament, but he urged me to try again and even talked about the day when I'd be dancing on ice like a ballerina. By the end of the first lesson, I had improved enough to do without the sled. Father was full of praise for me. I was pleased by my progress, but I was in tears because my feet were sore and frozen. At home, Mother rubbed my feet with snow, and a pleasant warmth began spreading through my body. After tucking me into bed, she brought me a cup of hot cocoa and sat near me for a while, kissing and caressing me. It was so nice . . .

Absorbed in my reminiscences, I had paid no attention to the people who were pushing themselves ahead of me. I now stood in thirteenth place but still wasn't unduly concerned. As the morning advanced, more and more people joined the line. Several placed themselves alongside me, while others were pressing forward from behind. Before long a double line had formed. At eight o'clock two policemen armed with clubs turned up and began introducing "order."

"What's going on here? A double line? Get off the steps,

everyone! Hey you, boy!" one of them shouted at me. "Down you go!"

"But sir, it's my place. I've been here since four in the morning. I was sixth in line!"

It was useless trying to talk to them amid the tumult and the jostling that was going on. I was constantly thrust downward until, in the end, I found myself at the bottom of the stairs. There was an uproar further along, and the policemen swung out with their clubs.

"Stop pushing, everyone!" they bellowed.

The door of the dispensary had opened up, and the lucky ones were already descending, each carrying a bottle of Wigantol. I looked after them enviously. By now it had become quiet, and the distribution was going in an orderly fashion. We moved up as the people at the head of the line came down. Another step and another. But the very moment I reached the door, it was banged shut in my face and the policeman announced the end of the distribution. He ordered us all to disperse and come back tomorrow.

At that point I started throwing a fit. I lunged forward toward the door, thumped against it with my fists, and kicked at it with my new shoes. I howled and I screamed. "I won't budge without the medicine! I was sixth in line and was constantly shoved down by others!"

I was beside myself with fury. The policeman grappled with me at first, then tried to persuade me to go home and return the next morning. But I grabbed hold of the door handle and screamed, "I'm not coming back tomorrow! The same thing's going to happen all over again! My father's terribly ill—he's stopped walking altogether. Only Wigantol can save him!"

Never in all my life had I bawled like that! I didn't know that I had it in me.

Just then the door to the dispensary opened, and another policeman came out. "Stop that racket once and for all! Get out of here, or else—" he shouted as he pushed me back.

I fell. But in my fall I had managed to thrust a leg through the opened door, and they were unable to close it again. As they tried to pull me away, I grabbed the door post and held on to it for dear life, yelling at the top of my voice, "It won't help you! I won't move without the

medicine, even if I have to stay here till doomsday! I was
sixth in line! The German soldier himself opened the gate
for me at four in the morning!"

Though my voice was getting hoarse, I kept shrieking
and struggling. At length, a man in a white gown came
out of the dispensary with a bottle in his hand. He walked
up to me and asked for my prescription. My hand
trembled as I held it out, and I almost snatched the bottle
away from him. Mad with joy, I ran down the stairs and
all the way home.

Father was astonished on seeing the bottle in my hand.
Not wishing to upset him, I didn't tell him about the manner in which I had obtained it. But my great struggle had
been worthwhile, for the Wigantol did, indeed, prove to be
a wonder drug. Four days later Father himself opened the
door when I returned from work. He was fully dressed
and radiant with happiness.

"Look at me! I'm walking again and will even be able
to run soon. I feel strong as never before!" he said, laughing and crying alternately like a happy little boy.

Everybody—Uncle Abraham, Aunt Faiga, Salek, Gucia,
Lola, and Avramek—gathered about us at the sight of
this miracle. Father strutted back and forth before them,
and I was like one hypnotized. Father was already full of
plans. In another two days, he'd finish the medicine and
return to work. Now, he said, he'd no longer have to deprive me of my soup ration.

But Father did not return to work as soon as he had
planned. Although he left the apartment, he still felt too
weak to undertake the long walk and returned almost immediately. If only Father's job were not so far away! I
tried to think of a way I could make things easier for him,
and suddenly I had an idea. I would ask Haim Rumkovski
for assistance! Our king had not been swept away by the
Shpera, and he was once again seen on the streets of the
ghetto. Surely he could get Father a job nearer home, in a
kitchen, perhaps, or a bakery. I determined to watch for
Rumkovski's carriage and to beg for his help.

Before I had a chance to turn to Rumkovski, the miracle wrought by the little bottle of Wigantol vanished like a
mirage. Once again Father's legs failed to hold him up,
and when he sat down, he was unable to rise again. Dr.

Kshepitzki prescribed another bottle of the medicine as well as two kilograms of potato peels. Once again I got up at the crack of dawn and was the first to pass through the gates at Sigorski Street. This time I didn't indulge in any fantasies but fought furiously for my rightful place in the line. True, I was forced down several steps by others who proved to be stronger, but I got my bottle. This time, however, it failed to have the desired effect. Father didn't leave his bed again. Full of despair, I again counted each spoonful of soup I took, but again I couldn't resist the awful temptation and often left Father far too little.

I began loitering about in the streets of the ghetto in the hope of catching sight of Rumkovski's coach. This time, I intended to beg for an increase in Father's food ration. "God," I prayed fervently, "give me the courage to stop his coach. Release me from my sense of shame and fear." Of course, even if I found the courage to speak to Rumkovski, there was no guarantee that he would listen. The capriciousness of our king had become common knowledge in the ghetto. He would respond to some of those who appealed to him for help but would drive off others with blows and insults. Rumkovski had decreed that Yiddish was the official language of the ghetto, and he forbade anyone to address him in Polish. So intense was his dislike of the Polish tongue that he would slap the face of anyone daring to use it in his presence.

I didn't speak Yiddish well. I had heard my grandparents use it when I was a small child, but everyone else had always spoken Polish to me. Now as I roamed the streets where Rumkovski was likely to turn up, I kept rehearsing in Yiddish the few phrases I meant to address to him. As soon as I heard the beat of horses' hooves, I stepped onto the road, but it was Dr. Leider's coach. The next day, when Rumkovski's coach did appear, I was seized with a kind of paralysis of the will. I wanted to step out in front of it, but something held me back. Before I could make up my mind, the coach drove by and was gone from sight. The third day came, and again I couldn't screw up enough courage to stop the coach. As before, I put it off to the following day. But on that day the coach passed by without Rumkovski in it. I drew a sigh of relief. This time I didn't have to reproach myself for having wavered and therefore missed my chance.

This went on for several days, and I was unable to overcome my aversion to the act of begging, which I knew was caused by my vanity. It was a failing that haunted me for many nights while I continued to rehearse the sentences I meant to address to Rumkovski. Yet no sooner did a chance present itself than I bungled and put it off from one day to the next.

Then our neighbor Avramek came unexpectedly to my assistance. He worked as a messenger boy for Rumkovski's secretary, and he arranged an interview for me with her. Avramek did not know about my inability to act, but he was aware of the tragedy being acted out daily in our little room. Despite the terrible suffering in the ghetto, the feeling of compassion for one's fellows had not yet vanished altogether, although it sometimes seemed to me that those who could best afford to help others were so engrossed in their own welfare that they were insensible to the distress and squalor around them.

Avramek accompanied me to Rumkovski's office and encouraged me to be bold in begging for an increased food ration for my father. I walked beside him with a thumping heart, praying to God to give me strength. When my turn came to see the secretary, I entered the office on shaking legs. A young woman with a severe frown on her face was sitting behind the table opposite me. She was scribbling away at something and didn't bother to look up. I had meant to tell her about my mother's death and my father's illness, but the woman's stern look made the words stick in my throat. My chin started quivering, and I burst into tears. Startled, the secretary raised her head, looked at me, and asked, "What is it you want, girl? Why are you crying?"

Since my tears prevented me from speaking, the secretary called in Avramek to explain. Avramek did his best, but he did not say what I had meant to say. She handed him a coupon for an additional soup ration—valid for only seven days. It was far too little! The week would be up in no time, and what then? But I was still in the office and I could still beg for a month's ration. If I didn't seize this chance, I would never have another. I couldn't do it. Someone else already stood at the door—my interview was over. The secretary's impatient gaze swept past me to the next one in line. "What's that girl still doing here?" she asked. "She got what she came here for, didn't she?"

I left the office and cried bitterly all the way home. I had failed.

The following week was a good one for us, even though it was all too short. For seven whole days, I didn't have to count the spoonfuls of soup I ate but could finish my ration to the last drop. After work I hurried to the public kitchen on Dvorska Street, where my pan was filled with three-quarters of a liter of hot broth for Father. Father relished every spoonful of this generous portion of wholesome food.

But the days went fast, and each one that passed increased the fear in my heart. Before I knew it, the seventh day had come and gone. That night I hardly closed my eyes. With the morning my torments would begin anew. Should I go back and ask for more coupons? What if I should burst into tears again and stand there as if struck dumb? I was already trembling at the thought of it. What could I do? Then suddenly I thought of a way out of my dilemma.

Earrings and Lottery Tickets

I owned two pairs of earrings studded with diamonds that had belonged to my maternal grandmother. One pair had been put among the valuables hidden in the safe in Genia's garden and later confiscated by the KRIPO. The second pair was kept with several other pieces of jewelry at the bottom of the linen basket in our room. It now occurred to me that I might be able to trade my earrings for an additional day's soup ration for Father.

Taking care not to arouse Father's suspicion, I removed the earrings from the basket. The following day during the lunch break, I finished all of my soup and then hurried

with my pot and the earrings to the public kitchen on
Dvorska Street. This place, the hub of the ghetto's bartering trade, was already swarming with people offering their
soup in return for bread, their bread for sugar, their sugar
for whatever else happened to be in demand. I took up a
stand at the entrance to the courtyard, and people approached me to ask what I had to exchange. Most of them
turned away indifferently on seeing the earrings; diamonds
were a worthless commodity in the ghetto. I was beginning
to despair. My lunch break was drawing to an end, and I
had been unable to make the desired trade. I was about to
leave when a man came up to me.

"Show me those earrings again. You sure they're genuine diamonds?" he asked.

"Of course they are," I answered eagerly. "They're heir-
looms handed down to me by my grandmother. We kept
them for an emergency, and now it has come."

"Keep your pot steady," said the man, and he poured
the soup from his own pot into mine. I hurried home delighted with my success. When Father looked dubiously at
the soup, I invented a tale about how, amid the uproar in
the public kitchen, I had gotten my soup yesterday without
handing in the last coupon. I couldn't tell Father the truth,
but I was bursting to tell someone about this successful
venture of mine. When I described it to Salek, his response
startled me. "You did right in getting the soup for your father," he said, "but we'll have to retrieve the earrings after
the war, even if we have to offer a price far in excess of
their value."

Salek's remark struck me as inconsistent with all his socialist theories. The loss of the earrings didn't bother me in
the least, for I was happy to have obtained another day's
soup for Father. I reminded Salek how, a few weeks ago,
he had talked so contemptuously about the wealthy who
wasted their money on priceless jewelry for their wives.
Now his words made no sense at all.

I also told Rosie about my bartering of the earrings,
mentioning in passing Salek's response. Childish, doll-faced
Rosie measured me with the superior gaze of an all-know-
ing adult and said, "Sala, don't you see that Salek's in love
with you?"

I burst out laughing. "Stop talking nonsense! We're first

cousins and feel like brother and sister toward each other."

But Rosie stuck to her opinion, convinced that I didn't know what I was talking about.

Of course, the earrings had bought only one day's ration of soup, and the sleepless nights returned as I racked my brains over how to get more soup for Father. One morning I was so immersed in my thoughts that when I got to work, I was at first unaware of the hubbub about me. Talking all together in their excitement, several girls told me about the lottery that was about to begin in our workroom. The lucky winner would be entitled to an entire month's work in a bakery!

I held my breath. For some inexplicable reason I was deeply convinced that God would help me draw the lucky ticket—maybe because all our soup coupons had run out, maybe because I had bartered away my precious earrings for a last pot of soup.

"Almighty God," I whispered, raising my eyes to heaven, "please help me!"

Trembling all over, I sat down at my machine but was unable to do any work. Ignoring the excited bustle about me, I entered into a parley with God, trading away ten years of my life in return for one month's work in the bakery and promising solemnly to observe all his commandments and to follow his ways for the rest of my life. I tried to convince God that my case merited his special favor. True, I argued, all of us in the workshop were equally hungry, but most of the others still had their families. I, on the other hand, had only a father who was critically ill. I beseeched God to help me and preserve Father's life for me. So absorbed was I in my communion with God that I already imagined myself the lucky winner. When I worked in the bakery, Father would finish his daily ration for breakfast and my own for lunch. I would eat my fill at work, and in the evening we would dine on the loaf I brought home with me.

While my imagination was running riot, Shula, the supervisor, entered. She wasn't going to participate in the lottery but her face was flushed with excitement. Shula tore up several sheets of paper, making thirty-six tickets, and wrote the word "Bakery" on one of them. After folding the tickets carefully and placing them all inside a hat, she called on one of the girls to shake up its contents. The drawing began.

Deep silence reigned in the hall. Beginning at the far end, Shula passed from one girl to the next. Our eyes were glued first on Shula and then on each girl in turn, as we waited with bated breath for her to unfold the paper. There were four rows of benches with nine machines to each. Neither the first, nor the second, nor the third row had come up with the prize. With clenched and trembling fists, I watched each girl take her pick and sighed with relief when she drew a blank.

Thirty-two girls had drawn blanks, and the coveted prize still lay at the bottom of the hat. Shula had almost reached me. It was Tola's turn. She took her time unfolding the piece of paper—it was a blank. My turn now. "Dear God," I prayed, "please guide my hand. Father's life depends on it. Which of the three am I to choose?" With closed eyes and a pounding heart, I fumbled for a ticket inside the hat, conscious of all eyes on me. I unfolded it very, very slowly. And then . . . my heart missed a beat. I had drawn a blank! I sank heavily into my seat and wept inside. "Oh God! Why did you do it to me! Why did you let me down? I had set such store on winning!"

Before I had time to collect myself, a shriek split the air of the workroom. "Bakery! I won it!" Rosie shouted. She fell on my neck laughing and crying at the same time. It never occurred to her how utterly miserable I was. But her delight was so infectious that I couldn't help smiling, and for a moment I even forgot my own wretchedness.

That day I didn't touch my soup but brought it all home for Father. I didn't tell him anything about the lottery, but when I told Salek, he gasped on hearing how the prize had eluded me by a hair's breadth. That same day, too, I made up my mind to step in front of Rumkovski's coach, confident in my ability to make him listen to me. I loitered in the streets of the Baluti Market for many hours, but, as if to spite me, he didn't appear anywhere that day. I saw him drive past the next day, though, and on several days after that, but my timidity had returned. As before, I couldn't screw up enough courage to stop the coach.

Rosie's machine stood idle for a whole month. While

eating my soup, I kept thinking of her and imagining the many loaves of bread she was now able to take home to her family. I was bursting with envy.

It was Rosie who eventually told Father about the lottery when she dropped in two weeks later with a loaf of fresh bread whose delicious fragrance filled our little room. Father, scarcely able to believe his eyes, didn't want to accept it at first, telling her that she ought to save it for her own family. But Rosie insisted that he take it; her relatives had plenty of food, thanks to her job at the bakery.

From Rosie's account of the lottery, Father realized why I hadn't breathed a word to him about it. He understood the distress I had felt, having been so close and then losing it all.

Death at Passover

After the second bottle of Wigantol failed to put Father back on his feet, he despaired of ever getting over his illness. He tried hard to conceal his true feelings, pretending to believe me when I talked about the war coming to an end soon and his eventual recovery. When I came home from work, he would greet me with a smile and his usual quips, but his dull, sorrowful eyes gave the lie to his cheerful exterior. I tried to keep my own despondency from him. The only thing I could do to help him was to supply him with books—plenty of them—to make him forget his hunger for a while. Though he read a great deal, the books could not ease his agonizing hunger pangs.

One day Father gave up reading altogether and no longer bothered to conceal his deep despair. He spoke openly to me about having given up all hope of ever leaving his bed alive. I burst into tears on hearing him talk like that and tried desperately to convince him that his weakness was due only to hunger.

"No, my child," Father said. "It's no use fooling ourselves. I won't hold out much longer. Even if this war ends
soon, I won't be here to see it. My only consolation is that
you might survive this hell. Somehow I'm sure you will.
You're young and have youth's staying power. I remember
how it was when I was a youngster during World War I.
The thought that you'll be happy and whole one day is my
only hope. As for myself, all I want is to eat my fill for
once before I die."

I buried my face on Father's chest and cried bitterly.
Then a thought occurred to me.

Daddy! I'll get you into the hospital. There they'll give
you plenty to eat and all the Wigantol you need. That will
put you on your feet again. Why didn't I think of it before? Why didn't Dr. Kshepitzki mention the possibility of
hospitalization?"

This idea gave me new hope, and I did my best to talk
Father into agreeing with me. I reminded him of the time
he had dysentery and was in an even worse state than now.
Only in the hospital, I assured him, did he have a chance
of recovery.

Father was silent for a while, absorbed by thoughts of
his own. It was obvious that he wasn't enthusiastic about
the idea, but he did nothing to oppose it. "Perhaps you're
right" was all he said.

When I made the proposal to Dr. Kshepitzki, he didn't
seem as hopeful as I was. In fact, his response was rather
evasive. Finally, he said dryly, "Well, if that's what you
want, there's no harm in trying."

As soon as Dr. Kshepitzki left, I hurried to the hospital
with his letter of recommendation. The receptionist informed me that they'd have Father admitted within a day
or two. I was overjoyed at the good news.

It was springtime and four days before Passover, which
would coincide with the next bread allotment. This time,
each person would receive eight *matzot*, the unleavened
bread eaten at Passover, instead of the usual weekly loaf. I
managed to collect Father's *matzot* ration and his monthly
ratzia before he was taken to the hospital. Pleased with
this stroke of luck, I told Father that, in addition to the
three meals a day he'd get in the hospital, he would also
have the food that I would bring him. Father made no re-

sponse, and I couldn't understand why he was so apa-
thetic.

Before leaving for work, I fixed him something
special—coffee mixed with a lot of marmalade to take
away its bitter taste. Father took a sip but was unable to
swallow it. I suggested that he eat some bread first and
wash it down with coffee. When he couldn't even swallow
the bread, I was thoroughly alarmed. Setting my mind at
ease, Father said that the sweetness of the coffee had probably deprived him of his appetite. He promised to eat it all
a little later. I left for work intending to look in two hours
later, but I returned within an hour. Father still hadn't
touched the food. Back at work, I waited impatiently for
the distribution of the soup ration, all of which I meant to
take home for Father today. The hot broth would, I felt
sure, stimulate his appetite, and he could then soak the
bread in it.

I had barely settled down at my sewing machine when
the caretaker of our workshop came to tell me that the
Red Cross wagon was at our house, ready to take Father
to the hospital. I raced down the street and reached the
wagon just after the two attendants had pushed the
stretcher into it. I told them that it was my father they
were taking away and asked them to let me kiss him
good-bye. But they thrust me rudely aside, grumbling that
they had no time to wait until everyone had done with
kissing and leave-taking. I caught a glimpse of Father in
the ambulance, smiling feebly and waving his hand. Then
the door banged shut, and the ambulance moved away. I
stood in the street a while, looking after the white wagon
until it disappeared from my view.

The thought of Father's smile and the wave of his hand
was encouraging, and I returned to work in a good mood.
Knowing that Father was in good hands and would even
reach the hospital in time for the midday meal made me
so happy that I began humming to myself, something I
hadn't done since Father fell ill. I started a song, and the
girls smiled at me as they picked up the tune and joined
in.

After work I made a parcel of my own and Father's ration and hurried to the hospital with it. This time Father
had been taken to the hospital in Marisin where I, too,

had spent the days of my illness. The receptionist knew me quite well by now and even remembered my father. He was like an old friend, so I chatted with him for quite a while about myself and about my father. I told him how lucky I was to have collected Father's weekly and monthly rations before handing in all his food coupons and re- marked with a teasing smile, "I'll be here to pester you day after day. I've brought Father's ration for today so he can eat it before going to sleep tonight. Tomorrow I'll be back with some more, and I'll come again the day after that. I'll bring him his *matzot* ration every day of Passover."

The receptionist listened patiently to my excited chatter. He promised to hand the food parcel over in person and to tell Father about his talk with me. When I said good- bye to him and to several members of the staff who knew me, I was aware of their kindness and their sympathy. It made up for the rudeness of those stretcher bearers who had refused to let me kiss Father that morning.

It was a gorgeous spring day, and the warm breeze that was blowing made me believe that everything would work out all right after all. I went to the cemetery to share with Mother the happy events of that day. Sitting on her tomb- stone, I raised my eyes to the sky and watched a little cloud floating there. A sense of lightness filled my whole being, as if I had been released from a heavy burden. There was such peace and beauty about me. Surrounded by the fresh green of spring, I offered up a prayer of thanksgiving for the favors shown to me.

All the way home, I hummed to myself and walked with a light step. When I saw Rumkovski passing by in his coach, I sent a forgiving smile after him and thought with satisfaction that now I didn't need any of his favors or the few miserable coupons his secretary had so stingily granted me.

The following day, the hospital receptionist told me that Father was fine and no longer felt hungry. When I called at the hospital the next day, however, the receptionist was not so friendly. I waved and smiled at him as I entered, but he didn't respond as usual and even seemed to ignore my presence. By the time I reached the desk, he had his back to me. He answered my greetings with a slight nod of his head and busied himself once more with what he had been doing. He's probably in a bad mood today, I thought.

"Sir," I said timidly, "I've brought Father's last portion of bread. Tomorrow I'll be back with his first day's ration of *matzot*."

Without saying a word, the man bent down, took two parcels from beneath the counter, and placed them on the table. Something trembled inside me. They were the two portions of bread that I had brought for Father yesterday and the day before. Why hadn't the receptionist handed the packages on as he had promised me? Hadn't he told me only yesterday that Father was well and not hungry any more? He had told me a lie. A lie! What had I done to deserve it?

"Why didn't you give the bread to my father?" I shouted. "He must have been waiting for it all this time! Father will be worried and wonder what's happened to me!" I burst into tears. "Why did you lie to me? Why?"

The man didn't look at me. Keeping his eyes fixed on the counter, he said quietly, "Listen, my child, I know I did wrong to tell you a lie. I did it because I hadn't the heart to tell you the truth. I felt so sorry for you. Your father died the day he was admitted. I couldn't bear to tell you that when you came in looking so cheerful and full of hope. I remembered your father standing at the gate and praying for your recovery that freezing night not so long ago. I just couldn't bring myself to spoil your happiness and tell you the sad news."

For a few moments, the receptionist's words failed to register. I kept thinking that Father was still hungry. He didn't get the bread I had brought for him.

Then the realization cut through me sharp as a blade. Father's gone! I'll never see him again! Never! The receptionist was still talking. "Forgive me for not telling you about it right away. I thought it would do no harm if you went on thinking for another day that everything was all right because you'd have plenty of time to weep for your father afterwards. But I couldn't keep it from you any longer. Tomorrow morning at nine they are coming to take him for burial. You should wait outside the cemetery at that time."

I stood motionless by the counter, no longer taking in what the man was telling me. My feet seemed to be nailed to the ground. The thought that Father was dead, that I'd never see him again, that all my hopes had vanished, kept pounding inside my head. As if from far away, I heard the man say, "Sit down, child. Here, take a sip." Finally something broke loose in me, and I was able to move again. I took several steps backwards and then broke into a run, heedless of the man's shouts, "You forgot the bread, little girl! The bread!"

The bread was the last thing in my mind just then. One purpose drove me on and made me run as though pursued by a demon. Before long, I had reached the far end of the ghetto, where the barbed-wire fence separated it from the outside world. A German guard with a rifle on his shoulder was marching to and fro. Another sentinel was marching past him in the opposite direction. One of them caught sight of me. He halted abruptly and, pointing his rifle at me, shouted, *"Halt! Stehen bleiben!"*

The second soldier rushed to his side, also pointing his rifle at me and calling on me to stop where I was. I ran on, praying for the bullet to deliver me. But the bullet didn't come. Sounds of shouting and whistling reached me from all sides. Then two Jewish policemen suddenly appeared near me as if they had popped up out of the ground. They chased me as I made an all-out dash for the fence. I had almost reached it when they caught up with me. I struggled and kicked and bit but was soon overpowered and dragged back in the direction of the ghetto.

"You fool! What do you think you're doing? The Germans were trying to get you! They would have killed you!"

"Please let me be. I wanted them to kill me!" I screamed, attempting to break loose. I pleaded with them to let the Germans kill me because my father was dead. He'd be buried the next day, and I wanted to be buried with him.

"Calm down, child," one of the policemen spoke soothingly. "I'm sure your father wouldn't want that—he would want you to live on. You're still so young, a mere child."

It took a while before I came to my senses. Gradually my strength waned and, with it, the will to go on struggling. The policemen seated me on a stone.

"Who have you got left, my child?" one of them asked. That question brought forth my tears, which had refused to flow on hearing that my father was dead. Now I wept and wept as I had never done before in my whole life.

"There's no one left of my family," I sobbed. "No one to live for. I wanted to be with my Daddy, and you stopped me. Why did you have to interfere?"

One of the policemen stroked my head. "Cry, child, cry. It'll make you feel better. Taking one's life is a sin. Your father can't have wanted you to do that. You've got to go on living for his sake."

The policeman left me for a moment to bring a cup of water. After I took a few sips, he poured the rest of the water into his hand and bathed my face. He remained standing beside me, while the other policeman returned to his post. I have no idea how long I sat on the stone, but it was beginning to get dark when the policeman finally asked where I lived. He said that he would walk me home. There was no need to watch over me, I told him, since I no longer had the courage to take my own life.

"I believe you," he said, but he insisted on taking me home all the same.

Uncle Abraham opened the door of the apartment and stared at us in amazement. I rushed past my uncle straight to my room, where I fell crying on my bed. After the policeman told him what had happened, Uncle Abraham came in and sat down beside me. He patted my head, and I heard him say softly, "My poor girl. How much trouble you have known. But so long as I'm alive, I'll look after you. Now I'll have two children again."

During the long night, Uncle Abraham dozed in a chair beside my bed, but he opened his eyes in alarm at the least movement I made. Finally it began to get light. I sat up dry-eyed.

"I'll come to the cemetery with you," Uncle Abraham said.

"No, Uncle," I said firmly. "I want to be alone with Father. It's the last time. Don't worry about me any more. I won't do anything. I haven't the will left to do it."

Uncle Abraham nodded, then took Father's *talit* and detached its ornamental collar. He put the collar away in the linen basket, saying to me, "Look after it. If you survive the war and get married, give this collar to your husband. Tell him that your father embossed it with his own hands." His voice broke and he began to sob. I wept with him. After some time, he handed me the *talit* and told me I must ask the grave diggers to wrap it around Father's body.

It was still early when I got to the cemetery, and I had to wait a long time before the black wagon arrived. The first body taken down was my father's. A tin plate with the name Anshel Kalman Plager was attached to his feet—my beloved father, who had always been an inseparable part of me. Two men were carrying him on a stretcher. Father's face had changed, and his eyes were wide open as if frozen in the midst of a fearful question. The men pressed his eyelids shut. Then they took the *talit* and wrapped it around the body, but they didn't do it properly and the legs were left exposed.

I walked dry-eyed behind the stretcher. Even when the body was lowered into the grave, I didn't cry. Something kept choking me, but I didn't cry. How strange!

One of the grave diggers took a pocketknife and cut the traditional *kriya* into the lapel of my jacket. They flung a few shovelfuls of earth into the grave and were about to leave. I protested, demanding they finish their job, but they were in a hurry, for it was Passover, and they were working only half a day. Besides, there were more bodies on the wagon waiting to be buried. They shrugged me off. Father was just another dead body to them, another job to be quickly disposed of.

The grave diggers left, and I stood there helpless and bewildered. I suddenly felt that Father needed me, that he didn't want to be left like that, partially exposed and shamed. I burst into tears. One of the men returned and lent me his shovel, but only for a short time, he said, until they had laid the other bodies out in their graves. I began covering Father's body with dirt. How horrible it was to cast dirt down on his body! "Dear God," I prayed, "give me strength but take away my understanding so I won't know what I'm doing!" Every additional shovelful made our separation more final. Soon Father would disappear from sight forever. Don't think . . . don't think. Finish the job quickly before the man returns for his shovel.

In the midst of my labor, I suddenly remembered that today—the first day of Passover—was my birthday. What a bustle there used to be at home on that day—what presents and feasting!

"Daddy, dear Daddy. Do you know it's my birthday today, the birthday of your only child?" No! No! I mustn't think about such things. I mustn't feel sorry for myself. I have to go on living even though Daddy is gone.

After I had filled in the grave, I stuck the nameplate on the little mound that I had made for that purpose. As I turned to go home, my legs almost buckled beneath me. I had no strength left to visit Mother's grave.

That night it rained hard. I lay in bed weeping and thinking of the rain seeping through the earth into Father's grave. My mind went back three years to the snowstorm that had raged the night after Mother's funeral, and I remembered how I awoke in terror thinking of Mother lying out there all by herself. But Father had been beside me soothing and kissing me. Now there was no one who could console me.

The next morning, I didn't get out of bed. I heard the hushed voices of the Milewskis, of Salek and Aunt Faiga. Uncle Abraham tried to make me something to eat, but I refused. After everyone had gone to work, I remained all alone in the apartment. The hours crawled by very slowly, and my loneliness began to depress me. I longed to be near people. After pacing about restlessly in my room, I went out into the street, which was deserted at this hour. I was drawn to my workshop, but for some reason I was ashamed to face those who knew me and had known my father. Twice I walked by the workshop before I finally mastered my sense of shame. I mounted the staircase with downcast eyes, keenly conscious of the looks of pity directed at me by the janitor and all those who passed me. Standing outside our workroom, I could hear singing. As I hesitated there, the door was flung open by one of the girls. "Sala!" she cried out.

The singing tapered off, and all eyes turned to me. It was an awful moment. Though my eyes were glued to the floor, I felt their looks of compassion boring through me. It made me wince. As I walked toward my machine with downcast eyes, I wished for the earth to open up and swallow me. I felt so ashamed. Strange as it may sound, I was deeply ashamed at the death of my father. But why? Could it be, I asked myself, that everyone felt like that after suffering a loss?

While I was concentrating on my work, Shula, our supervisor, came up from behind. I heard her choke back a sob as she bent down and planted a kiss on my cheek. Next to me, Rosie was crying softly. A girl started humming, but she was quickly hushed. "Oh, sorry," she whispered. The feeling of being the focus of pity became unbearable. I was on the verge of tears. Then for some reason, I started singing. Scarcely a day after Father was buried, and I found myself singing! I began softly at first, and then I sang much louder, while the tears streamed down my face. Finally the others joined in, and at last I could stop. Thus passed the first day after I had buried my father.

Even at home, I couldn't rid myself of the inexplicable sense of shame, which was aggravated by the furtive glances cast at me by the Milewski kids and by Salek. But here I could at least escape into my room and pretend to be asleep.

Going to work the next day was already much easier. I looked at no one, greeted no one, and passed along the benches with downcast eyes. Unlike the day before, I was not disturbed by the glances of the girls, and my presence no longer bothered them. Intent on their work, they sang and hummed as usual. I myself did not sing for a long time afterwards. When the lunch break came, I no longer counted the potato cubes or the spoonfuls of soup I took. I felt as if I were enclosed inside a shell, completely isolated from my fellow workers.

My Encounter with Rumkovski

Several days after my father's death, something happened that forced me out of my apathy. I was at work, and while my hands were busy at my sewing machine, I was trying to decide to whom I could give Father's *matzot*. I couldn't bear to touch any of his food rations; I couldn't forget that Father's wish to eat his fill just once before he died had remained unfulfilled. Nor did I offer the *matzot* to Uncle Abraham or Salek, knowing in advance that they wouldn't accept it. All at once I thought of someone to whom I could give the bread—Mr. Shor. I had seen him on the street several weeks ago but had slipped past unnoticed, appalled at his terrible appearance. The extra food, I thought, would do him good, and it would make me happy to be able to do something for this old friend of my parents.

In the midst of my musing, I became conscious of an excited bustle in our workroom. Rosie told me in a low voice that Haim Rumkovski was expected at any minute. All the girls around me had stopped working, and from their agitated whispers, I gathered that our king was coming to choose one of us for a job in a kitchen or bakery. Many of my fellow workers started touching up their hair and smoothing down their dresses. Each hoped to be the one to gain Rumkovski's attention; each prayed to be granted the coveted privilege that would relieve the hunger in their homes. As for myself, I went on working at my machine. Rumkovski's visit had nothing to do with me. Then a thought flashed through me like an electric current, and I had the feeling that something unusual was about to take place.

"Oh, God," I prayed fervently, "don't let him notice me. I know it was my fault when I couldn't beg Rumkovski for help though I knew that Father was starving to death.

Yes, I acted like a coward when I couldn't pluck up the courage to beg for more coupons. But don't punish me now. Haven't I already paid enough?"

The dread that I would be singled out by Rumkovski was overwhelming. I tried to dismiss it, taking refuge in the thought that he'd probably pay no attention to a girl whose cropped hair stood on end like the bristles of a brush. I had made up my mind to go into the washroom and stay there until the visit was over, but Rumkovski arrived before I could make my escape. The door was flung open, and though my head was bent, I caught a glimpse of Rumkovski's tall and imposing figure standing on the threshold. He was accompanied by Gonik and Berman, the managers of our workshop. Our supervisor, Shula, her face flushed with excitement, came forward to welcome him.

The hall was plunged into a momentary silence. All the girls raised their heads to acknowledge the visitor and then set to work busily at their machines. Some fidgeted nervously in their seats, others smiled to themselves, each hoping to attract Rumkovski's attention.

Rumkovski surveyed the hall and then turned to the nearest bench of machines, where I happened to have my place. I forced myself to work on calmly, to keep my mind on what I was doing. Rumkovski and his retinue passed from one machine to the next. He cast a brief glance over the shoulder of each girl and went on. He reached Tola. I winced and wished fervently to become invisible. Then Rumkovski came to a halt behind me. I went on working for all I was worth, praying for him to move on to my neighbor, Rosie. But Rumkovski remained behind me. I was ordered to stand up—next to Rumkovski I felt tiny indeed. He measured me from top to bottom and noticed the *kriya* on the lapel of my jacket. Then, the thing that I had desperately wanted to avoid came about. Addressing me in Yiddish, Rumkovski asked, "Who in your family has died recently?"

I felt the blood rushing to my head. I'll show him how little he scares me, I said to myself. I'm going to reply in Polish even if he slaps me because of it.

"My father," I said, anticipating the blow.

But contrary to expectations, Rumkovski continued our conversation in fluent Polish.

"Who have you still got?"

"No one," I said. Silence reigned in the hall.

"Would you like to work in a kitchen?" Rumkovski asked in a soft, gentle tone.

My throat contracted. It took all the strength I could muster not to burst into tears. "God!" I said to myself. "Why do you torment me? Why didn't you send this opportunity only a week ago?"

My mind in a whirl, I heard myself say, "No. I don't want to work in a kitchen."

Raising one eyebrow in disbelief, Rumkovski asked, "Then in a bakery, or in a grocery store?"

I swallowed spittle and felt my heart thumping violently. My fists were clenched so hard that the fingernails cut into the flesh, and I looked at our king with undisguised loathing.

"No, sir," I said in a harsh voice that scarcely seemed to be my own. "There's no need for me to work in a bakery or a grocery. The food I get here is quite enough for me now that I'm no longer sharing it with my father. Your offer has come too late to save him. Help those who can still benefit from it!"

Rumkovski's face flushed a deep red. Used to tears and servile pleading, he could hardly have anticipated such a reply. I, too, was greatly upset and on the verge of losing control of myself. Running unceremoniously between Rumkovski and Gonik, I rushed out of the hall. Only in the washroom did I let myself go and burst into the tears I could no longer withhold. At the same time, I was glad Rumkovski didn't see me crying and felt proud to have turned down his tempting proposals. When I returned to the workroom some time later, the machines were still idle, and all I could hear was the excited chatter of the girls. Rosie told me that after my outburst, Rumkovski had cut short his visit and had left our workshop furious.

What I had done that day was not soon forgotten. I didn't tell Salek, but of course he heard of it from his parents, who were both employed in the same workshop. For weeks after the incident, people kept pointing at me. While standing in line for the daily soup, I often heard them remark, "That's the little fool who passed up a chance to eat her fill." Yet despite their ridicule, I couldn't help feeling proud of myself at having had the courage to resist this temptation. I had no regrets about it even at moments when I had hardly anything to eat.

On the day following my encounter with Rumkovski, I took the parcel of *matzot* to Mr. Shor. His daughter Sabcia opened the door and welcomed me inside with a sad look on her face. Mr. Shor was sitting on a chair with his enormously swollen legs stretched out in front of him. His face was so bloated that the eyes looked like two slits cut into it. The news of Father's death shocked Mr. Shor and Sabcia, since they had always known him as a strong and healthy man.

"And now you're all alone," Mr. Shor commented sadly.

When I told them why I had come, both Mr. Shor and his daughter declined my offer of the *matzot*, insisting that I alone was entitled to them and that I needed the extra food. That must have been my father's wish, they argued. Nothing could make them change their minds. But I was just as determined that they should have the *matzot*, for the Shors' situation reminded me forceably of the experience that I had just been through. Mr. Shor, who was much older than my father, had never managed to find any employment. He was by now so weakened from lack of food that he could scarcely drag himself about on his swollen legs. I knew that before long they would fail him altogether. In Sabcia, he had a devoted daughter who was struggling futilely to prolong the life of her father as best she could by sharing with him every morsel of the food she received for herself.

The look in Mr. Shor's eyes on seeing the *matzot* was one of hungry desire mingled with irresolute resistance. It reminded me of my father in similar circumstances, when Rosie had brought him the loaf of bread from the bakery. When I said good-bye to the Shors, I dropped the parcel of *matzot* on the table and rushed out of the room. Sabcia ran after me, calling for me to come back, but I was already far away.

My Cousin Salek

After the encounter with Rumkovski, my depression returned, and again I lost interest in my surroundings. I withdrew into myself and hardly exchanged a word with my fellow workers. My indifference extended to my relatives at home, and even Salek's attempts to rouse me proved futile. My cousin would not give up, however. He would bring home books and leave them lying about on my table. I'd try to read but rarely got past the first couple of pages. I often caught myself leafing through a book without taking in what was printed there.

Salek was away from home most of the time after work, but he always had a few minutes each day to spend with me. He began telling me about the formation of a resistance group in the ghetto. I shrugged it off, looking at Salek with disbelief. Resistance? How? With what? We were totally isolated from the outside world. No German soldiers were seen within the ghetto, but they patrolled its boundaries armed to the teeth. The smallest sign of resistance was enough to flood the ghetto with thousands of troopers and cause the death of hundreds of its inhabitants.

"You don't understand," Salek explained patiently. "That's not what I mean. I'm talking about some sort of resistance to a future action like the *Shpera*. We'll oppose any further deportations of that kind. We'll kill every German soldier who searches our homes, even if we have to pay for it with our lives. They, too, will pay dearly. Besides, the end of the war is already in sight. Then we'll avenge ourselves for everything the Germans have done to us."

"You're crazy!" I shouted at him. "The war is never going to end!"

Salek was startled at the fury of my outburst. He didn't

119

know, of course, that since Father was no longer alive, I didn't care whether the war was going to end soon or ever.

My days were empty now. At the end of my five hours at work, time hung heavy on my hands. I was hungry and slept badly at night. Finally I took up reading seriously and before long became absorbed in the fictitious world of my books, living the lives of their heroes and heroines. I began a new book almost every other day, and reading made me forget my hunger for a while.

One day, however, something occurred that jerked me back into reality. I was sitting in my room, reading; the book was *Anna Karenina*. Completely immersed in it, I hadn't noticed anyone entering, but suddenly I became conscious of someone standing behind me. I was about to turn my head when I felt myself caught in a passionate embrace and lips closing over mine. It was Salek. Rising abruptly, I disengaged myself by pushing him violently away from me. He stood there trembling and blushing deeply with embarrassment. "If only you knew how much I love you," I heard him whisper.

A wave of anger surged over me. "Love! Of course, that's all you have on your mind! You've still got your parents, and apart from hunger, what do you know of real suffering?"

I made a dash for the door and raced down the stairs. I could hear Salek calling after me, "Sala! Salusia! Come back! I won't touch you again!" But I was already outside. I roamed the streets for a long time, thinking about Salek. Although my cousin was a year and a half older than I, I considered myself more mature because of the hardships I'd been through. Yet Salek insisted on treating me like a baby, just as he had when we were children. In the past, he had always been kind to me and had given in to all my whims. Even when I hit out at him during our childish squabbles, he never raised his hand against me. Of course, in those days Salek and I had always been arguing. I was sure that he resented the crush I had on his handsome brother Moniek. But he had stopped teasing me after Moniek had died.

I remembered Salek's response when I told him what I had done with my precious earrings, and then I recalled Rosie's observation. Of course. Salek *was* in love with me! And what was my reaction? I begrudged him his parents and even blamed him for not knowing the meaning of distress at losing them! Now I deeply regretted the cruel words I had flung at him earlier.

"Dear God," I whispered, "forgive me. I don't want Salek to lose his parents." After all, they were all I had left myself. Hadn't my beloved Uncle Abraham always treated me like a child of his own, dividing his ration equally between Salek and me? I recalled that terrible night when Uncle Abraham soothed me, saying that now he had two children again. "Oh God, don't punish me for my envy of Salek. Please, don't take his parents away from him. I'll never envy him again."

Thoroughly ashamed of myself, I returned home and entered the room with my head bowed. Salek was still there. "I was so worried about you," he said.

"There was no need for that," I replied, looking away.

"I'll never touch you again."

"Forget it."

On the face of it, our relationship returned to what it had been before. Salek still confided in me and shared all his experiences. Though we made no allusions to this incident again, neither of us was able to forget it.

One day Salek told me about the mother of one of his fellow workers who was very ill and had lost the use of her legs. The son shared his meager food ration with his mother, who could not go to work anymore. Salek called a meeting of all the young people in his workshop and appealed to them to help a comrade of theirs who was in great distress. All that was required was that each of them contribute one spoonful of their daily soup ration to make up an additional portion. Salek's proposal was adopted, and his friend's mother had her soup each day without anyone feeling the worse for it. Encouraged by this successful act of charity, Salek also persuaded each of his fellow workers to contribute a teaspoon of sugar from the monthly *ratzia*. Salek's idea of mutual aid was prompted by his memory of my own frustrating efforts to share my rations with Father. How different things might have turned out had someone done at my work place what Salek did at his!

When the mother of one of my fellow workers fell ill, I followed Salek's example. I gathered the girls of the workshop together and told them about the mutual aid scheme, explaining how important it was for us to help one another. Speaking from personal experience, I told them about my own futile struggles to save half of my soup for my father. After gaining their approval, I passed from one girl to the next with a pot in my hand and each put a spoonful of soup into it. Our act of charity was rewarded. The girl's mother regained her health and returned to work.

Salek was pleased by the success of his mutual aid plan and by the news we were receiving about the progress of the war. As 1943 drew to a close, every week brought more reports of German defeats on the eastern front and the steady advance of the Russian army. I had mixed feelings about these developments. The realization that Father had not been allowed to see the end of the war filled me with great sorrow. I was terribly afraid of facing the future alone.

The Little Girl Who Had Never Seen a Flower

It was Rishia, Genia's little girl, who eventually lifted me out of my apathy and my fear of the future. She was five years old by now, and the time I spent with her filled me with a new will to live. It was for her sake that I began to hope for a speedy end to the war so that I could show her the beautiful things that existed outside the world of the ghetto. I pitied her for never having had the chance to see any of those things. I myself had beautiful memories that I could recall at will: a happy childhood, loving parents, wonderful vacations spent at my uncle's country estate, and many other pleasant experiences. Rishia couldn't even recall her father, brother, or sister.

My close relationship with Rishia began one day when Genia asked me to take care of her daughter while she supervised the dispatch of a large consignment of goods from her factory. Genia usually worked at night so that she could be with her little girl throughout the day, but this job required that she work the day shift. During the hours I spent with Rishia, she asked me all sorts of questions. At first she wanted to know where my father had disappeared to. My stories about his having gone far away didn't satisfy her; she insisted on knowing how he had managed to get out of the ghetto. If he had escaped, she thought, he could bring her own father to her. Finally, I had to tell her the truth. I explained that I would never see my own parents again but that her father, sister, and brother would return to her after the war because they were still alive. Rishia listened attentively to everything I said, and I was happy to have someone I could talk to without restraint.

From that day on, we became very attached to one another. When I went to visit, Rishia was always waiting for me impatiently, while I could scarcely wait for my workday to end so I could spend the rest of the afternoon with her. The hours I spent with Rishia made it possible for Genia to give up working night shifts, which was wrecking her health. She could now work during the day like everyone else.

Rishia was a very bright child but different from those few other children of her age who had miraculously survived the *Shpera*. She was a pretty girl with shining blue eyes, flaxen hair braided into two wiry plaits, and round, rosy cheeks. Although Rishia had forgotten the taste of milk, eggs, fruit, and other nutritious food, she had never actually suffered from hunger, for her mother, as an important manager, was entitled to an increased food ration that was ample for both of them. Genia rarely took her daughter out into the street, for this pretty, healthy little girl attracted the attention of all the undernourished inhabitants of the ghetto.

Rishia was a happy child since she didn't know about any world other than the one she lived in. I began to open her eyes by telling her of a life beyond the barbed-wire fence of the ghetto. She listened with rapt attention, taking in every word I said. I talked to her about the countryside, about forests, rivers, fields, and animals, and made drawings for her of apples and pears, flowers, hens and cats. When I explained to Rishia how a cow was milked and what milk looked like, I couldn't help thinking of Helen Keller, the blind, deaf, and dumb child whose teacher patiently introduced her to the wonders of this world. Although little Rishia was in possession of all her five senses, she was less fortunate than Helen Keller, who could at least touch a flower and smell it. Rishia, like all other Jewish children growing up in the ghetto, lived in a world without flowers. Everything here was barren and desolate, a mixture of squalor, filth, hunger, and grinding poverty. For Rishia and children like her, the traditional fairy tales about Little Red Riding Hood, Cinderella, or Snow White had little appeal. These children wanted to hear about concrete, real things that existed outside the ghetto and of which we Jews had been deprived.

Sometimes I took Rishia for a walk on Zgierska Street, alongside the barbed-wire fence and across the bridge that spanned the two parts of the ghetto. Standing on the bridge, I told Rishia about Liberty Square, at the far end of Zgierska Street, and about the monument of the great Polish hero, which the Germans had blown up. There, I told her, only three houses off the square, had been my parents' home, where I had been so happy.

One day while we were standing on the bridge, Rishia asked whether Jews had looked different before the war from the way they looked now and if they had ever looked like the gentiles. When I didn't understand what she was driving at, she became irritable and demanded that I describe to her exactly what a Pole and a German looked like. After hearing that there wasn't any real physical difference between non-Jews and Jews, she sank into thought for a while and finally asked, "Then why did they separate us from them?" I could not give her an answer, for I, too, kept asking the same question.

Rishia loved to hear me tell stories, and her favorite was Hans Christian Andersen's tale of the Little Match Girl. She would make me repeat it over and over and never tired of hearing how the lighting of each match revealed to the little girl scenes of a world she longed to live in. It puzzled me why Rishia was so enchanted with that story and preferred it to all others. Then one day, as I was about to enter her room, I smelled something burning. I rushed in and saw Rishia sitting on the floor surrounded by burnt-out matches.

"Rishia!" I shouted at her in alarm. "You could have burned the house down!"

She burst into tears. "You lied to me!" she sobbed. "I've burned up all the matches and didn't see my daddy or Halinka or Kuba!"

I took the girl into my arms and kissed her. The Little Match Girl, I consoled her, was only a story, but when the war ended she wouldn't need any matches to conjure up her relatives. She'd be able to see them all in reality.

From that day on, Rishia never asked me to tell her the story of the Little Match Girl again.

1944

Girlfriends from Happier Days

As the weeks and the months passed, conditions in the ghetto deteriorated rapidly. More and more people died of starvation. Rosie's father had lost the use of his legs, and Rosie was now in a constant state of dejection. She no longer sang at work, and the days when she used to demonstrate tap dances were long over.

I, too, came down with a curious illness. Every month with great regularity, I suffered fits of breathlessness that lasted for three days. On these days, I couldn't go to work and therefore forfeited my daily soup ration.

Dr. Kshepitzki couldn't diagnose this ailment, ascribing it at first to an attack of asthma. Finally, because of its punctual reappearance every month, he thought it might be connected with my having reached the age of puberty. I was already sixteen but had not yet begun to menstruate. The doctor thought that there was a link between those fits of breathlessness and the delay of my menstruation. He told me that it was a common occurrence in the ghetto for women to cease menstruating due to acute malnutrition. Like most of the ailments of the ghetto, this problem had only one real cure—food. All that Dr. Kshepitzki could do was to give me pills against asthma, which did much to ease my breathlessness. I also suffered from pains in the back, which the doctor alleviated by draining surplus water from under my skin with a big hypodermic needle.

During the early months of 1944, deportations from the ghetto were resumed, but the tactics had changed. Now the managers of all the workshops were required to supply

126

lists of people whose work could be dispensed with. These people were to be deported from the ghetto. It was a harrowing task, for the managers were compelled to select a specified number of people from each workshop. To their credit, they sifted their staffs with utmost consideration, checking and rechecking the family status of each worker to avoid breaking up family units. Those who had no special family ties were usually the ones picked out for deportation.

Each deportation list was read with great trepidation. Whose turn to go was it this time? People did not want to leave the ghetto, despite the terrible living conditions and the tempting loaf of bread granted to each prospective deportee. Families who had already lost many of their loved ones refused to be decimated any further, holding on desperately to those that were still left.

One day Rosie failed to turn up at work, and I learned that her father had died. On my way home from paying a condolence call, I ran into Heltzia, a girl friend from my prewar schooldays whom I hadn't seen for over four years. Heltzia had sat at the desk in front of me in elementary school. She had been nicknamed Giggling Sue because of her outbursts of uncontrollable laughter, which were so infectious that they often started me laughing. Then we would both be punished for disrupting the class. Heltzia and I had been close friends, and seeing her now brought back happy memories of those wonderful days.

I often walked home from school with Heltzia and another close friend, Irka. Our way led through Sienkiewicz Park, enchanting in its beauty no matter what the season. In the fall, when the new school year began, the park was steeped in gold, yellow, and purple, and we waded through thick layers of golden leaves that covered the ground. Under the chestnut trees, we would gather the ripe chestnuts, peel the prickly shells, and fill our coat pockets to bursting with the brown nuts. When we had gathered up enough chestnuts, we'd clear a spot of leaves, dig a small pit, build a fire, and toast the nuts in it.

In winter we would walk through the park with slow and deliberate paces, leaving the deep imprint of our footsteps in the white carpet of snow. Occasionally we were hit by a volley of snowballs thrown by our classmate Romek and his buddies, who had been lying in wait for us behind the trees. Heltzia, Irka, and I were never slow in retaliating, but the battle usually ended in our turning tail in defeat. During periods of ceasefire in the war of the sexes, we would build a snowman together, which then became the common target of our snowballs.

Sienkiewicz Park was lovelier in the springtime than at any other season. Then the trees were blooming in a multitude of colors, and the fragrance of the purple lavender bushes reached us from afar. In the spring we would fling our satchels onto a nearby bench and lose ourselves playing hopscotch or jumping rope. Every day we'd be late coming home, and every day we'd be reprimanded, but to no effect. The beauty of the park was too fascinating—it confounded our sense of time.

The park was also beautiful in the summer, shimmering with multicolored flowers in the scattered beds, but at that time of year we were too preoccupied with our homework and preparations for final exams to do it justice.

My friend Heltzia had changed greatly from the plump and laughing schoolgirl who used to share my adventures in the park. Now she was thin and haggard, and her eyes had the look of a hunted animal. Her mother had received a deportation order, and the police were after her, so she had gone into hiding. Neither Heltzia nor her mother could return to their home or to work, and all their ration coupons had been withdrawn. Heltzia's brother, who worked with the fire brigade, was doing everything in his power to get the deportation order cancelled.

Heltzia's family had already had its share of trouble. Her older sister and brother had been separated from the rest of the family when the ghetto was closed, and her father had died from hunger and exposure two years ago. Heltzia's mother had almost been deported, but her son had rescued her by pulling her down from the wagon on which the German soldiers had placed her. Now that she had received an official order of deportation, her children were determined not to hand her over.

I suggested to Heltzia that since she could not go home, she might come and stay at my place. She accepted my offer and remained with me for several days until her brother succeeded in getting the deportation rescinded. During the first evening of Heltzia's stay with me, I had my periodic fit of breathlessness. Alarmed, Heltzia watched me fighting for breath but was unable to help me. After my attack passed, we began to talk about our school days and all our old friends. Heltzia told me that Irka was living in the ghetto and was very ill.

In those days before the war, Irka had been one of my closest friends. She was the fattest pupil in our class and had been nicknamed the Bomb. I remembered that Irka had two younger brothers. Heltzia now told me that both of her brothers had been deported during the *Shpera*, along with her mother, who had joined her two youngest children of her own free will. Irka had been left alone with her father, who died some time later of malnutrition. Irka herself contracted tuberculosis and was now in a sanitorium in Marisin. Except for Heltzia, nobody ever came to see her there.

When I offered to join Heltzia on her next visit, she told me that I would not recognize Irka. Though I was prepared for the worst, I was aghast at what I saw. I could hardly believe that this skeletal, shrunken creature lying on the bed in front of me was the same ball of fat I had once called the Bomb. Two sickly-looking red spots were burning on her hollow cheeks, and even her eyes had changed. Formerly light blue, they now had a sheen that made them look almost black. It was only with a great effort that I restrained my tears. Irka was overjoyed to see me, and despite her own misfortunes, she wept on hearing of the death of my parents.

After that day, Heltzia and I made it our duty to visit Irka regularly and to try to bring a little happiness into her life. Twice a week we went to the hospital, and despite the scarcity of food, we never came without something. Heltzia's mother sent a slice of bread or occasionally made a single cookie from what she could spare of the precious monthly flour ration. I was also able to bring bread, since at that time I was receiving extra food from Genia in return for my care of Rishia. I also supplied Irka with lots of books. These visits were Irka's happiest hours. She seemed to live exclusively for them, and she would be frantic with anxiety if we didn't turn up on time. Anticipation of our visits had become Irka's sole purpose in life.

One day when we arrived with our small package of food, we were told that Irka had died early that morning.

Heltzia and I were the only mourners at the burial of our
sixteen-year-old friend Irka, the last member of the Katz
family.

A New Zest for Life

Salek was shocked to hear of Irka's death. He clenched
his fists, and his large black eyes lit up with a vengeful
gleam. "The Germans will pay for it," he said, gritting his
teeth. Salek was filled with an ardent desire to avenge the
humiliations of our people, the death of my parents, all of
our suffering. He still believed it was possible to change
the world, and the determined look on his face left no
doubt as to the seriousness of his resolve. I was more
willing to listen to him now than I had been in the past.
Though I didn't know how to go about it, I was ready for
any sacrifice.

Salek now told me the reason for his mysterious ab-
sences from home until late at night. Something was happening in the ghetto: a resistance group was being
organized to set off a rebellion when the opportunity arrived. In preparation, the members of the group were busy
manufacturing homemade explosives and firearms. Salek's
fervor affected me, and I, too, wanted to be involved. I
was ready to join Salek's group, to be assigned to the most
dangerous missions, and to accept the consequences. I was
ready to lay down my life for the cause.

"I knew I could count on you," Salek said in the gentle
voice so familiar to me. "What you can do first is to enlist
the support of the girls in your workshop. Bring up the
subject of a resistance group very gradually, and choose
your candidates with utmost care. See to it that they don't
breathe a word about it to their parents."

The task that Salek had given me infused me with a
new zest for life. I began by inviting several of the girls to
eat their lunch in my room, which was conveniently close

to the workshop. They came bringing their pots of soup, and the first thing we did was count the pieces of potato each had received that day. Gradually, more and more girls came, and as the circle grew, the room became crowded; my friends sat on the bed and the floor or just stood about.

Soon, I began to introduce the subject of resistance into our lunchtime chatter. I talked about the end of the war, which had to be coming soon in view of the defeats the Germans were suffering on all fronts. Even so, there was no knowing what the Germans still had planned for us. If something like the hunt during the *Shpera* were ever repeated, we had to fight it no matter what the consequences. That was why we had to organize, as many other youngsters in the ghetto already had. The moment would come when each of us would be given his or her task. Meanwhile, we had to bide our time and keep in constant touch with one another.

The majority of the girls were in favor of joining the resistance group, though some expressed reservations, as I had in the past. I repeated what Salek had said: we would fight only if the Germans carried out searches in our homes in order to deport the weak and the sick. It was in our power to do it, I said, if we were well prepared. It might upset the Germans' plans and give us a chance to kill some of them and take their weapons. As instructed, I didn't say anything about the secret manufacture of arms that Salek and his comrades were engaged in.

The idea of resistance brought new life to our workshop, and once again the robust sound of singing voices could be heard. The windows rattled when we broke into the song *Der Veg Forois*. As for me, I was so happy with the work Salek had given me that I told little Rishia about it. When I was with her, I no longer dwelt on the past but began to talk about the future, when the war would be over. Then she would be able to see the other members of her family without having to burn matches, and she would find out what forests, fields, and flowers looked like.

"But remember," I said, "the flower you'll see for the first time in your life will be the one I shall bring you the very day this war's over."

These days I saw Salek only very late at night. He had turned seventeen and was now working a full day like all adults. Right after work, he would meet with his friends, and he rarely came home before midnight. I often waited up for him. When he arrived, he would sit down on my bed and tell me how the resistance plans were coming. I shared fully in his enthusiasm and determination.

The Final Deportation

Before Salek and his comrades had time to get organized, rumors began to circulate about the transfer of the entire ghetto population to labor camps in the country. All our plans for rebellion were thrown into confusion by the news, for this deportation seemed to be different from the earlier ones. Since no separation of the aged, the sick, or the children was planned, our suspicions were not aroused.

I myself was overjoyed at this new turn of events, happy at the chance of getting out into the countryside and the fresh air. There couldn't possibly be any barbed-wire enclosures in the country villages, I reasoned. So impatient was I at the prospect of setting out on what seemed to me an exciting venture that I could barely wait for the moment when I would leave the ghetto behind me.

The rumors soon turned into facts, and posters appeared announcing the elimination of the entire ghetto by August 1944. The announcements included detailed instructions on what each individual was entitled to take along, setting the weight limit at exactly 12½ kilograms. Soon we heard that workshops considered indispensible to the Germans were to be transferred lock, stock, and barrel, and that the employees of such shops could be accompanied by the members of their immediate families. Salek's repair shop was considered essential, and he told the officials that he would be joined by his parents and his sister—me.

But Salek was not sure that he wanted to leave the ghetto. He had little faith in the Germans; he didn't believe that they meant what they said. The day that the deportation was announced, he sat up with me until very late, trying to talk me into accepting the scheme he had in mind for both of us. We should defy the orders of the Germans and stay in the ghetto. The Red Army was advancing on Lodz, and the Germans were deporting its inhabitants indiscriminately, to who knew what destination. His parents, he argued, had no other choice but to leave; because of their age and their exhaustion from malnutrition, they couldn't possibly lead the life of fugitives. He and I, on the other hand, were still young and stood a good chance of pulling through. We could hide in the cemetery during the day and forage for food at night. Salek assured me that he wouldn't be alone. Some of his friends had prepared special hideouts and were storing up food to tide them over till the Red Army arrived. He wanted us both to join this group.

But my thoughts ran in a totally different vein. They had already taken me far away from the ghetto and its barbed-wire fence. In my flight of fancy, I saw myself sitting in the compartment of a train, speeding past villages, fields, and forests, breathing the fresh air of the country. All I could think of was getting out of this accursed place once and for all. I felt sorry for Salek.

"If you want to stay on, that's your affair," I said. "I personally won't remain here a moment longer than necessary. Besides, I have no intention of leaving your parents. How can you, their only son, turn your back on them and leave them to their fate?"

Salek gave me a pained and helpless look. "You still don't understand a lot of things," he said. "Don't you realize that my parents can't hold out much longer? You and I are still young and able to face up to hardships. We've got to try. It's our only chance for survival."

But my mind was made up, and I wouldn't let anyone divert me. Anything was preferable to staying on in the ghetto.

"If you go, then I'll come with you," Salek said finally in a tone of resignation.

The deportations got under way speedily. All workshops except Genia's were closed down, and practically no one went to work anymore. Food was distributed ahead of the usual schedule. All public kitchens were closed, and the public utilities ceased to function. Garbage quickly piled up, creating an unbearable stench. The whole situation was chaotic.

Notwithstanding all that, there were many who resisted leaving the ghetto. They hung on with a desperate persistence, as if it were their last stronghold. Genia was one of those. She refused to budge from her room and pleaded with me to remain with her and Rishia. She greatly feared this new separation.

"Believe me," she said, "since the death of your father I've looked upon you as my own daughter. Who knows if I'll ever see my other children again? Once this war's over, you'll have a home full of love with me. I still have my money, and I'll send you to school as your parents would have done. I've no strength left to bear this separation from all of you. Rishia will be sick with longing for you."

Genia did her best to talk me into staying in the ghetto with her. She would find me a job in her workshop, which was protected and safe from deportation. It would not be for long, she reasoned, since the Russians were advancing fast and would conquer Lodz very soon.

Though Genia's words moved me to tears, I said that I couldn't leave Uncle Abraham. It was my duty to remain at his side. I told Genia that even Salek, who had wanted me to go into hiding with him, had decided not to break up the family. And if the war was coming to an end, wouldn't we all meet again in any case?

Of course Salek had not quite given up hope of persuading me to stay. He harped on the subject until the very day we had to leave our apartment, but I was deaf to all his arguments.

"Do as you see fit," I told him. "I don't want to hold you back. As for myself, I'm leaving together with your parents, and that's final."

Salek then repeated the same words he had spoken a day or two ago. "If you go, then I'm coming with you."

That morning I had taken leave of my parents. I went to the cemetery to tell them that I was, at long last, leaving the ghetto, but I promised to come back after the war to tell them how I'd been getting along. On my way out, I passed a black marble tombstone in the shape of a tree whose branches had been lopped off. I was startled to see that it was Moniek's grave. As I stood in front of it, a wave of envy passed over me. "How lucky you are," I thought, "to have been spared all the horrors we've had to endure because we were born Jews. Rest in peace. Nothing can harm you anymore."

Early the next morning, I packed my knapsack with the things we were allowed to take along: a pot, two plates, a knife, a fork, a spoon, underwear, socks, two blouses, a skirt, a dress, two towels, a sheet, and a small pillow. I also added a few articles that had been an inseparable part of my life: Father's ornamental *talit* collar; the doll that had been with me since I was two; an album presented to me on graduating from elementary school that contained, in addition to inscriptions by my classmates, dedications from both my father and my mother; and finally, the book of poems by Adam Asnyk that Father had given to me. One of the poems, "The Orphan," still moved me as it always had whenever I read it during moments of deep sorrow. When I finished packing, Uncle Abraham lifted my knapsack and, checking its weight by suspending it from his hand, decided that I hadn't exceeded the stipulated 12½ kilograms.

I now removed from the family album the photos of my closest relatives—my mother and father, Uncle Abraham and Aunt Hanushka, my two favorite boy cousins, and Aunt Tsesia's family. The laughing, happy faces of my beloved parents gave no hint of the horrors and the grueling deaths that would soon overtake them. I wrapped all the photos up and put them into a pocket of my coat. I added Mother's golden spangle and two of her rings but decided to wear her golden wrist watch. Then I took Father's gilded cigarette case, put the pills for my recurring asthmatic fits into it, and slipped it into another coat pocket.

Uncle Abraham and Salek were also busy packing. Salek kept fighting with his father over the number of books he wanted to take along. Uncle Abraham removed many of the books as soon as Salek shoved them into his bag because they took up precious weight that was needed for more essential things.

Finally we were ready to go. Uncle Abraham was the last to leave the apartment. He locked the door and dropped the key into his coat pocket. Aunt Faiga was in tears, and Salek was thoughtful. I alone was cheerful. Though fully aware that we were setting out for an unknown destination, I couldn't disguise my excitement. I have nothing to be afraid of anymore, I thought, since I have already lost all those dearest to my heart. What else could happen to me? Was there anything worse than living in this ghetto? Worse than hunger, sickness, and death?

Before long, I would discover that there were torments infinitely worse than these.

Leave-Taking

It was still early when we arrived at Salek's workshop, which was to be transferred in its entirety. We spent two whole days there, sleeping fully dressed on the floor along with many others. Only on the second day did it occur to me that I'd forgotten to say good-bye to Genia and little Rishia. The thought kept bothering me, and finally I told Uncle Abraham that I had to go and see Genia and Rishia before we left. He objected strenuously. It was rumored, he said, that many quarters of the ghetto had already been cordoned off by the Germans for the purpose of house-to-house searches. Those caught were being transferred to the prison on Czarniecki Street for instant deportation.

"If you go out now, you're sure to get caught and sent off all by yourself. Here we're together and will go to the same labor camp. You can't risk a separation now. Genia will understand, and after the war you can explain everything."

I ignored my uncle's remonstrations and went out into the filthy and deserted streets. On the point of crossing Koscielna Street, I stopped short, hearing the sounds of screeching wheels, of soldiers running and cursing, and people shrieking. A truck packed with people stood at the corner of the street, and scores of soldiers were blocking the other end.

"Good God," I thought in alarm. "I must have run right into a trap! Serves me right! I should've known better than disregard Uncle Abraham's warning. What am I to do now? If they catch me, I'll be packed off all by myself without any luggage, without Father's *talit* collar, without the photos and my pills!"

Panic-stricken, I surveyed the area, my brain working at top speed. I was standing near a church surrounded by a high wall with broken glass all along the top. The image of Jean Valjean from *Les Misérables* flashed through my mind. I began climbing the wall but kept slipping on the brown bricks, which offered hardly any footholds. Somehow I managed to reach the top, and I didn't even feel the chips of glass cutting my hands. Without thinking twice, I leaped down and fell onto the soft soil of the churchyard. Getting to my feet, I ducked behind some thick bushes and crouched there, listening to the terrible noises outside the wall.

For several hours, I stayed hidden, scared out of my wits that the Germans would find me. But they didn't search the churchyard. When darkness came, the tumult outside subsided. Only then did I become aware that I wasn't the only one to have sought refuge here. Shadowy forms crawled out from behind other bushes and moved toward the wall. I crawled after them. Finding a small opening at the far end, I managed to wriggle through and run to Genia's place, which wasn't far away.

Genia was not at home. I'd forgotten that she was working night shifts again so she could be with her little girl during the day. Rishia was already asleep. I stood beside her bed and looked down at her, my heart aching at the sight. Rishia had grown up before my very eyes, and the hours spent with her had been some of my happiest in the ghetto. Now she was probably angry with me for having left her despite all my promises.

I went to the drawer, took out pen and paper, and wrote a parting letter to Genia, asking her forgiveness for leaving her and Rishia. I begged her to understand why I couldn't stay here any longer, how I yearned to get outside the ghetto no matter what the consequences. Maybe working in the countryside, breathing the fresh air, would make me forget what I had been through. I asked her to explain it all to Rishia and to tell her that I'd be back right after the war to bring her the promised flower. The words got so blurred with tears that I had to write the letter all over again. Concluding with "I love you both more than anything in the world. See you after the war, Sala," I folded the letter and left it on the table.

I bent over Rishia and planted a light kiss on her cheek. She stirred, and I held my breath. God forbid that she should wake up and see me, for then I wouldn't have the strength to tear myself away. Rishia slept on, with a smile flitting across her face.

It was close to midnight by the time I got back to Salek's workshop. Both Salek and his father were waiting for me outside in the street, frantic with anxiety, having almost given up hope of ever seeing me again.

The next morning, all the people in the workshop were ordered to pack up their belongings and report to the deportation center in the prison courtyard on Czarniecki Street. Here our documents were processed, and a loaf of bread, along with a small quantity of sugar, was handed to each person. Then we were herded toward the railway station in Marisin.

Men, women, and children burdened with their bundles trudged along in a seemingly endless line. They were leaving the ghetto with conflicting emotions. Some hoped to improve their lot in a new place, while others couldn't conceal the fear they felt at this venture into the unknown. Aunt Faiga lamented the loss of her bed, where she could at least lay down her tired body after a day's work. Who knew what awaited her now?

When the gate opened and I stepped outside the ghetto, my heart missed a beat. I considered myself lucky to be leaving. I felt a momentary pain at the thought that my father wasn't here to share this joy with me, but nothing, not even the heavily armed troopers guarding us, could destroy my elation. All that mattered to me was that I was finally outside the ghetto's barbed-wire fence.

Our way led alongside the railway track. How long was it since I had last seen a train? If only I could get a seat by the window, so I could look at checkered fields and forests rushing past, see little cottages, winding creeks, and grazing cattle. What a shame little Rishia wouldn't be sitting beside me so I could show her the wonders of nature!

Trembling with excitement, I moved forward in the midst of the throng in front and behind me. My uncle and aunt and Salek and I were walking abreast of each other.

We could already hear the huffing of the steam engine and see its smoke spiraling upward. But what was this? It wasn't a passenger train puffing toward us but a long line of freight cars used for transporting cattle. Each car had only a small barred window at the top. A horrible fear took hold of me. I saw soldiers using brute force to shove the people onto the cars. Now, for the first time, the thought flashed through my mind that Salek may have been right: we ought not to have left the ghetto. Too late!

The freight cars filled up with exemplary order. Exactly thirty-two persons to each car, regardless of whether a child, father, or mother were left stranded outside. Pleading with the soldiers was futile. The heavy iron doors clanged shut, the thick bolts were shot across, and two troopers with drawn bayonets sat down on the steps of each locked freight car.

The train seemed endless, and the long column of people stretched ahead of us. As soon as one car filled up, we all moved to the next one. The embarkation proceeded rapidly. The crowd was thinning out as the compartments filled up one after the other. We had reached the very last of the cars. The soldier standing on the steps was counting, *"Eins, zwei, drei . . ."* The four of us stood close together holding onto one another. We mustn't be separated. Aunt Faiga was the first to mount the steps. They were very high. Her pack was heavy; she stumbled and almost fell down. The soldier pushed her up brutally. "Thirty-one," we heard him count. Uncle Abraham was next. "Thirty-two! Enough! No more!" the soldier shouted. Uncle Abraham protested. "Sir, my children! They're my children! Let me get off! Take two other persons! Let us be together. Please!"

The butt of the rifle came down heavily on my uncle's head, and he fell backward into the car. Salek sprang forward, but I stopped him.

"It's no use, Salek. You'll get shot trying to interfere. We're sure to join them again tomorrow."

The iron door shut, the bolt fell into place, and two armed soldiers took up their places. Soon afterward, a whistle rent the air, and the train started up, moving slowly and heavily at first, then quickly gathering speed. Before long it disappeared from sight.

The remaining deportees were returned to the ghetto to

await their own dispatch the following day. On our way
back, I was tormented by thoughts of unspeakable re-
morse. I walked with my head bent and didn't dare to
look Salek in the face. He didn't say a word but held on
to my hand all the way. My conscience gave me no rest.
It's all my fault. Why did I ignore his distrust of the Germans' intentions? Why didn't I agree to go into hiding
with him? Now we're stranded without his parents, and
he's in this mess because of me!

I looked around. If only we could still escape and hide
somewhere inside the ghetto. But it was too late. What was
done couldn't be undone. Heavily armed German troopers
and Jewish policemen were watching every step we took
on our way back into the ghetto.

The barred iron gate of the prison on Czarniecki Street
fell shut behind us. Our separation from Uncle Abraham
and Aunt Faiga had left us both deeply depressed, and we
wandered aimlessly about the huge prison courtyard,
feeling like two frightened and abandoned children. We
didn't let go of each other's hand.

Then Salek said, "Look who's here!" pointing out a
young man to me. "It's Fulek Zelver. He was the moving
spirit of our resistance organization. He seems to be with
his mother, sister, and brothers. Come, let's join them."

I looked at the people Salek had pointed out. I knew
Mrs. Zelver quite well. She was a native of the town of
Kalisz, like Uncle Abraham, and often used to visit at our
place. The gentle face of this woman and the kind look in
her eyes had always drawn me to her; she reminded me of
my own mother. Mrs. Zelver was accompanied by her
only daughter, Surtcha, and her four sons, the youngest no
older than ten. Salek went up to them.

"Hello, Mrs. Zelver. Do you mind if we join your
family? They wouldn't let us go with my parents, and now
we're all alone here."

Mrs. Zelver looked at us, and a warm smile spread over
her face. "By all means, dears. Do come and join us. Instead of five children, I'll have seven now."

We remained with the Zelvers during the one night that
we spent in the prison. Before going to sleep, Salek and I
cut two slices from one of our loaves of bread and decided
to keep the other loaf untouched until after we reached

our new destination. We slept fully dressed, using our knapsacks as pillows, and both of us dreamed that we were together with Salek's parents.

Early the next morning, we were aroused by the tumult in the huge prison hall. In order to delay our next meal as long as possible, Salek and I went outside to walk about the courtyard. But hunger drove us back inside. We had just entered the hall when we heard a policeman calling our names. He informed us that we were wanted by someone standing outside the prison gate. With pounding hearts, we ran back outside. Were we perhaps to be released in some miraculous way?

On the other side of the prison gate stood Dr. Leider and his wife. They had seen our names on the list of persons returned to the ghetto from the railway station and had come to say good-bye, bringing us a parting gift. The doctor pulled something out of his pocket. It was a sausage! A whole sausage!

Salek reached out through the bars and took the gift with many words of gratitude. I couldn't utter a word. Tears filled my eyes, as I remembered the wonderful evening I spent with the doctor and his family, and the help he had given to my sick father.

After Dr. Leider and his wife had left, Salek broke the sausage into two equal parts, gave me my share, and suggested that we eat it then and there. "A windfall of this kind," he said, "will never come our way again! Let's make the best of it now."

An hour after eating the delicious sausage, Salek and I were again on our way out of the ghetto.

The Iron Door Closes

Once again we passed through the gate in the barbed-wire fence. Another long line of cattle cars was waiting for us at the train station. Salek and I got into the same car as the Zelvers and seated ourselves on the floor around the walls. The small vent holes at the top of the car let in hardly any daylight so it was almost dark inside. Soon the iron door was slammed down with a heavy bang, a shrill whistle sounded, and the train was set in motion.

The rhythmic clatter of the wheels and the familiar sounds I always loved to hear while sitting in a speeding train induced in me a pleasant sense of anticipation. I hadn't the slightest doubt that we were soon to join Salek's parents in the labor camp. One thing, however, puzzled me. Why were there so many people among us who seemed to have no connection with the essential workshops? I made up excuses, supposing that these other people would be separated from the workshop employees and their next-of-kin on arrival. After all, hadn't a special list of our names been compiled before we left the assembly point?

After we got under way, I looked around the car and saw in its center two pails, one of them full of water, the other presumably serving as a toilet. Did the Germans really expect us to behave like the cattle transported in these freight cars and to relieve ourselves in full view of everybody else? I hoped that all of us would be able to hold out until we reached our destination.

The hours passed, and the train was still rushing on. Salek and I were getting hungry but tried to put off eating in order to save the bread for as long as possible. We tried to convince ourselves that the sausage we had eaten in the morning would keep us satisfied all day long. But the sight of the many people around us eating made our mouths

142

water and weakened our resolve not to eat anymore that day.

Salek and I had made an agreement about the food we had with us. Since we didn't know how long this journey was to last, we had to go very easy on our bread. Salek entrusted all the bread left—a loaf and a half—into my care, knowing it would be safer with me, since he lacked the willpower to withstand his hunger pangs.

"Promise me," he said, "not to give in, even if I beg you on my knees."

I, on the other hand, couldn't resist the temptation to take an occasional lick of sugar. So I put my share into his keeping and begged him, likewise, not to yield to any of my requests.

When evening came, we gave up our struggle. I cut off a slice of bread for each of us, and Salek sprinkled some sugar over both. We took care to eat the bread very slowly so that it would last as long as possible, hoping desperately that the train would reach its destination before we had finished. But far from stopping anywhere, the train seemed to be hurtling on at an increased speed. We washed down our "meal" with water that I ladled from the pail into my small soup bowl.

We had been traveling for many hours now, and the pressure on my bladder was becoming unbearable. I looked at the people about me, wondering whether some of them didn't also need to relieve themselves. Up to now, no one had dared to use the toilet pail in view of all the others; even the few children among us had managed to restrain themselves. But how long was it possible to withstand the urge?

I heard Fulek whispering something to his mother, who nodded in agreement. Fulek then took a sheet out of his pack and looked up at two hooks fixed to the ceiling in a corner of the wagon. Since the hooks were too high for Fulek to reach, his brothers David and Leizer, along with Salek, formed a pyramid, enabling him to climb up on their backs and to tie the sheet to the hooks. The pail was put behind this screen, and people now began to line up to use the makeshift lavatory. I sighed in relief and looked with admiration at the four boys. They had been mere children when they entered the ghetto, had grown up in it, had witnessed the degradation of their people, yet they had not lost their sense of human dignity.

It was getting dark, and the air inside the crowded car was stifling on this warm summer night. Most of the people were sitting in silence; some were dozing while others stared straight ahead. I was sunk in thought, feeling proud of all of us in this compartment for striving to retain what little dignity we had left. Suddenly, overcome by a sense of defiance, I began humming the song *Der Veg Forois*. People looked up in wonderment. Ashamed of my sudden impulse, I was about to stop singing when I felt the pressure of Salek's hand on mine. This encouraged me to sing the song to the end.

It was completely dark by now, and the train went on speeding into the night. The clatter of its wheels combined with the darkness became oppressive. I began humming the sad song *Vander Ich Fun Land Tzu Land* (I Wander from Land to Land), and before long Salek and the Zelvers joined in. The train seemed to accompany our singing with its own rhythmic music.

As our journey continued, the train would occasionally slow down while it was being shunted onto another track. Then it would regain speed and move on. When the toilet pail became full in the course of the night, Salek and the Zelver boys emptied it through the narrow chink between the floor and the iron door. The morning light had begun to filter through the vent holes, and the train was still rushing ahead. "What a frightening journey this is!" I thought to myself. "Not to have any idea of where you're going or what's awaiting you there."

"I'm hungry," I said to Salek. "Let's eat something." I cut four slices of bread and sprinkled sugar on each. As before, we washed the food down with water from the pail. About two hours later, Salek asked me to show him how much of the bread was left. I showed him the full loaf and the last third of the other one. Salek tried to persuade me to finish off the remaining third on the assumption that we were sure to arrive at the labor camp that day and would be given something to eat there.

"What makes you so sure of being fed there?" I asked, reminding him of the plight of all those people in the ghetto who couldn't make their rations last long enough. Salek didn't ask for any more bread, but after a while I took pity on him and cut off another slice just for him. He wouldn't take it unless I, too, ate a slice. Pretending not to be hungry, I only took a few grains of sugar and drank some water. Before long the second evening of the journey was upon us, and still we were on the move. When Salek asked for another slice of bread, I refused on the grounds that it was wasteful to eat at night. We had to try to forget our hunger and go to sleep. We'd eat again the next day.

In the morning we finished the last of the first loaf, and I had a hard time resisting Salek's pleas to break into our last loaf. Once we did that, I said, we risked running out of food, since we had no notion when this journey would come to an end. Finally we reached a compromise: if we didn't reach our destination within two hours, we'd eat something. Meanwhile, I permitted Salek to take a little of the sugar to quiet his hunger for a while. Salek said no more but sat licking his sugar dolefully. I asked him to make it last as long as possible, but, seeing his sad face, I relented and said I would break into the last loaf if he still insisted after finishing the sugar.

Nightmare

Even before we had a chance to break into our last loaf of bread, the train slowed down, huffed and puffed as if exhausted from its long journey, and finally came to a halt. After the train's clatter stopped, a thunderous noise reached our ears, as if great numbers of people were gathered outside.

"Great God!" I thought. "How will we ever find Uncle Abraham and Aunt Faiga in such a huge crowd!"

The racket outside increased, and all of us in the car sprang to our feet.

"Salek," I whispered in alarm, "there must be thousands out there. How on earth are we going to find your parents?"

The noise was earsplitting, not unlike a roaring wave about to engulf us. I began trembling, and Salek grasped my hand. What was going on out there? What *was* that terrible noise? Could it really be an ocean wave rolling toward us? No, people were making those sounds—thousands of people screaming in terror!

We heard the bolt of our car being removed and the heavy iron door being shifted aside. When I looked out, I thought for a moment that I was having an hallucination. Was I sick again, a victim of fantastic visions? The spectacle before us was almost impossible to comprehend.

From our elevated position in the freight car, we had a clear view of a mass of people caught up in a bedlam of confusion, a kind of hell let loose. Heavily armed S.S. troopers and men in blue-and-white-striped jackets were running through this crowd, swinging truncheons and rifle butts right and left, smashing people's heads amid bone-chilling wails and shrieks. At a distance we could see a barbed-wire fence and many watchtowers, in each of which stood a soldier with a machine gun. And what was that beyond the barbed-wire fence? Strange creatures who looked as if they had been lifted straight out of horror films! It was impossible to tell if they were men or women, for their heads were shaven and their clothes consisted of shapeless black rags. Similar tattered rags seemed to be strung out along the barbed-wire fence.

"It must be a lunatic asylum we've been brought to," I said to myself. Though I had never seen such a place before, I imagined that this was what it must look like. Before I had time to recover from my bewilderment, a group of the muscular men in their striped jackets burst into our car. All of us stood there stupefied, clinging to members of our families. Salek and I held one another in a terrified embrace. He pressed me close as if to protect me, but he himself was trembling like a leaf. One of the thugs tore us apart and thrust us violently toward the exit. "Forward! Get off!" he barked.

Salek reached out for our packs. A blow came down on his arm, accompanied by an ugly laugh. "You don't need that anymore," the man said. No one was allowed to take the luggage we had packed so carefully. I shall never forget how at this moment of horrible confusion I had only one thought in my mind—I was losing Father's *talit* collar, the last remnant of my ties with a glorious past. The thought was blotted out at once by the breakneck speed of the events taking place. We were being pushed down the steps. A woman near me stumbled and fell off. Blows hailed down on her until she got up again. I went down the steps, clutching the bread in my arms, and before I even touched the ground, I was yanked violently to the left by a soldier with a bayonet who was shouting, *"Frauen links, Männer rechts!"* ("Women to the left, men to the right.")

"Salek!" I shouted, looking around. "Where are you?" I couldn't see my cousin anymore; I had lost sight of him in the crowd. In vain I stood on my toes, turning my head in all directions. Salek had vanished. I was being swept along among the women, when all of a sudden it struck me. The bread! All the bread had remained with me! I tried to push my way back toward the right, calling out at the top of my voice, "Salek! Salek! Take the bread! Salek! The bread!"

My voice was swallowed up in the turmoil around me, and another voice bellowed, *"Frauen links!"* A truncheon blow descended on my back, and I was flung brutally to the women's side. There I saw heartbreaking scenes as children were taken from their mothers, brothers from sisters. Wails of "Mummy! Daddy!" filled the air. I witnessed the youngest Zelver being torn from his mother's arms but immediately lost sight of both of them.

Amid curses and bellowings, the women and girls were pushed and prodded into groups of five, and the fantastic procession got under way. In the midst of this huge crowd, I felt frightfully alone, a kind of aloneness I had never experienced in all my life, not even when Father died. Then I still had Uncle Abraham and Salek, Genia and little Rishia . . .

As I walked, I pressed the loaf of bread to my breast. The thought that I hadn't allowed Salek to eat when he wanted to, that he must be ravenously hungry while the entire loaf remained with me, almost drove me mad.

The procession now moved onto a wide road bordered on both sides by a long barbed-wire fence. Before us a large arch came into view. It bore the inscription *Auschwitz*, and below it the words *Arbeit Macht Frei* (Work Will Make You Free). By now we were quite close to those curious-looking creatures we had seen from afar. They were making signs to us, gesticulating, opening their mouths wide, trying to tell us something. Poor lunatics! I thought to myself. Look at them! Who can understand their signs and the sounds they're making?

We trudged along without any idea of where we were headed or what was going to happen to us. Hadn't the Germans assured us that the entire ghetto population was being transferred to the countryside where the essential workshops would be reassembled? Hadn't they told us that all families would stay together? With very few exceptions—Salek among them—we believed what the Germans said! But families were being torn apart brutally. Why? What difference would it make to the Germans if relatives remained together? Hadn't we turned out good products in the ghetto while living with our families?

The ghetto! I had deluded myself, believing there could be nothing worse than the ghetto. I had wanted to get away at all cost so I could breathe the fresh country air, see trees and flowers again. I had even persuaded Salek to join me, against his own better judgment. If only I could get word to Genia not to leave the ghetto, to hide away somewhere!

Then it occurred to me that perhaps this was only a horrible nightmare. Such things couldn't be real. I pressed my nails into my flesh and felt the pain, I bit my lips until they bled. There was no doubt about it. It was all happening now.

As we got nearer the barbed-wire fences, I noticed signs at varying distances: "Danger! High Tension Wires!" Every step we took brought even more horrible revelations. What had earlier looked like black rags spread out along the fence turned out to be dead bodies of people who had been electrocuted by touching the wire. I thought that in their madness they had probably been unable to read the warning signs and had paid for it with their lives.

The nearer we came, the more distinctly we could hear the shouts of those crazy-looking creatures on the other side of the fence. They were trying to talk to us, calling out in a welter of tongues—Polish, German, Yiddish, and many others unfamiliar to me. They wanted us to throw over to them some of the bread we had brought along. We wouldn't need it any more, they told us; it would be taken away from us in any case, as would all our clothes. We'd look exactly like them before long, they shouted, and we would all go up in smoke.

The woman next to me started to eat her bread with frantic haste, swallowing it in big chunks. The loaf in my hand began to feel heavy and seemed to burn me under the gaze of all those hunger-crazed people. I hesitated for no more than a second. I meant to throw my loaf across the fence, but it slipped from my hand and fell to the side of the road. The grotesque-looking forms started forward in the direction of the bread, pushing each other aside in their effort to get at it first. When it hit the ground, the loaf rolled away and came to rest near the barbed-wire fence. I saw the people's faces twisting horribly and heard them cursing as they raised their clenched fists. None dared to reach out through the electrified fence; the bread remained lying nearby, just beyond their reach.

The slow advance of our column had now brought us to a group of S.S. men who were confiscating all the valuables still in our possession. I cast about desperately for some way of preventing them from taking away my mother's jewelry, each piece of which reminded me of precious moments in the past. They were my last links with what I held dear. Father and I had kept the jewelry throughout our years in the ghetto and in the most trying of circumstances. Now that I had lost contact with Salek and had to leave all my belongings behind, those few things I still had with me became a thousand times more precious. I could not let them go.

I hastily removed the golden chain from my neck and put it beneath my tongue, hoping it would not be found there. I slipped Mother's gold watch from my wrist and held it in my closed fist. By now the woman in front of me was being searched. A paralyzing fear took hold of me on seeing the brutal treatment given her by the soldiers. She was ordered to open her mouth, and one of them looked into it with a flashlight. On spotting a gold tooth, he took a pair of pincers, and within an instant, the tooth was gleaming in his hand. This tooth must have served as a dental support, for as soon as it was removed, several other teeth fell out after it. The woman began vomiting. Revolted at the sight, the soldiers kicked her forward violently.

Feeling close to retching myself, I moved forward to be searched. The soldier's hand ran up and down my body and dipped into all my pockets. He pulled out the package with the photographs. I held out a trembling hand and said, "Please let me keep these photos. They're all I have left of my dead parents."

The soldier gave me a look of contempt, and I was appalled to see him tear the pictures into tiny pieces and toss them up into the air with a mocking smile. I sobbed quietly while the soldier kept groping about in my pockets. He found the two rings—Mother's wedding ring and the one with the diamonds that she used to love so much. During all my years of hunger and privation, I had never dreamed of giving up these treasures. Now they disappeared into the pile of jewelry heaped up on the big table. The soldier proceeded with his search. He pulled out Father's gilded cigarette case, in which I kept my asthma pills.

"Sir," I begged him, "take the case but let me have the pills inside it." But the pills were flung about in all directions and the cigarette case was thrown onto the table. Now I was ordered to open my mouth. The soldier, wise to all the tricks that might be used, pulled out the chain from beneath my tongue. My attempt at cheating them earned me a resounding smack across my face. Finally my fist was forced open, and Mother's golden wristwatch joined the rest of the jewelry on the table.

I had only one thing left. It was the heart-shaped golden ring on my finger engraved with my initials, S.P. I had received it some time before the outbreak of the war and hadn't removed it since. In fact, it had become a bit tight and I couldn't take it off anymore. The soldier tried unsuccessfully to force the ring off. Then another soldier came up with a pair of large scissors. Good God! He was going to cut it off together with my finger! But he didn't do that. He simply cut through the band and threw the ring onto the table. I was yanked aside to make way for the next woman in line.

I stumbled forward, my legs buckling beneath me. I had been robbed of everything: my pills, my jewelry, my parents' pictures. I might have been able to gaze on their beloved faces in moments of despair, and they would have given me strength. Now I had nothing, and I might even forget what they had looked like.

The column next stopped at a large wooden hut, where we were confronted by a number of frightfully stout female guards called *Kapos*, each with a club. We were ordered to strip and be quick about it, leaving on only our shoes. In vain had I worn my two blouses and winter coat, enduring the discomforts of the hot August weather so as to be able to stuff a few additional articles into my bag! Now I had to take everything off and leave it on the growing mound of clothes on the floor. Standing stark naked and trembling with fear and shame, I saw the women ahead of me, naked like myself, filing by several other *Kapos*. Each *Kapo* held a pair of hair-clippers and passed it rapidly through the women's hair, transforming their appearances within seconds. The *Kapos* worked with a devilish precision, obviously enjoying the task. The women moved up one after another, standing quietly while their shorn hair fell down around them. After their heads were shaved, their body hair was removed as well.

Once again I pinched myself and bit my lips to make sure that this wasn't some recurring nightmare. The pain that shot through me was enough to convince me that it was real. Then I thought that perhaps it was the reality of some other world, of life after death. Was I in hell? Was I being punished for my sins? For occasional disobedience of my parents? For ignoring the warnings of Salek and Genia? Surely such punishment should be reserved for those who had stolen or killed. But I had never committed these crimes. Could the women around me be guilty of such things?

Such were my thoughts while I advanced step by step toward the *Kapos*. When my turn arrived, one of them, grabbing my hair from underneath, exclaimed ecstatically, "What a gorgeous mass of hair! It'll easily make two beautiful wigs!"

"Please, madam," I beseeched her, "don't shave my head. It's only one year since I was sick with typhoid, and it was shaved then. You can see for yourself, my hair is perfectly clean. Please, don't shave it all off."

The *Kapo* looked at me from top to bottom and then burst into uproarious laughter. "What do you need any of your hair for? You're not going to be around for long.

This way, your beautiful blond hair will remain behind as a souvenir."

The clippers passed back and forth across my scalp, and all my hair—once the pride of my parents—dropped about me on all sides. Dear Daddy! I thought. Can you see what they are doing to your daughter? Then all of a sudden—even while the woman was busy shaving my head—an inexplicable calm descended on me and a sense of strange elation passed through me. I felt happy, as if God had granted me a special favor. "I'm grateful to you, great God," I prayed silently, "for having taken Father in time and sparing him all these degradations, and for saving my gentle mother from enduring any of these ordeals. Thank you, Almighty God, for finally releasing me, too, from the tormenting thoughts of what they would suffer if they were here with me."

Now that my scalp was shaven, I no longer cared what was happening to me. In complete apathy I raised my arms and spread my legs while the clippers did its work efficiently. Finally, giving me a violent push, the *Kapo* barked, "Go to the right, over there to the *Kapo* standing with the young girls. She's going to be your teacher. You kids will have a lot of learning to do here." She shouted across to her colleague with a sardonic smile, "Here's another pupil for you!"

I walked off to the right, wondering what I was to be taught here. How to tear a child from its mother's arms? How to beat people on the head with a truncheon? The art of extracting teeth for the sake of a piece of gold?

The *Kapo* I was sent to received me rather kindly. She handed me some sort of black rag to put on and confirmed her colleague's words by saying, "You young girls will soon begin going to school. You can consider yourselves lucky. All the others are being sent to hard labor. Only you are going to study." She repeated this little speech whenever a few more girls joined our group.

I put on the ragged garment, pleased to have something to cover my nakedness. It was a loose, tattered robe twice my size, with openings for the head and the arms. It occurred to me that these were exactly the same sort of rags worn by those grotesque-looking creatures I had seen earlier alongside the barbed-wire fence. And I had taken them for lunatics! They were nothing of the kind. They merely wanted to tell us that before long we, too, would look like them. And now we did, and we would ourselves be taken for lunatics by those arriving after us. Perhaps we *were* all lunatics and Auschwitz an asylum from which we would never escape.

The First Night in Auschwitz

After a large group of girls had been gathered together, our *Kapo* began arranging us into rows of five abreast. She was now joined by several other guards, stout like herself, their hair short and stubbled as if it, too, had been cropped not long ago. These women's dresses were so short that they barely covered their hefty thighs. Escorted by the *Kapos*, our procession set out in the direction of the so-called school building. Fortunately I never reached it, though how it happened I hardly knew myself. Perhaps my dead parents interceded with Divine Providence on my behalf. . . .

As we moved along the broad road, I was conscious of a keen sense of aloneness, of being surrounded by strangers, each of whom was utterly alone in her own misfortune. Then I saw a column of ghastly-looking figures coming toward us. Like ourselves, they were bald and clad in loose, black garments. They were also ranked five abreast but, unlike us, were walking barefoot over the sharp gravel on the ground. A large number of *Kapos* guarded them on both sides. Suddenly I caught sight of a familiar face in the group. Who was it? Surtcha, of course! Mrs. Zelver's daughter, with whom I had spent the last couple of days in the cattle car! Surtcha was walking at the outer edge of a row of five. A thought flashed through my mind. I must join her at all cost! Anything but this unbearable loneliness. There was little time to lose. Within seconds, I had slipped out of my column and joined hers.

I was now walking in the opposite direction from the group I had been with.

In looking back, I cannot help but think that this sudden impulse of mind had been inspired from above. How else can I account for the fact that not a single *Kapo*—and there were many of them there—noticed what I had done? I did have a momentary doubt about my action and wondered why we had been allowed to keep our shoes on while they were walking barefoot. But it was too late for regrets. My former group had passed on and was now some distance behind me. They were heading for the "school building," which, I found out later, was nothing but a gas chamber. Not a single member of the group would survive. If I had not left them, I would have shared their awful fate.

"Surtcha," I whispered to the girl walking beside me. "Surtcha!" She turned her head toward me, and fear gripped my heart on seeing the look of dull incomprehension in her eyes. Had she lost her reason?

Suddenly a gleam of recognition crossed her eyes. "Salusia!" Her face lit up as she grasped my hand. "Salusia!"

"Surtcha!" My tears began to flow, tears of happiness at meeting someone I knew. "Where's your mother and all your brothers?"

"I don't know. Don't know a thing. I was pushed away. I just caught a glimpse of Mother and Yanush before they disappeared from sight. I don't know what happened to them, what's happening to me, or to all of us here."

"Surtcha," I said, "let's try and stick together." I squeezed her hand while the tears streamed down my face.

"What's going on here!" the shrill voice of a *Kapo* sounded beside me. "There should only be five in a row! Everyone on this end step back one row!"

I moved back with all the others, and no one noticed that I didn't belong. I remained with the group chosen for hard labor but destined to live.

The group was led into a huge wooden barrack with a large red-bricked oven running across the middle to the other end. The *Kapos* began to count us: 1,000 women to each barrack, 500 to each side of the oven. Although the room was of enormous dimension, it was too small to accommodate all of us. We were squeezed in like sardines in a can, standing practically on one another's toes. So that all 1,000 women could be shoved into the barrack, we were ordered to sit down with legs spread wide apart and to push ourselves up against the woman in front of us.

At first it was comforting to sit down and rest our weary limbs. But the relief was short-lived. We were pressed so hard against one another that our positions soon became unbearably painful. Surtcha and I, sitting together, held each other in a close embrace. Our eyes met, and all at once we burst into hysterical laughter, tears streaming down our faces. Our laughter lasted barely a few seconds, coming to an abrupt end as we looked at one another with eyes wide in horror. Was it possible that we had both gone mad?

Night descended, and we began our first night in Auschwitz. On the ceiling high above us, a small electric bulb was kept burning. Surtcha and I were shivering with cold despite the warm summer night and the stuffy atmosphere of a room occupied by a thousand women. The cement floor was very cold, and we were sitting on it wearing nothing but our loose garments. Half sitting, half reclining, everyone tried to sleep, if only to forget for a while the horrors we had been through. But even that relief was denied us as our limbs grew numb from prolonged sitting in the same position. At first people quietly asked their neighbors for permission to shift a leg or stretch an arm, but soon the requests turned into abusive squabbling and violent jostling. The hall was filled with the sounds of moaning and outcries of pain.

In that hall, surrounded by all those forlorn and stupefied women, I first began to doubt the existence of God. Never before, despite all the hardships I had undergone, had I ever dared to let such ideas enter my mind. But now I wondered if there could be a God in heaven who looked down and saw everything. If there was such a God, wouldn't he have acted to bring deliverance to us, his chosen people? Hadn't God's wrath been brought down upon Pharaoh and the Egyptian hordes who tormented his people? Our suffering was incomparably worse than that of the Israelite slaves. Why, then, didn't God punish Hitler and his henchmen instead of allowing them to torment us for so many years? Perhaps God himself had begun to despise his own people.

I was roused from these painful thoughts by the sound of someone behind us crying softly. Surtcha and I turned our heads to the pale, weeping girl.

"What's the matter? Are we pressing too hard against you? Are we hurting you?" we asked.

"No, it's not that," the girl sobbed. "If only I knew where my little sister was. All our family died in the ghetto; only the two of us were left. I always believed that we'd see this thing through together. Now they've separated us and put my sister in with another group."

I felt sorry for this pale girl, whose name was Blumka. "Don't worry," I consoled her, "your sister will be all right. She's probably in the group I was with earlier and is being sent to school. She's even been allowed to keep her shoes on. Surtcha and I will be your sisters. Let's try and keep together."

By now the noise in the hall was great, and the *Kapo* guarding us was becoming angry. She was keeping an eye on us from a narrow, raised platform on which there was a bed covered with a pink blanket. To those of us crowded together on the floor, the *Kapo*'s "room" looked like an enchanted castle in a legendary world. Before she had climbed the ladder to her platform, our *Kapo* had ordered us to keep quiet and let her get some sleep, but the continuous noise was disturbing her.

Suddenly, a curious silence descended on the hall, and I raised my head to see the fat *Kapo* climbing down the ladder, club in hand, her face livid with anger. She gave a long shrill whistle, and within an instant, two other *Kapos* armed with clubs burst into the hall. One of them, a tall, thin woman, had long red hair that looked like a tongue of fire. All three *Kapos* ran wildly about, wielding their truncheons and striking blows on the heads of anyone near them. The red-head flailed her victims with almost ecstatic fury. This furious action lasted no more than a few minutes. The *Kapos* swept through the hall like a hurricane and were gone as suddenly as they had come.

"Didn't I warn you to keep quiet!" our *Kapo* yelled. "Maybe I'll be able to get some sleep now!"

During the day, I had heard it whispered that these women were Jews, not unlike the Hebrew overseers of the slaves in Egypt. This made their cruelty all the worse.

Couldn't our *Kapos* see that it was impossible to keep quiet in our situation? If only one person in a hundred wanted to straighten out a leg, it would cause a lot of noise. Didn't she know that it was excruciatingly painful to sit like that for hours on end?

I got to my feet. Surtcha and Blumka tried to pull me back. "What are you going to do! She'll kill you on the spot!"

I pulled my black garment from their grasp and walked across to our *Kapo*. She was on the point of mounting the ladder when she caught sight of me. Standing with her legs spread and leaning on her truncheon, she looked at me curiously with a malicious glint in her eyes.

"What do you want?" she asked in German.

"Do you understand Polish?" I asked her in the same language.

"Yes. I'm from Slovakia."

"That'll make it easier for me to talk to you. You're Jewish, aren't you?"

"So what," she said in a mocking tone.

"If you're Jewish, why do you help the Germans torture us? Why do you beat your own sisters? Haven't you any feeling of pity? Haven't we all gone through enough, torn from our relatives, deprived of everything we possessed? And now we haven't even enough room to put down our heads. We're pressed against each other, with hands and legs completely numb. How can a thousand women in such positions keep quiet all the time? You don't understand it since you have a bed all to yourself."

The *Kapo* didn't move. Leaning on her truncheon, she seemed to be listening patiently to every word I said. When I stopped talking, she said in heavily accented Polish, "Finished?"

"Yes," I replied.

"Turn around," she commanded. I did and immediately found myself in a pitch black world with stars swirling about my head. I seemed to be floating among thousands of stars, and I seemed to hear a soft, soothing melody that gave me a sense of wonderful tranquility. Suddenly I felt water on my face. I opened my eyes and realized that I was lying on the floor, with the enormous *Kapo* standing over me and dousing me with a strong jet of water from a hose. I was terribly thirsty. Water! I opened my mouth to take a drink, but the moment the *Kapo* noticed me moving, she turned the hose aside.

"Get up!" she commanded. I got to my feet wearily. My head was heavy and a dull noise sounded in my ears. "Climb onto the oven and get down on your knees!"

The *Kapo* took four large bricks, placed two in each of my hands, and ordered me to raise the bricks above my head. I couldn't do it—they were too heavy. Blows fell on my back until, with a superhuman effort, I managed to raise my arms. I felt as sore as if every bone in my body was broken. I don't know how long I was kept there holding the bricks above my head. All I remember was a command finally coming from somewhere far away—"Get back to your place!"

I dragged myself back and either passed out or fell into a deep sleep. On awakening, I had an experience so strange, such a combination of the heavenly and the horrifying, that it seemed a kind of hallucination. I heard the sound of a voice, crystal clear and maddeningly sweet, soaring up into the vast expanse of the hall, high above us wretched creatures writhing painfully on the floor. It was a voice utterly at variance with the gruesome spectacle around us, and the song it sang—"Ave Maria"—also seemed strangely exotic in this setting. The beautiful melody filled the air, penetrating into the inner recesses of my soul and making me momentarily oblivious to the horrors I had undergone.

I raised my head to see where this divine voice was coming from. On the flat top of the oven, I saw standing the pale and haggard form of a young woman clad in the black cloak worn by all of us. It was Estusio Kenner, a singer well known to us from the ghetto in Lodz. I didn't know what it was that had made her get up and sing, whether she had been prompted by some request or inspired by an impulse to give all of us, floundering in a sea of despair, something to hold onto.

The singer continued with a song about the suffering endured by our people throughout the ages, which ended with a message of hope and consolation. The words failed to give us any relief. All we could do was weep silently as if in accompaniment to the sweet voice. The *Kapos* themselves, falling under its spell, suspended their cruel activities for a while as they too listened to the singer whose voice seemed to rise in prayer from the depths of hell.

Lineup

I must have dropped off to sleep again that night, for I remember distinctly the sounds of earsplitting shrieks and prolonged whistling breaking in on my consciousness. Like a pack of hounds after their game, a large number of *Kapos* stormed into our midst, stepped all over us, and brought down their clubs with full force upon our heads.

"*Appell!* (Roll call!) *Appell!*" they shouted. "Everybody get out! Quick! March!"

Holding onto the hands of Surtcha and Blumka, I was swept forward in the stream of bodies. It was still dark outside, but I could see thousands of dazed, barefoot women pouring out of many large barracks like ours. Driven by an unceasing hail of blows, we reached an open square of enormous dimensions that was packed to capacity within minutes. In the distance appeared the outlines of several smokestacks spitting flames and smoke and red sparks up into the sky. A curious smell—an indefinable mixture of something burnt, singed, and decomposing—hovered in the air.

The *Kapos* lost no time lining the women in the square up again in groups of a thousand, five to a row. We were ordered on our knees and warned to keep our bodies stiffly erect. I couldn't tell how long we were kept kneeling, but it seemed to be an eternity. Anyone trying to sit back on her heels to relieve her aching knees was immediately pounced upon by one of the *Kapos*. I now longed for my former sitting position, and all memory of numb limbs vanished in my fervent desire to have something to lean my weary body against. There was an eerie stillness all around. Every now and then somebody collapsed, but no one dared to come to her rescue or to utter a word. The only sounds were those of the *Kapos* screaming abuses or blowing their whistles.

Gradually the darkness faded to make way for the first rays of the morning sun. It almost seemed as though the sun halted momentarily in its upward journey, astonished at the spectacle it shone upon. Looking around the square, I could see nothing but row after row of kneeling forms that resembled scarecrows or black-cloaked skeletons. The scene looked like a gruesome painting that only the sick imagination of a lunatic could have concocted.

Soon after daylight, a group of tall S.S. officers arrived, resplendent in black uniforms and highly polished jack-boots. They walked in gay self-confidence, swagger sticks under their arms and holstered pistols in their belts. Compared to the kneeling monsters in the square, they seemed like creatures from another planet. The officers passed at some distance from us without so much as glancing in our direction, as though we were not present at all. But their appearance set all the *Kapos* into a flurry of agitation, and they made their reports with the obsequiousness of slaves. The *Kapos*, too, were ignored by the officers, who talked among themselves as they strutted past. Once more the air was filled with whistling and shrill orders as the *Kapos* drove us back into our barracks. The roll call was over.

As soon as we were lined up and on our knees, a number of women prisoners entered the hall, dragging baskets full of dry, sliced bread. One of them made a hollow in each slice, another filled the hollow with honey, and a third passed the slice on to be shared by a row of five. The distribution of food was carried out with speedy efficiency under the supervision of the *Kapos*.

Only now it occurred to me that none of us had eaten anything since we were taken off the train; the numbing horrors we had experienced had driven all thought of hunger out of our minds. At the sight of food, however, we found we could scarcely wait. We fell upon the honey, a delicacy not tasted since the start of the war, with unimaginable greed. But we did not enjoy its sweetness for long. The Germans had devised a new torment, and the sweet, thick honey was part of the plan. No sooner had we finished eating the dry bread spread with honey than we were seized by a hellish thirst that nearly drove us out of our minds. But no water was brought to quench our thirst. I tried to swallow spittle, but my mouth was dry and sticky. So great was my torment that it drove all other thoughts—even my anxiety for the rest of my family—out of my mind. I had to have water! My mind conjured up pictures of all the springs, rivers, and waterfalls I had ever seen.

Now I also became aware of the soreness of my back, the after-effect of the murderous blows I had received the previous night. Every movement I made shot pain through me. The sweltering August heat was beating down on the stuffy building, increasing our misery.

God! Was there no end to evil? Whenever it seemed that I had reached the limits of my endurance, convinced that nothing could be worse than my present plight, all the outrages of the past diminished in the face of what we were made to endure next. If only I could let myself go— scream, hit out with my fists! But all I did was bite my clenched fists until they bled.

At noon they brought us soup, and the aroma set our heads spinning. Something to drink! We would take anything so long as it put out the fire that was driving us into insane frenzy. Cauldrons filled with the steaming soup were carried in by more women prisoners. One small dish was ladled out for each row and had to be shared by five women. The first person in a row had scarcely managed to carry the dish to her lips before it was snatched away by others unable to await their turn. They lunged forward, biting and scratching in a desperate scuffle to get possession of the coveted soup. It was a horrible spectacle watched with demonic glee by the German officers, while the *Kapos*, who seemed to have been waiting for this opportunity, assaulted us again furiously under the pretext of restoring order.

In my row Blumka was the first to taste the soup; it was scalding hot, very thick, and extremely salty. We didn't hurry her. But as soon as she brought the dish to her lips, she almost dropped it, for it was so hot that she burned her mouth. Her eyes were watering as she handed the dish on to me with a warning to take care. My fingers, tongue, and throat scalded. Surtcha didn't take any of the soup and quickly passed it on to her neighbor, Bronka, a tall, thin girl who hadn't exchanged a word with any of us until now. She handed the dish on to *her* neighbor after taking no more than a sip. The dish was back to Blumka. Now we were more careful, blowing to cool the soup before taking our share, passing the dish back and forth among us. But the soup didn't still our hunger, and it only increased our thirst.

The building was unbearably hot. My back was aching and my insides were twisting and turning. Time seemed to stand still. I don't know how long we were kept on our knees before it was announced that we were being taken to get a drink. It is almost impossible to describe the uproar in the hall when we heard the word "water." We jumped to our feet and lunged forward as if infused with new life. Like animals, we surged ahead, hitting out, biting and scratching as we elbowed one another out of the way in a mad stampede to be among the first to reach the water. Even the truncheon-wielding *Kapos* lost control over us.

Throughout all the years in the ghetto, under the most gruesome conditions, we had managed to preserve a semblance of our humanity. Now that vanished. Here in Auschwitz, the Germans had created the ideal conditions for transforming human beings into wild beasts within the shortest possible time.

When we reached the water, we found two long pipes with many faucets attached to them. The sight and sound of the splashing water drove us absolutely crazy. To get to the water! Just to wet our lips! The crush was terrible, and women were knocked down and trampled underfoot. In the wild scramble, I was knocked to the ground just as I got near the faucets. I pushed my head under the flowing stream, opened my mouth, and drank and drank and drank, unable to satisfy my terrible thirst. Before I had drunk my fill, I was shoved away, and soon all of us were driven back into our hut.

We had hardly settled in when our *Kapo* decided that this was the time for all of us to go to the latrine, which was located in another building. When my turn came to use one of the holes cut into the long wooden board, my bowels would not move. I could do nothing but look with envy at those who succeeded in relieving themselves when ordered to do so. In Auschwitz, the Germans not only manipulated our tortured souls but also regulated every function of our bodies. Eating, sleeping, elimination—all were under their control, causing us physical torments impossible to describe.

Not long after returning to our hut from the latrine, we were chased outside again for a new kind of inspection. This intermittent activity was continued, and we spent the next five days lining up, kneeling in the square, being chased back and forth, until we had reached a state of stupefied exhaustion. Early on the morning of the sixth day, we were aroused by the *Kapos* shouting; "Selection lineup! Selection lineup! Everybody out!" Again we were driven back to the square, where we learned that not all of us were to be allocated to a labor gang. The number of women available exceeded the requirements, and a sifting operation was to be undertaken.

A group of S.S. officers soon appeared on the scene, and the *Kapos* shouted, "Strip! Everybody strip!" I hesitated. I had not yet overcome my shame at being seen naked by those of my own sex, let alone by all those German officers! "You deaf? Strip and be quick about it!" I heard the shrill voice before I felt the painful blow on my head. Quickly I pulled off the ragged cloak, and at that moment all sense of shame vanished as I realized that we were anything but sex objects in the eyes of those Germans who were surveying us with obvious expressions of disgust. We Jewish women belonged to a "subhuman species," and we were utterly repulsive to the German officers.

The selection was to be made by only one of the officers. I can't recall his face because I was too scared to look up, but from a furtive glance, I got the impression of jet black hair and a toothbrush moustache in the style of Adolf Hitler. What I remember most vividly was the monocle through which he cast a brief glance at each woman placed before him. The officer was Dr. Mengele. He was sparse with words, using his raised forefinger to make his intentions clear. After a cursory glance at the naked figure in front of him, his finger moved to the right or to the left in unspoken command. Women whose limbs were slack and whose skin sagged about the belly and buttocks or young girls appearing to be nothing but skin and bones were sent to the left, while all those whose bodies were covered with sufficient flesh went to the right.

Once again we witnessed atrocious scenes of separation

as sisters, mothers, and daughters who had remained together until now were brutally torn from each other's arms. Nothing made any difference, neither tearful pleading nor an attempt to join a loved one who had been sent to the other side. All without exception were beaten back mercilessly by the *Kapos*. The decision made by a flick of the doctor's finger was irrevocable.

It was Surtcha's turn now. She was sent to the right, as were Blumka and Bronka. Though they were very lean, they did not yet look like living skeletons. Now my turn had come. I wished fervently to join Surtcha and the others, to be together with my newfound sisters, no matter what was going to happen to them—anything rather than being alone again. I trembled with fear that I would be directed to the side of the weak and the sick, for I was thin as a stick and as yet completely flat-chested.

A confusion of thoughts filled my mind. I was sure to be taken for a child incapable of hard work. My back was full of blue welts from the beating I had taken, which would certainly count against me. I covered my chest instinctively with my black robe, but a *Kapo* leaned forward and tore it away. Now I stood stark naked in front of Dr. Mengele and his group of aides. A brief glance through his monocle, a quick movement of his finger, and I found myself walking off to the right. I sighed in relief, as did my three friends, who had watched my processing with bated breath. We were still together. At the time, none of us knew we were among those who were destined to live and that those who had been sent to the left would die.

All of us standing to the right of the doctor were ordered to put on our black robes. We filed past several *Kapos* who dipped paint brushes into a red liquid and ran them over our backs from top to bottom. This was our identification mark.

While the four of us were standing together in a huddle, a tall, thin, olive-skinned girl was pushed to our side. Seeing Surtcha, she embraced her, kissed her over and over again, and kept murmuring tearfully, "Surtcha, dear Surtcha!" It was Faiga, the sister of Surtcha's best friend. Her joy at meeting someone she knew was boundless.

From that moment on, the five of us—Surtcha, Blumka, Bronka, Faiga, and I—became inseparable, like five faithful sisters. Being an only child, I had never known what it meant to have a sister. Even if I had had a real sister, I doubt whether I could have loved her any more than I loved each one of those girls—my four sisters from Auschwitz.

The Mittelstein Labor Camp

All those who had been selected for the labor camp were lined up five abreast and herded along the road leading out of Auschwitz. Once again I saw the electrified wire fences with the black-clothed corpses clinging to them. I no longer mistook these people for lunatics who hadn't heeded the warning signs. Now I envied them the courage—which I lacked—to put an end to their unbearable torments. When we reached the railway tracks, we found a train of cattle cars guarded by soldiers. The sight left me completely indifferent now. I no longer expected that this train would take me to rejoin Uncle Abraham and his family. I was indifferent to our destination. All I was concerned with was not being separated from my four friends.

On boarding the train, each of us was given a piece of bread to last us for the trip. Once again two buckets were placed in the center of the car, one full of drinking water, the other serving as a toilet. We no longer hid the toilet pail away in a corner, nor were we squeamish about relieving ourselves in public. A single week of degrading treatment in Auschwitz had reduced us to the level of animals.

After many hours of travel, the train came to a halt. During this arrival, no unusual sounds reached us from outside. Everything proceeded with calm efficiency. The doors were opened, and armed guards pushed us out of the cars. I got down without raising my eyes, certain that what awaited us was the familiar drab scene of barbed-wire fences and watchtowers with machine-gun barrels pointing in all directions. But when I did look up, I saw a landscape of breathtaking beauty. In the distance, red-roofed cottages gleamed on forested hillsides, and checkered fields spread out in all directions. It was the kind of view I thought I would never see again. I bit my lip and pinched myself, as I had done so often in Auschwitz, to find out if I were dreaming. This time, a violent thrust from the rifle butt of a soldier behind me left no doubt that I was awake. Before we left the platform, I saw the name of this beautiful place written on the station building. It was Mittelstein.

At the far end of the railway track, we were handed over to a group of women soldiers in smart green uniforms. With their blond hair fluttering in the breeze, those good-looking, rosy-cheeked young Germans fitted perfectly into the enchanting landscape. We, on the other hand, stood out like something belched forth from beneath the earth. The young women, who were our *Aufseherins* (prison wardens), stood chatting and flirting with the soldiers who were guarding us. But in their dealings with us, their faces became hard and cruel, and their language turned to violent abuse.

As we began our march to the labor camp, I fell under the spell of the gorgeous scenery. It made me forget momentarily that I was one of those hideous-looking creatures being driven along by heavily armed soldiers and cursed unceasingly by the *Aufseherins* running back and forth alongside us. I wanted to fill my sight with the beauty around me and inhale the fragrance of the clean air. I conjured up scenes of my childhood in the Tartar Mountains; I saw Mother and Aunt Hanushka sitting by my bedside telling me that all those awful things I had been raving about were only the result of an illness from which I had just recovered . . .

"Links! Zwei! Drei! Vier!" The shrill command of an *Aufseherin* broke the web of my fantasies and wrenched me back to reality. I knew that the beauty of this natural setting was not meant for any of us to enjoy; not even a flower were we permitted to pick on our wearisome march. After what seemed an interminable time, we reached a small glade completely encircled by hills. There, within a huge compound surrounded by electrified

barbed-wire fences and watchtowers, we were to live from now on.

Exhausted from our long march, we sank to the ground of the huge prison yard. In constant dread of being separated, my four friends and I sat huddled close together near the grilled prison gate, on the other side of which stood two armed sentries. From my resting place, I had a clear view of the lush scenery surrounding our camp. Now its beauty was intensely painful and opened up new wounds in my heart. I began to brood about the fate of my loved ones.

I thought of Salek. Where was he now? Was he still thinking of me lovingly or was he perhaps cursing me for persuading him to leave the ghetto? Surely he understood that I had done it not just because of my intense desire to leave but also because I thought it was for his own good. How could I possibly have known that things would turn out the way they did? Despite these morbid thoughts, I was somehow convinced that, under the worst of circumstances, Salek was still thinking of me and worrying about me. This, at least, was comforting.

But what about Uncle Abraham and Aunt Faiga? Where were they now? How had they survived our separation, the brutal breaking up of their family? The very idea that they might still be in Auschwitz and at the mercy of those German beasts nearly drove me out of my mind. I recalled Aunt Faiga's unhappiness at having had to part with her bed in the ghetto. A bed! The very word had now become almost meaningless. To think that only seven days had passed since we had all slept in our own beds between clean sheets. Only one week ago! And now, after Auschwitz, we were stripped of everything we had called our own.

Not everybody was sunk as I was in morbid thoughts about their loved ones. With unconcealed amazement, my friends and I looked on as two of our neighbors ripped off wide strips from the bottom of their robes and tied them around their shaven heads. This headgear gave them a totally new look, and their shortened gowns seemed almost attractive on them. Now these two young women began loitering about the prison gate, trying to attract the attention of the sentries. It was not long before they succeeded

in doing so and were ordered to enter the sentry box outside. A short time later, they emerged escorted by several
soldiers and *Aufseherins*, who now began assigning us to
our various huts. We were told that the first of those
women—named Hella Rochverg—was to be the
Lagerälteste (head of all the prisoners in the camp) and
that the other one—Hanka—would take charge of the
work in the kitchen. A third woman, who was a doctor,
was also taken out of the ranks.

These three women were put in the very first hut, which
had three large rooms in it. The first room, in which there
were three separate bunks, was to be their common sleeping quarters. The other two rooms, containing twenty
bunks each, were set aside as the infirmary.

The rest of us prisoners were accommodated in the
other huts, fifty women to each. Our group included
women from both Poland and Hungary, and the Germans
took care to put twenty-five Polish-speaking prisoners together with twenty-five Hungarian-speaking ones in each
hut. Their evil intent soon became obvious; they hoped to
cause bad blood between the two groups, neither of which
would be able to understand the language of the other.
The Germans did not realize that many women in both
groups could speak or understand Yiddish and that this
language would play an important role in our communica-
tion with each other.

The huts in Mittelstein were similar to those we had
known in Auschwitz, except that these were furnished with
three-deck bunk beds and a long wooden table running
across the middle of each hall. My four friends and I were
put into the very last hut. We were relieved on seeing all
those bunks, for they made us think that living conditions
here were a great deal more bearable and revived our
hopes of perhaps getting through the war alive. On entering our hut, we immediately rushed forward to take possession of five bottom bunks and threw ourselves on the
straw mattresses. These bunks became for each of us the
most cherished of places—a private corner, something we
could look upon as our very own.

An earsplitting whistle soon had us back on our feet as
several *Aufseherins* burst into the hut. Unlike our former
Kapos, these women were pure Germans. They were much

more brutal in their attitudes toward us and performed their tasks with typical German thoroughness. The *Aufseherins* lined us up again in rows of five abreast and led us out into the huge yard, where we had to stand at attention for about two hours before the *Kommandoführerin* (camp commandant) arrived.

Her appearance was compelling indeed. She was unusually tall, with blond hair gathered into a thick bun. Her well-tailored uniform was that of a high-ranking officer. At her appearance the soldiers at the gate and all the *Aufseherins* leaped to attention with abrupt salutes. Holding a whip in her hand and accompanied by a huge Alsatian dog, the *Kommandoführerin* strode into the square, coming to a halt in front of the assembled prisoners. After surveying us with a look of hatred and undisguised contempt, she launched into an address that she was to repeat unvaryingly throughout our stay in the Mittelstein labor camp.

"You who are assembled here are pieces of shit taken from a nation of shit! If any of you here has illusions of ever leaving this place alive, just forget about it. If any of you think that you'll be released at the end of the war, forget about it. For mark my words well, if the war comes to an end at twelve o'clock, five minutes before noon, not a single Jewish *Schweinehund* will be alive. We'll see to it that you get killed one by one! But until that time, you have to serve the German master race, to work hard and to obey orders. Don't think that any of you filthy Jewish females will be fed for nothing!" Her voice—strong and clear—carried across the glade and re-echoed from the hills surrounding it. The words struck terror into our hearts. All our hopes were shattered once again as we heard what the Germans had in store for us.

The *Kommandoführerin* now turned to more practical matters. Our status here, she said, was that of *Häftlinge*—common convicts—and from now on, we would be identified solely by number. At the lineups in the morning and evening, each of us was to respond when her number was called; our names no longer meant anything here. The next day, the *Kommandoführerin* concluded, we would begin to work in a factory where French, Dutch, and Russian prisoners of war were also employed. She warned us under pain of severe punishment never to have any dealings with them. We were strictly forbidden to voice any complaints, and all talk was to be limited solely to the job at hand.

At the end of the *Kommandoführerin's* speech, each of us was assigned her number. Mine was 55091—my new name from now on. After we were tagged with our numbers, the *Aufseherins* selected the kitchen personnel, and a *Stubenälteste* was put in charge of the distribution of bread rations and the maintenance of the huts.

When we got back to our huts, the bread was brought in—one loaf for every eight prisoners. We fell on it like wild beasts, and like wild beasts we devoured it ravenously. On that day, too, we were given shoes—tattered cloth clogs attached to heavy wooden soles. Mine were several sizes too large.

I quickly took off my own leather shoes, opened a seam in my mattress, and shoved them inside the straw. I'll wear them again when the war's over, I said to myself. I shall never part with them so long as I live. They were the shoes that Father had paid for with his daily crust of bread, and they were now my most precious possession. I couldn't help but see the hand of Providence in letting me keep them, for among all my fellow prisoners I was the only one still wearing something brought here from a former life, something that had been touched by my mother and father. I often talked to the shoes as if they were living beings.

My new clogs kept slipping from my feet, and they made it difficult for me to walk. I didn't care, so long as they enabled me to preserve my own shoes until the war was over.

The Factory

I was torn from sleep by whistles, yelling, and the frantic barking of dogs.

"Aufstehen! Aufstehen! Raus! Appell!"

I opened my eyes. It was the dead of night, and I found it difficult to wake up. Because of my sore back, I had been sleeping on my stomach. How good it had been to sink onto the straw mattress and inhale its familiar smell, to stretch out my leaden limbs for the first time in over a week, to sleep and to forget. Now that sleep was interrupted. All the electric bulbs along the ceiling of our hut lit up simultaneously, and several *Aufseherins* rushed back and forth blowing whistles and yelling: *"Aufstehen! Aufstehen!"*

Not yet fully awake but thoroughly frightened, we were hustled outside. I caught a glimpse of an *Aufseherin*'s wristwatch and saw that it was not yet 4 A.M. Our camp was the only illuminated spot in the sleepy world about us. We stood in the compound fully two hours, shivering in the chilly mountain air until at 6 A.M. sharp, the gate opened and the *Kommandoführerin* passed through, followed by her huge Alsatian hound. Flipping her whip to and fro, she strode in with her head held high and a cruel smile on her lips. Heels clicked together as she was greeted by her saluting subordinates. Hella, our *Lagerälteste*, began calling out our numbers, each of which was answered with a loud "Present." At the conclusion of the roll call she reported the number of prisoners to her superior, who passed the word on to the *Kommandoführerin*.

By now the sun had risen, and its rays stabbed through the crags of the mountain ridges. I held my breath on seeing everything about me steeped in golden light. As on the day before, I fell under the charm of the scene, despite the chilling air, despite my hunger and my drowsiness.

171

The chief of *Aufseherins* now reported to the *Komman-dofuhrerin* about the routine arrangements she had made: how many of us were to work in the factory and how many had been picked for work in the kitchen. Then we were on our way out of the camp.

Our route led through one of the most enchanting villages I have ever seen. Along its streets were dainty red-roofed cottages whose windows were enclosed by green shutters with heart-shaped peepholes carved into them. The shutters were closed, suggesting that the inhabitants of the cottages were still asleep at this early hour. Or were they, perhaps, already up but keeping the shutters closed to shut out the sight of the ugly creatures marring the beautiful view? There were some signs that the village was coming to life, for smoke was beginning to curl up from chimneys here and there.

Stomping through the village that morning in my cumbersome clogs and trying not to lag behind my fellow marchers, I tried to picture to myself the interior of such a cottage. I saw the farmer's wife standing by the kitchen stove, getting the breakfast ready for her family; saw her rousing her children. They would all be seated around the large kitchen table before long.

I began thinking about the *Aufseherins* and the young soldiers who were driving us forward as though we were dangerous convicts. Had it ever occurred to them that I, too, might once have had a mother who used to be up early in the morning, preparing my breakfast, rousing me with a gentle kiss, urging me not to be late for school? Had they ever thought that their prisoners were once students in school, studying geography and history, math and literature? I myself could hardly believe that I was once a schoolgirl absorbed by such things. Look where it had gotten me!

"*Links! Zwei! Drei! Vier!*" The monotonous voice of an *Aufseherin* broke into my reflections. My feet inside the loose, heavy clogs were becoming extremely sore, and still there was no sign of reaching our destination. Finally we came to a dense pine forest concealing a small ravine; within it was a sprawling building topped by several towering chimneys. An iron gate guarded by many armed soldiers swung aside, and we were admitted into a big courtyard. The few men and women standing about in it stared at us in shocked amazement. It was obvious that they had never seen creatures like us before—shaven monsters of indeterminant sex, clad in shapeless black rags.

We were herded into a hall filled with machines and placed under the supervision of men called *Meisters*. I was assigned to a workbench on which a heap of rubber-like discs lay next to a big stapler. The stern-faced *Meister* who was the supervisor of my group picked a disc out of the pile and showed me how to punch five equidistant holes all around its edge. This process was to be repeated over and over again. Faulty handling of the stapler, he said, would cause the discs to burst, and he warned me against that happening too often.

The work was fairly easy and the punching of holes went fast, but as soon as any of us slowed down, we became aware of eyes spying on our every movement. The *Meister* himself popped up beside us every few minutes, urging us to speed up the tempo but raising hell on discovering even the smallest number of burst discs. In addition to the *Meisters*, many *Aufseherins* kept a close watch on us, ready to pounce at the slightest opportunity.

On the wall above the entrance hung a big clock, which soon turned into my worst enemy. Its hands didn't seem to be moving at all! Hoping to make the time go faster, I tried to slow down the tempo of my work when I thought that our *Aufseherin* wasn't watching or after the *Meister* had just walked past. But on looking up after what had seemed to be a long time, I was appalled to see that only a few minutes had passed. We had been told that our workday was to last for twelve hours, with a short break at noon for the distribution of our soup ration. When I next looked up at the clock, it was only 8:20 A.M.—there was still more than eleven hours of work ahead of us! I decided to stop checking the time from then on. Looking down the hall, I caught a glimpse of Bronka, who seemed completely dwarfed beside the huge machine she was attending. Blumka was not far away from her, but I saw neither Surtcha nor Faiga, who must have been working somewhere behind me. Just then a painful blow descended on my back. It was the heavy hand of my *Meister*. "No time for daydreaming here! Get a move on! Or else!"

Taking a new disc from the heap beside me, I broke my resolve and threw a rapid glance at the clock. Only ten more minutes had passed! Now the punched discs came out fast from under my staple. When I looked up again, I supposed that it was close to 10 and that the lunch break was only two hours away, but it was only 8:45. My war with the creeping hands of the clock lasted all morning. During that time, one of the *Aufseherins* took a sandwich from her bag and began to eat. I now also had my gnawing hunger to contend with. I looked back with longing to the workshop in the ghetto, where the five-hour workday had rushed by. I had been in the company of my friends then, and I used to chat and sing while at work. Here I was in the midst of my people's worst foe, under the prying eyes of *Aufseherins*, a *Meister*, and the no less hostile face of the clock on the wall.

After what seemed an interminable morning, I heard the bell ringing for the lunch break. In rows of five, we were led into a huge mess hut furnished with long tables and benches. On tressles in the center of the hall stood two big cauldrons full of steaming soup, its savory smell filling the air. Two women prisoners of the kitchen staff were in charge of doling it out, while two *Aufseherins* next to them kept a close watch on the precious broth. So starved were we that, had it not been for the heavy guard, we'd have rushed headlong toward the soup, for we had not had anything to eat since the bread distribution of the day before. The early morning air, the two-mile trek, and the many hours of work had made us frantic with hunger at the mere smell of the soup.

A tall, blond, good-looking man in breeches and highly polished riding boots entered the mess hut. He was Herr Klein, the general manager of the plant where we were working. Placing himself beside the two *Aufseherins* guarding the cauldrons, he first looked at us with a scornful sneer on his face, then burst into a thunderous peal of laughter as he watched us grotesque creatures fighting, scratching, cursing, and squealing in a desperate attempt to be among the first in line for the soup. So infectious was his mirth that all the *Aufseherins* in the hall soon joined him, holding their sides while the tears streamed down their faces. The spectacle we presented must have proved to them beyond a doubt the justification of their "Master Race" theory.

Surtcha and I were among the last to receive our portion of soup. Herr Klein stood looking down upon us. All at once, he grabbed Surtcha's head, pushed it inside the still steaming cauldron, and said in a laughing voice, "Take a good look! It's yours for the asking!"

This became a favorite sport of Herr Klein. From then on, he would turn up daily at the mess hut and pounce upon a victim as unsuspecting as Surtcha had been. He also invented other amusements for his own benefit and that of his fellow Germans. Entering the hut with his hands full of small pieces of bread, he would fling the bread beneath one of the tables and call on his audience to watch how the ravenous women prisoners scuffled for it like a pack of hungry wolves. Day after day, my portion of soup would be mixed with the salty tears of humiliation.

At the end of our twelve-hour workday, we were marched back to our camp. Only then I became aware of the ache in my arms and hands caused by the endlessly repetitious movement of the stapler. To make matters worse, my feet, tired and sore inside the heavy clogs, could barely drag my body back to the camp.

When we finally arrived, we dropped down on our bunks too exhausted even to eat the bread ration doled out to us. It seemed that only minutes had passed before we were roused again by the all-too-familiar sound of whistles. Again it was only 4 A.M., and shouts of *"Appell!* Get up! Everybody out!" rent the silence in our hut.

As on the day before, we were driven outside to stand motionless in the chilly night air for two hours before it pleased the *Kommandoführerin* to appear on the scene. When she turned up eventually, she began bellowing commands to stand up straight, to close ranks, to turn right, turn left. Then, in order to teach us a lesson, she loosed her Alsatian on us. Anyone in the front rank who stood the least bit in front of or behind the white line was bitten or toppled to the ground by the ferocious beast. A wild scramble for the back ranks ensued, during which we all came in for our share of truncheon blows. No one wanted to stand in the front line within easy reach of the dog.

After this early morning drill, we were compelled to listen to the *Kommandoführerin's* abusive speech aimed at our "race of shit." At the conclusion of her address, we set out again on the long march to the plant where we worked

twelve hours at our maddeningly tedious jobs, broken only
by the short lunch period and Herr Klein's humiliating
games. Then back again to our camp. This routine went
on invariably, day after day.

We all looked forward anxiously to our first Sunday at
the labor camp, hoping to be allowed to stay in our bunks
all day long and catch up on our sleep. Sunday arrived,
and at 6 A.M. we were roused and lined up as if for our
usual march to work. Instead of going to the factory, however, we were taken to the place where a truckload of coal
had been dumped outside the camp. We were ordered to
cart the huge pile of coal to the other end of the camp
and to get the job done by the end of the day.

With despair in our hearts, we began lugging heavy
pails full of coal past a gauntlet of *Aufseherins* who kept
pushing and prodding us forward, trying to make us work
faster. Time seemed to stand still, and the pile didn't seem
to get any smaller. My arms and legs barely obeyed me—
my whole body felt as if it were broken into pieces. It was
almost with longing that I now thought of the work I did
at the plant every day. Very late that night, we finally finished carting all the coal to the other side of the camp.
Thus ended our first day of rest at the Mittelstein Labor
Camp.

Soon our daily work schedule was made even more unbearable by the establishment of a twelve-hour night shift,
which we worked every other week. Doing such tedious
work during the day was bad enough; doing night shift
was absolute torture. At night, we came in for a greater
share of blows from both the *Aufseherins* and the *Meisters*
since we couldn't keep our eyes open when the irresistible
desire to sleep overwhelmed us. I tried to fight off my
drowsiness by calling up all sorts of pleasant childhood
memories. But I could never dwell on them for long before they were replaced by morbid thoughts about the fate
of the various members of my family. I couldn't rid myself of the feeling that Aunt Hanushka was no longer
alive. On the other hand, I often had hopeful thoughts
about Aunt Tsesia, Uncle Shimshon, and their five children—maybe during the deportations of 1941, the Germans had not yet begun tearing whole families apart . . .
But I knew I was deluding myself.

Full of apprehensions, my mind turned to Genia and

little Rishia. Had they managed to hide away somewhere in the ghetto? If only there were a way to warn them of what was going on outside of it! The ghetto now seemed to me to have been a paradise, where we still had our own home, our beds, clothes, books, and, above all, our relatives and friends. But I recalled the Germans' intention to eliminate the entire ghetto. If they had done that, then all its remaining inhabitants must also have been brought to Auschwitz. A shiver ran down my spine. Genia and Rishia in Auschwitz! No! I mustn't think about it! But try as I might, I couldn't think of anything else during the long hours of the night shift. I also brooded about Uncle Abraham and Aunt Faiga. Where were they now? Had they too reached Auschwitz and been subjected to the same inhuman treatment as the rest of us? "Dear God," I prayed in my heart, "be merciful to them!"

But most often I thought of Salek. I did not worry as much about him, trusting in his resourcefulness and ability to stand up to any hardship. Yet I couldn't shake off a gnawing sense of guilt about what I had forced him to do, coupled with a deep longing to talk to him about everything that I had been through since the moment we were torn apart and I had remained alone holding onto his loaf of bread. I wanted to feel the gentle pressure of Salek's hands and to hear his soothing voice again . . .

Could these have been signs of love?

My Four Sisters

The summer of 1944 was over, and fierce autumn winds had begun to blow. In addition to the normal hardships of hunger and exhaustion, we now had to contend with exposure to increasingly cold weather. As the days grew shorter and the hours of darkness longer, we scarcely noticed the golden-red hue of fall in the countryside around

Mittelstein. It was dark when we set out for work and dark when we returned.

The only time my four friends and I could meet and be together was on a Sunday, for Surtcha and Faiga never worked the same shifts as Bronka, Blumka, and I. We occasionally caught glimpses of each other in the course of the week when our heavily guarded columns passed on the way to and from work, marching to the rhythm set by the monotonous voices of *Aufseherins*.

When we had to work night shift, the seemingly endless week brought us to the limits of our endurance. Too exhausted even to touch the bread ration distributed in the morning, we would shove it into our mattresses to guard against it being stolen, intending to eat it on waking. I would push my bread deep down where I kept my shoes and would fall asleep with my fingers touching both of these precious things. All I wanted to do was to get to sleep as quickly as possible and to sleep as much as I could before we were roused again.

Even during our twelve hours off from the factory, we rarely got enough sleep; the *Kommandoführerin* and her legion of subordinates made sure of that. We seemed barely to have dropped off when the great whistle sounded, accompanied by shouts of "Get up, you lazy bitches! *Raus!* All of you!" Those of us doing night shift were often assigned to haul vegetables from the gate of the camp, where they had been dumped, to the camp kitchen. At first I wondered why the trucks couldn't dump the potatoes, carrots, and turnips right in front of the kitchen, but I quickly understood that it was part of our *Kommandoführerin*'s evil design to deprive us of our much-needed rest. We were kept busy at this back-breaking toil day after day, in addition to spending every Sunday clearing up the coal heap left purposely outside the camp gate. It goes without saying that after days of rest like these, we couldn't keep our eyes open during the night shift.

Surtcha and I always contrived to haul the coal or vegetables in each other's company, which made the time go by faster. Taking a pail too big to be carried by a single person, we would fill it up and, while lugging it along, would snatch a few minutes of talk about the past. Only on seeing an *Aufseherin* would we stop talking and step up the tempo of our work. It was not the distant past we discussed but our days in the ghetto and the friends we knew then. I told Surtcha about Genia and Rishia, and she told me the story of some people very close to her—Talka Zyskind and her family. It was a tale all too familiar to anyone who had spent several years in the ghetto, but it would come to have special meaning for me in the future.

The Zyskind family—the parents and their two children, Talka and her older brother, Eliezer—entered the ghetto in 1942 when the Jewish population was being expelled from the small country towns around Lodz. Fifteen-year-old Eliezer and one of Surtcha's brothers became close friends, and both joined "Bnei Akive," the religious Zionist youth movement set up in the ghetto. During the *Shpera*, Talka and her mother had almost been deported, but Eliezer moved heaven and earth to save them, and they were finally released. When malnutrition undermined the health of Mr. and Mrs. Zyskind, Eliezer took upon himself the care of the whole family, waiting in endless lines for food, coal, and medicine. Surtcha had helped to take care of Talka, teaching her arithmetic, Hebrew, and Jewish history, along with a few other children in the ghetto. She had become quite attached to the little girl.

"You should've seen her," Surtcha reminisced fondly. "What a beauty she was, despite the fact that she was all skin and bone. She had large grayish-blue eyes with a perpetual look of puzzlement in them. Talka was very intelligent for her age and often asked me questions to which I had no answer."

"Surtcha, I was asked such questions too!" I said. "I couldn't explain to five-year-old Rishia why we Jews, God's chosen people, had to suffer so much."

Our conversation was interrupted by painful blows landing on our backs. "No talking! D'ye hear! Get on with the work! Don't let me catch you at it again!"

Other than interludes such as this, the dreary routine of our daily life went on unchanged for months on end. We were completely cut off from the world around us. The French, Dutch, and Russian POWs working in the plant were strictly forbidden to have any dealings with us, but they tried to keep up our spirits in various ways. They managed to show us the "V" sign whenever they were unobserved, or they made the movement of a knife cutting their throats, a symbol of the fate awaiting our common

enemy. We understood from their gestures that the war
was going badly for the Germans and that they were on
the verge of total defeat.

Our fellow workers at the plant had got accustomed to
us by now, especially since we were beginning to look
more human as our hair grew out. We had also improved
the appearance of our garments by ripping off narrow
strips from the bottoms and turning them into belts. There
was even enough extra material in each robe for a pair of
panties, which we sewed with a needle someone had pro-
cured from God knows where. We would all stand patiently in line waiting to use this treasure, and when we
got our hands on it, we would spend every minute of our
spare time making the precious underwear.

In the midst of our hellish lives, small gains such as this
helped us to survive from day to day. Even more important to me was the kinship I felt for my four friends; it
was like a glimmer of light in the darkness that enveloped
us. The five of us had been thrown together by the flick of
a finger in Auschwitz, and we had stayed together as if we
were really sisters. It seemed to me that our friendship and
our care for one another enabled us to preserve something
of our humanity despite the inhuman condition of our
lives. The five of us did indeed behave differently than
most of the prisoners; we didn't curse or fight with any of
the others, and we always took the last places in the lineup
for soup rations. Our devotion to one another gave us the
inner strength to turn a blind eye to much of the vicious
behavior of our fellow prisoners.

In time our forbearance even seemed to affect the others
around us. They stopped squabbling with us about every
paltry thing, and their language became less abusive even
toward one another. The atmosphere in our hut also became more peaceful as the initial hostility between the
Hungarian and Polish groups gradually subsided. Many
friendships were formed between prisoners, but the bond
that existed among us five was unequalled anywhere else
in the camp.

One way that my friends and I expressed our concern
for one another was by sharing everything, even to the
point of depriving ourselves. Each additional crumb of
bread that came our way was immediately divided into
five equal parts, even though each portion was too small to

benefit any one of us and, more often than not, aggravated our hunger pangs. Such extra bread was sometimes obtained from the *Meisters*, who took pity on their half-starved slave workers and "forgot" to pick up a slice of bread placed on the workbench during an inspection. Before doing this, they would cast furtive glances about them, afraid of being caught at their act of charity.

The *Meisters* who supervised Faiga, Blumka, and Surtcha often left them extra slices of bread, but it never occurred to the three girls to eat the bread themselves. Each slice was duly divided among us five, and though it never sufficed to still our gnawing hunger, it gave us the spiritual strength to bear our ordeals. On returning home from a grueling bout of night work, crushed by the unceasing torments of the *Aufseherins*, I would discover deep inside my mattress, next to my beloved shoes, a small crust of dry bread that one of the girls working day shift had left for me. When I found such a token of love, I was moved to tears, and all the abusive invectives hurled regularly at us by the *Kommandoführerin* dissolved into thin air.

Something to Share

My *Meister* never "forgot" and left any bread for me. This made me unhappy, for I, too, wanted to have something I could share with my friends instead of constantly receiving things from them. I finally did get the opportunity, though it almost cost me my life.

One morning on returning from night shift, I was sent to the kitchen along with several other prisoners to get our hut's daily ration of hot coffee. (This dark, bitter brew hardly deserved to be called "coffee"; in fact, we also used it to wash ourselves.) As I entered the kitchen, Hanka, the head of the kitchen staff, called me aside. "I've got some-

thing for you," she said, "but step outside first and tell me
if the coast's clear."

I returned with a pounding heart to report that there
wasn't anyone in sight.

"O.K.," she said. "Give me your pot. I'll fill it up with
boiled potato peel, so you'll have something to share with
your friends. I've been watching the five of you for quite
some time. The *Lagerälteste* told me that you are the
youngest of all the prisoners."

Hanka filled my pot with the steaming peels and cautioned me not to rush back with it. "Carry it as though it
was coffee so it won't arouse suspicion."

My joy was boundless as I walked back with my pot of
potato peels. At last I, too, had something to share with
my friends. I already saw myself dividing the peels into
five equal portions and heard the delighted cries of the
others when they discovered this rare treat inside their
mattresses in the evening.

I had already turned onto the path leading to our hut
without meeting anyone when suddenly I saw the entrance
gate to the camp swing open to admit an *Aufseherin* accompanied by the commandant's Alsatian. My heart
missed a beat. It wasn't the *Aufseherin* I feared at that
moment, for she was too far away to prevent me from
reaching the hut and hiding the pot beneath a mattress. I
was in mortal terror of the dog. The *Kommandoführerin*
called her vicious pet "Mensch" (man), in contrast to us
prisoners, whom she always referred to as "filthy dogs."
Mensch had now spotted me and was bounding toward me
in long leaps. I froze in my tracks, feeling my stubbled
hair stand on edge. There was no place I could conceal
the food from the animal's keen nose, and I could not run
fast enough to escape. The dog was sure to catch me. A
special inspection lineup would be called. I'd be beaten to
pulp unless I revealed where the potato peels came from,
and if I did, it would surely be the end of Hanka's work
in the kitchen. They might even kill me to set an example.
No! I don't want to die—not like that!

Mensch had almost caught up with me. I heard the
dog's rapid panting, saw the fangs in its opened mouth,
felt it clawing at my robe. I closed my eyes . . .

Then a shrill whistle and frantic shouts of "Mensch!
Mensch!" rent the air. The *Aufseherin* was calling the dog

to her. Though unwilling, the animal let go of me and raced back to the guard's side. I was saved.

I barely made it to the hut, where I collapsed onto my bunk, sobbing hysterically. Bronka was beside me, and she kissed and comforted me until my terror subsided. Then she divided the peels into five portions, shoved Surtcha, Blumka, and Faiga's shares inside their mattresses, and fed me my own slowly and patiently.

The shock of my experience with the dog had completely unnerved me, and I was unable to sleep all day long. True, the potato peels had been so delicious that they almost made up for the terror I had felt. But from that day on, I was never able to rid myself of a morbid fear of dogs.

That night at work, my eyelids kept drooping, and the *Aufseherin*, angry at having her own peace constantly disturbed, hit out at me with increasing fury. Not even my *Meister*'s frequent backhanded whacks were able to keep me awake for any length of time. My eyes simply wouldn't stay open. Suddenly I felt a hard bang on the head. Was it another of those murderous blows to wake me up? No. My head, lolling forward, had struck the machine. I was losing control over myself. I thought with dread of the interminable night ahead—how on earth will I get through it? I've got to ask the *Aufseherin* for permission to go to the toilet so I can shake off this drowsiness in the freezing night air outside.

I held up my hand. Forbidden to take care of our needs at will, we had to stand up like schoolchildren, raise our hands, and repeat word for word the sentence "Please, may I go outside?" If the *Aufseherin* nodded her head, we'd stand beside her and wait for five others to do the same. Only then were we led outside under her supervision. But there were times when the *Aufseherin* refused to let us go. Then we simply had to hold back and wait for the next opportunity.

When I stood up, the *Aufseherin* cast a hateful glance at me and shook her head vigorously. In desperation I looked around and met Bronka's gaze. Her cheeks were flushed and there was a gleam in her eyes. Half an hour later Bronka raised her hand and stood up. The *Aufseherin* nodded. Another woman joined Bronka, and I was next in line. Before long three more women had joined us, and we were led outside. I drew the keen night air into my lungs and soon felt its invigorating effect. Bronka whispered, "Let's go in together. I've got a surprise for you."

"Bronka," I whispered as soon as we were alone, "is that an apple I smell?"

"Yes, it is!" Bronka said in great excitement. "That's why I wanted you to come out with me." She was talking very fast. "What luck! When my *Meister* came up to my bench, I saw that he had an apple and a knife in his hand. He sat down near me to peel the apple, and I saw him wrap the rinds in a piece of newspaper and throw them into the garbage can. As soon as he turned his back and the *Aufseherin* was busy with something else, I sneaked up to the can—and look what I got!"

Bronka reached into the front of her dress and pulled a small package from it. Inside it were—incredible!—the rinds of a fresh apple. Just then we heard the *Aufseherin* calling us from the yard. "Come on out, you two! What's keeping you in there! *Raus!* And be quick about it!" We gobbled the rinds up hurriedly so that she wouldn't find them.

The next few hours flew by. My drowsiness vanished, and even the feeling of terror that had haunted me subsided. The tangy flavor of the fresh apple peels lingered in my mouth and somehow filled me with the strength to see the shift through to the end.

In the morning when we lined up for the long march home, I managed to slip in beside Bronka. I had an overwhelming urge to be near her, to exchange impressions and relive the wonderful event of the night. We talked all the way home, ignoring the repeated warnings of the *Aufseherin* and even the occasional blows on our backs.

My good fortune lasted throughout the day. After the morning lineup, Hella, the *Lagerälteste*, dropped me a hint to come and see her in her room immediately afterward. When I arrived, she handed me what was left of her ration of bread. Her privileged position entitled her to an entire loaf a day, but since she had free access to the kitchen, she wasn't dependent on her daily ration. Hella often gave one or another of us prisoners the food she had left over.

"Because you are the youngest of the prisoners," she said, patting my head, "I want you to come here once a week for an extra piece of bread."

Now I would have something to share every week! I took the piece of bread Hella had given me and went back to my hut. After breaking the bread up into five equal portions, I put a piece beneath each of the mattresses of my four friends—my sisters.

1945

My Shoes

It was now the depth of winter. Despite the fierce snow-storms and the low temperatures, at times falling far be-low zero, we were compelled to line up for morning and evening inspection dressed only in our black robes, without socks or coats. Standing in line during the frosty nights and looking up at the black velvety sky lit by the moon and stars, I often wondered about the limits of human en-durance. In normal times, the least draft of air would have given me a severe catarrh or bronchitis, but now I never had so much as a cold. Even the asthmatic condition that had caused me so much discomfort had disappeared.

But exposure to the cold had taken its toll on me and my fellow prisoners. Our limbs no longer seemed to be-long to us; they felt like wooden extensions screwed onto our bodies. Out legs were dark purple, streaked from knee to ankle with red lines that were caused by coagulated blood oozing through the cracked skin. While we were outside in the cold, our chafed limbs were numb and senseless to pain. It was only when we warmed up and the blood began to circulate that our real torments began. This happened most often when we tried to sleep. Each of us had been given a thin black blanket, and we slept in pairs, huddled close together beneath two blankets, in an effort to get warm. But as soon as we warmed up a little, we were kept awake by the maddening pain in our legs. Even if we managed to drop off from sheer exhaustion, the pain would soon wake us up again.

After such periods of broken sleep, we marched to work through the deep winter snow. Since my clogs were several sizes too large, every step I took became an ordeal. I

186

couldn't walk rhythmically, and the snow, sticking to the wooden soles of the clogs, turned immediately into lumps of ice. My ankles kept turning outward and prevented me from keeping in step with the others. The voice of the *Aufseherin* snapping "Left, two, three, four!" sounded like the demonic rhythm of a witch dance. "What's the use?" I thought to myself. "I can't stand it any longer! Tomorrow morning I'll start wearing my own shoes to work."

I made the same decision during every long march to and from work, but when I took the shoes into my hands, smelled the leather, and recalled how my father had had them made, I couldn't bring myself to wear them. "No," I'd tell myself, "don't weaken now. They're too sacred a possession. If I ever get out of here, marry, and have children, I'll show them these shoes. They will touch the leather once touched by my parents . . ." Then I'd kiss my beloved shoes and shove them back deep inside the mattress.

One winter day, a young girl died in our camp. It wasn't hunger or hard labor that killed her but a murderous assault by the *Kommandoführerin* and her dog. The girl had been called out of the lineup and accused of having taken some bread from the infirmary. The commandant had decided to make an example of her. Sobbing bitterly, the girl begged to be spared a flogging and swore solemnly that she was not guilty. But her pleas had no effect. The *Kommandoführerin's* whip lashed out over her head and around her body, while the dog Mensch, frantic at the smell of blood, set upon the girl, tore her dress, and bit her flesh until she was left lying mauled and inert at the feet of his mistress.

This was not the first time that the *Kommandoführerin* had amused herself during a lineup by choosing a prisoner at random and accusing her of all sorts of trumped-up charges: talking with a POW at work, stealing bread, complaining to a *Meister*. The accusations were followed by a flogging that served to satisfy the commandant's blood lust.

On this day, I couldn't shake off an indefinable sense of disaster extending beyond the horrible spectacle that had just taken place. My premonition was right. The *Kommandoführerin* now told us that the accusation against the girl was based on the discovery of bread hidden in her

mattress. The bread had been found during an inspection
of our huts conducted while we stood in the lineup. On
hearing this, my knees began knocking against each other.
Great God! Have they found my shoes? It can't have happened! Only last night I had tried them on to see if they
still fit my swollen feet and had almost made up my mind
to wear them to work the next day.

As soon as we were dismissed, I rushed into our hut.
My mattress was turned inside out, all the straw scattered
about. I felt my heart tearing within me as I rummaged
frantically for my shoes. They were gone! I wanted to
scream, to pound my head against the wall, to scratch and
bite myself, but all I did was collapse upon the scattered
straw and give vent to my grief in uncontrollable spasms
of weeping, which lasted for many hours.

My friends, especially Bronka, tried their best to console
me, but I was inconsolable. I mourned over my shoes as
one would mourn the death of a beloved person. I felt
guilty for grieving more over the loss of my shoes than
over the brutal killing of one of my fellow prisoners, but
my guilt changed nothing. The girl who was killed had always kept to herself. No one even knew her name.

Between Despair and Hope

Not long after the young girl was killed by the *Kommandoführerin* and her dog, two more women died. One
of them suffered from acute pains in her gums and teeth,
and for three whole days she was in the infirmary screaming at the top of her lungs. We wept for her on hearing
those anguished shrieks during our morning and evening
roll calls. At the end of the third day, the screams stopped
suddenly and forever.

The second woman died of consumption. At first she
coughed up only red mucus, but before long she was
retching her lifeblood away. Every now and then, we

heard of women with similar symptoms and knew that their days, too, were numbered.

I had started working night shift again and, as usual, the long week ahead filled me with great trepidation. During the first night, however, something happened that gave all of us a feeling of indescribable elation. At about 3 A.M. the air-raid siren went off for the first time in the camp. In their consternation the *Meisters* and *Aufseherins* scuttled about like poisoned rats. But our happiness knew no bounds. Let them bomb the plant! Even if we got killed, all the Germans would go down with us. Only now did I understand the real significance of Samson's prayer, "Let me die with the Philistines!"

All the people in the plant—the Germans, the POWs, and even we slave workers—were rushed into the air-raid shelter. We kept our faces blank so that the Germans could not see the joy we felt. Fifteen minutes later, the all-clear sounded. Nothing had happened. We went back to our jobs, yet things were no longer the same. It was obvious that the front line was moving closer. There were bound to be changes, and perhaps—we hardly dared to think of it—they would be for the better.

That same week there were two more air-raid alarms. Work at the plant proceeded as usual but changes did take place. Young *Meisters* were sent to the front and were replaced by older ones. Even Mr. Klein was drafted. We were overjoyed at this news and wished him a lingering death in return for all the indignities we had suffered at his hands.

One Sunday, we were assembled in the big square, and the *Kommandoführerin* entered with her Alsatian. She was accompanied by another woman in the uniform of a high army officer, who was introduced to us as our new commandant. In her final address, our former *Kommandoführerin* couldn't refrain from telling us once again that we were nothing but a "nation of shit and *Schweinehund*" and that if we still harbored any illusions about leaving the Mittelstein camp alive, we had better forget them. We scarcely paid attention to what she was saying, being much too happy at the prospect of finally seeing the last of her. We had no doubt that the commandant who was succeeding her couldn't possibly be as wicked as this woman. But we quickly learned that any evil can be replaced by another that is even more vicious.

The day that our former *Kommandoführerin* left the camp remains engraved upon my memory. The roll call began in pitch darkness and during a bone-chilling frost. Soon the first sun rays seeped through the low-hanging clouds to settle upon the snowbound mountains and the dark pines shrouded in purest white. The sight of this beauty brought me close to tears. I wanted it to last so I could forget my sorrow as long as possible.

We had been standing at attention for a long time when our former *Kommandoführerin* appeared, out of uniform and wrapped in a heavy fur cape. She emerged from the officers' mess and stepped into a horse-drawn sled. The driver's whip set the sled in motion, and before long it vanished among the trees, coming into view again intermittently. We could hear clearly the merry jingle of the bells on the horse's neck.

The sight of the elegant, fur-clad woman gliding away through the sparkling landscape reminded me of the fairy tales I used to love reading in my childhood. So captivated was I by the scene that I paid no attention to the speech made by our new *Kommandoführerin*. My thoughts lingered on that beautiful and savage woman, who had flogged more than one wretched prisoner to death. Why was she like a devil in human form? What was lacking in her own life that made her loathe us so unreasonably? Hadn't she unlimited freedom, health, and beauty? What was it that had unleashed such malicious instincts in her?

Our new *Kommandoführerin* was much older than her predecessor and had none of the other's good looks. We hoped that, being older, she would be a little more humane, but we were greatly mistaken. This woman was an alcoholic who became dangerously violent when she was drunk. During inspection lineups she would run amok, dragging women out of the ranks by their hair, assaulting them with drunken fury, and often torturing them to death while we watched.

During that long winter, we suffered not only from the commandant's savage attacks but also from the brutally cold weather. Then one day near the end of February, a truck piled high with boots, coats, and woolen socks was driven into our camp. We were overjoyed to receive the warm clothes and to get some protection against the fierce winds and piercing frosts. It wasn't pity that had prompted this gift but the complaints of our *Meisters*, who could no longer bear to look at our chilblained legs covered with pus and scabs.

There were women among us who, the moment they put on their coats and socks, never removed them again. They went to sleep fully dressed, not bothering even to take off their boots. Working the night shift, trudging for miles to and from work, and standing for hours during the lineup so fatigued them that they would throw themselves onto their bunks, mud-caked boots and all, as soon as they came in. Many of the women who neglected themselves in this way became infested with lice, but most of us tried to keep ourselves clean. We would take off coat, socks, and shoes before going to sleep no matter how tired we were, and even during the coldest weather, we would wash ourselves with the hot coffee we received on returning from work.

Somehow we survived during the long months of that terrible winter, and there were even occasions when the sound of laughter was heard in the camp. I remember particularly two amusing incidents involving my friend Faiga's nighttime visits to the latrine. Going to the latrine in the middle of a winter night was something we all avoided if we could, since the latrine hut was about a kilometer away from our quarters and located on top of an ice-covered hill. One night, however, Faiga woke up with an urgent need to relieve herself. When she got out of bed, she became confused and forgot that she was sharing an upper bunk with another girl in an effort to keep warm. Faiga fell to the floor and, thoroughly shaken, let out a prolonged howl. When the lights went on and I saw her sitting dazed on the floor, I laughed out loud. Another time, Faiga's confusion in the middle of the night led her into the closet where the bread for the next day was stored. An uproar ensued, and there were hysterical outcries—"A thief! Someone's stealing our bread!"—but of course the culprit was only poor, bewildered Faiga. This time I laughed until tears ran down my face.

Such moments of laughter were the only bright spots in the drab uniformity of our existence until the coming of spring finally brought some variety to our daily lives. The

snow on the mountains melted, and patches of green began to take its place. Now we stood at attention for hours
with the sweeping rains of March lashing our faces, and
we marched to work through quagmires of sleet and slush.
Except for the changing weather, things were just as before: the same routine, the same savagery, the same calcu-
lated Germanic precision. We still received smiles and
signs of encouragement from the POWs and "forgotten"
slices of bread from the *Meisters*. But the hope inspired by
these events was soon blotted out by a recurring sense of
depression and despair as we listened day after day to the
drunken ravings of the *Kommandoführerin*.

Eventually the driving rains stopped. The mud
hardened, and the wind had a caressing warmth to it. The
glory of spring was all around us, but it did not touch our
souls. Full of envy, I looked at the green fields on both
sides of the road. The sprouting leaves on the trees were
reaching out for the sun, for freedom; the birds were fly-
ing high in the sky, chirping and trilling. I, too, would
have burst into song had I been as free as they.

The First Day of Passover

My friend Faiga was a deeply religious person. She
never once neglected saying her daily prayers, a genuine
source of consolation for her, and she accepted her ordeals
submissively without ever voicing the least complaint. I envied her. Since Faiga had never missed out on a day of
prayer, she knew exactly when the religious holidays fell
due. One day she announced that it was the eve of Passover and that she had decided not to eat her portion of
bread the next day, thereby observing, at least for one day,
the commandment not to eat any leavened bread during
Passover. We attempted to talk her out of it.

"God will forgive you for eating bread this Passover,"
we argued. "He surely knows the state we're in. Besides,

how will you survive the lineups, the march to and from the factory, and twelve hours of work if you don't eat your bread ration?"

But Faiga had made up her mind—she would observe the first day of Passover by not eating her share of bread. At the time we did not know that all of us would be deprived of bread on that day.

We were assembled for our early roll call that morning when the *Kommandoführerin* came wobbling tipsily toward us on jackbooted feet, accompanied by her own huge dog. Cracking her whip in the air, she roared, "One of you filthy *Schweinehund* dared to tell a Dutch POW that you were being beaten up here in the camp!"

It seemed that stories about the floggings in our labor camp had begun to circulate among the POWs working with us at the plant. They had decided to intervene on our behalf with a petition demanding more humane treatment and better working conditions. The *Meisters*, naturally, transmitted the petition to our *Kommandoführerin*. Now she demanded to know who the informer was. The commandant said that she would show us the real meaning of a flogging; she'd teach us all a lesson before she made mincemeat of the informer. She called on the culprit to step forward and confess, but no one made a move. Then the *Kommandoführerin* began running among us like one demented, lashing out with her whip, dragging several prisoners forward by their hair. Finally, changing her tactics, she promised a double ration to anyone willing to point out the informer. No one stirred. If the guilty person did not confess, she said, all of us would have to pay the consequences. The *Kommandoführerin* gave us an hour to consider the matter and then staggered off beside her dog.

We stood there for fully four hours. It started to rain hard, and two women near me collapsed in the mud, but none of us dared to come to their aid. They were eventually removed to the infirmary. Finally the *Kommandoführerin* came running toward us, her uniform and hair in disarray. She had evidently just risen from a few hours of sleep. Possibly she had received an urgent call from the plant about our absence from work that morning, or she had sobered up sufficiently to realize her own mistake.

She began lashing about her furiously, bellowing at the top of her lungs and demanding to know who it was that had informed against her. Even though she increased the reward of the bread ration, nobody came forward. Running through the ranks, the *Kommandoführerin* picked out several prisoners at random, slapped their faces, and kicked them violently with her hobnailed boots. They were ordered to clean out the latrines with their bare hands as soon as they returned from their shifts at the plant. Then all of us were deprived of our bread ration for the whole day.

It was awful not to have anything to eat or to drink after our four-hour ordeal on the parade ground. That day we marched to work on the verge of total exhaustion. It was already eight o'clock in the morning, and the spring sun shone down upon us in all its glory. There was moisture in the air from the recent rain, which accentuated the fragrance of sprouting plants and blooming trees around us. In the village, the smoke rising from the chimneys of the cottages kept changing direction with every puff of the light breeze. The green shutters were now wide open, but the curtains at the windows made it impossible to see inside. As we marched through the village, a woman with a child appeared at the corner of the street. On seeing us, she grabbed the child and vanished as if she had seen a ghostly vision.

As soon as I had settled down at my workbench and picked up my stapler, I recalled that two years had passed since that first day of Passover when I had buried my father. If it had not been for the intervention of those two Jewish policemen, I might have been killed by the German guards and buried in a grave beside my father. Then I would have been spared countless torments to my body and my soul during those next two long years!

After what seemed an eternity, we were given a thin saltless broth for our lunch. With this tasteless meal, I observed the first day of Passover in the labor camp of Mittelstein.

A Flickering Hope

It was not long before we were aware of great changes taking place around us. The POWs no longer contented themselves with making the "V" sign or the throat-slitting gesture; instead they would pass close by us, whispering "Don't lose hope now. The war's about to end. The Huns are getting licked and are on the run everywhere." Where the Germans were running to and where from we didn't know, nor were we concerned with the particulars. What mattered were the messages of encouragement that fanned our flickering hopes.

Around this time, I caught a glimpse of the headlines of a newspaper my *Meister* happened to open up near my bench. "Red Army advances in Poland . . ." I managed to read this much before he noticed me, whacked me on the back, and snarled an order that I stick to my work or else. The bit of news that I had glimpsed gave me a thrill of joy. Poland was being liberated! Then thoughts of regret began to assail me. If Salek and I had hidden away in the ghetto, mightn't we have been liberated by now? And the same would be true of Genia and Rishia, provided they had been allowed to stay behind. Perhaps they had already rejoined Rishia's father, brother, and sister. No, the ghetto had been liquidated—there would have been no place they could have hidden.

My thoughts kept chasing one another, and finally I decided that only at the end of the war, when I would see my relatives again, would I find out how everyone had fared. But I might not survive that long if the *Kommandoführerin* carried out her threat to finish us off before the end came. Even that, I mused, wouldn't matter so long as the Germans went down with us. To know that their own bitter end was near was my greatest consolation.

Soon there were more signs of the changing situation.

One day, my *Meister* failed to turn up for work, and my *Aufseherin* kept leaving her post to go outside, scarcely bothering to keep an eye on us. That day I turned out countless burst discs. I looked around me and talked in sign language with Bronka. During the lunchbreak we heard from the kitchen staff, who had gotten it from the POWs, that several managers and *Meisters* had fled, that the Red Army was approaching. I was quivering with excitement.

The very next day, the plant was closed down. Even though we no longer went to work, the *Kommandoführerin* and the *Aufseherins* made sure that the routine within the camp remained unchanged. The lineups before dawn continued, and after them we were sent out to do work that was infinitely more arduous than any we had done at the plant. Its sole aim was to work us to death and to keep us from knowing what was going on outside the camp. We lugged coal and stones, felled and sawed timber, dug ditches and filled them up again. The work kept us on our feet almost nonstop for twelve hours each day, during which the *Aufseherins* drove us on incessantly with whip lashes and truncheon blows. Each day that passed, our soup got more watery. It still smelled faintly of potatoes but none could be detected in it.

Despite our suffering, we worked on with a sense of hope in our hearts, for we were well aware that the Germans were beginning to panic. We lived on in the consciousness that our tribulations were bound to end sooner or later, in one way or another. A kind of fatalism gripped us. Come what may, so long as it happened fast.

At roll calls the *Kommandoführerin* dinned into our ears her intention of killing us all off before the very end. We wouldn't be around to welcome the Russian liberators, she said. The very last German bullets were being kept in readiness to kill every dirty *Schweinehund* in the camp. Ironically, she was unaware of how her drunken ranting rekindled our hopes, for it revealed how close the Red Army was. While she spoke, we took great care not to show any emotion. She would scrutinize our faces closely and virtually foam with fury if she seemed to detect the slightest change of expression. She'd drag the unfortunate prisoner out of the ranks and flog her mercilessly in front of us, shave off her hair, and deprive her of a day's food ration. We dared not twitch an eyelid and almost ceased breathing in her presence.

We lived in a constant state of anticipation, but the days and weeks passed, and still nothing happened. Nothing—except that our hard labor brought us to the verge of death from exhaustion. Many prisoners fell ill, and the infirmary was filled beyond capacity. Our exhaustion deprived us of all ability to think. Order in the camp became a thing of the past, filth and neglect were everywhere, and the stench around us was unbearable. Though the days were getting warmer, I often found myself sleeping in boots and overcoat, too weary to remove them before turning in.

I felt I was coming to the end of my own endurance. The same urgency to get out that had assailed me during my last days in the ghetto took hold of me again. This time I knew that any change might be for the worse, but I no longer cared. All I wanted was to get away!

Then something finally happened. One night, a truckload of S.S. men drove into the camp. The troopers got down from the truck and surrounded the infirmary. They hustled all the invalids outside and hoisted them on the truck with inordinate haste. Again we witnessed those terrible scenes so familiar to us. The sick refused to mount the truck, claiming to be suffering from nothing but a common cold and scheduled to be discharged the next day. One woman screamed that she had only come to get something for a headache. Others pleaded with the soldiers to let them stay on with a sister, a mother, or a daughter in the camp. But all they got were murderous blows from truncheons and whips before they were flung into the truck.

I stood watching the scene in horror and disbelief. I myself had been discharged from the infirmary only a few hours earlier, after spending several days there. This is what had happened to me.

The kitchen staff had needed extra hands to assist with the distribution of the soup. I was standing nearby, and on hearing Hanka's call—"Two persons to carry the pot outside!"—I was one of the first to respond. Another woman and I were instructed to heave the huge pot of steaming soup from the stove, to carry it outside, and to begin ladling the soup out to the prisoners. The other woman be-

gan to lift her side of the pot, but it was far too heavy for
me. Suddenly I felt an excruciating pain and let out a
shriek. Boiling soup had spilled over onto my feet. Unable
to move, I kept screaming at the top of my lungs. Bronka,
who happened to be near the kitchen, dragged me out and
got me to the infirmary.

Because of the unbearable pain, the doctor couldn't remove my socks. She had to cut them away together with
the scalded skin while I screamed in agony. The infirmary
had no ointments for burns. All the doctor could do was
to lay bandages soaked in chlorine on the burned areas in
the hope of alleviating the pain for a while and to drug
me with sedatives. My legs had begun to swell up by the
evening, and I was running a high temperature. I didn't
sleep at all that night. Only in the morning, after another
dose of sedatives, did I fall asleep, and for the first time I
was able to ignore the "Great Whistle" for early-morning
roll call. I slept on and on. As through a mist, I was aware
that my four friends had visited me, that I had mumbled
something to them, and dropped off again into a deep prolonged slumber.

Every morning our *Kommandoführerin* made an inspection tour of the infirmary accompanied by her huge
dog and several *Aufseherins*. Passing from bed to bed, she
would turn to the doctor with the same sneering refrain,
"What about that lazybones there? Why isn't she up and at
work?" When she came to my bed, she pointed down at
me, saying "And what about that one there?" The doctor
lifted the blanket to show her my bandaged legs. Distrust-
ing the doctor's word, the *Kommandoführerin* made her
remove the bandages, which stuck to the scalded area,
causing me to cry out in pain. With a grimace of revulsion, the commandant glanced at the wounds and then
gave permission for me to stay another day.

When I left the infirmary, my legs were still swollen,
and each step I took was torture. I didn't know then how
fortunate I was to be discharged long before my legs had
healed. That same night all the patients were deported—
God knows to where.

From that time on, the infirmary remained unoccupied,
and the doctor was idle most of the time. The sick preferred to keep on working until their strength gave out
rather than risk another deportation. My friend Bronka

was one of those who stayed away from the infirmary, even though she was very ill. She grew skinnier from day to day, and her incessant coughing woke me up at night. Though she tried to conceal it, I often saw her spitting blood. Full of fear, I told my other friends; we knew full well, as did Bronka herself, that these were the symptoms of consumption.

The four of us decided to share our own bread rations with Bronka, but she wouldn't hear of it. Soon she began running a high temperature. It was hard to lie near her at night, for her body was aflame with the fever, yet she kept complaining that she felt cold. Since Bronka dared not go near the infirmary herself, I usually went there for her to ask the doctor for something to relieve a cough that wouldn't let me sleep. The pills I got from the doctor I handed on to Bronka.

Outside the Camp

The Sunday after the infirmary had been evacuated, I awoke early. It was quite a while before the Great Whistle would go off. What had roused me was another whistle, that of a train passing near our camp. When I heard the sound, something tugged at my heart. In my mind's eye I saw the passengers on the train sitting by themselves or in family groups, imagined their suitcases filled with nice clothes, underwear, pajamas, and scented soap among their toilet articles. I, too, had once had possessions like these tucked away in my suitcase—I had sat at a window seat and watched the train swallowing distances.

The shrill sound of the whistle summoning us to line up jerked me out of my reveries. Today, as on several previous days, we were able to hear the muffled sounds of booming, as if many cannons were firing simultaneously at a distant target in our direction. There was no doubt that the front line was approaching. Our hearts beat faster at

the sound. We wanted to cry out but dared not let on that
we had any idea of what was going on beyond our camp.
Our faces remained blank, and we pretended total indifference. The *Kommandoführerin* continued to take out her
fury on random prisoners during every lineup.

We had heard a rumor that our camp was to be liquidated and all the prisoners were to be transferred somewhere else. Although I keenly wished for a change, my
heart contracted at the thought of being removed from
here at a time when the Russians seemed so close and the
chances for liberation so real. A group of 150 prisoners
had already been transferred the previous week. My
friends and I had taken leave of them with a cheerful "See
you again after the war." The long period of common suffering here in the camp had created a bond and a sense of
camaraderie among all of us.

In addition to the 150 women who were transferred out
of the camp, other groups were being taken each day to
baths in a nearby town, where they could wash themselves
and be deloused. All of us were by now infested with these
pests, and I could scarcely await my own turn to get rid of
the beastly creatures. Apart from that, I was dying to get a
glimpse of the world outside the camp. Those returning
from the baths were full of stories about the wonderful
sights they had seen on their way.

My turn came, and I climbed into an open truck. Clinging to the wooden railing, I gazed about me while the
truck climbed hills and descended into valleys. We left the
village of Mittelstein behind us and drove along a broad
road cutting through a dense forest and past miles of
broad green fields. Finally we arrived at the small town of
Glatz, a place filled with two- and three-story buildings
and shops with big display windows.

Our way took us through the center of town, and the
appearance of the people I saw there shattered all my
hopes that the war might be ending soon. The German citizens walking about in the streets of Glatz seemed carefree
and well dressed. There were women pushing baby buggies
or holding their toddlers by the hand and youngsters riding bicycles to school. We saw a policeman directing the
traffic and a postman delivering the mail. Just as in the
village of Mittelstein, there was nothing to indicate that a
war was raging not far away. On catching sight of our

truck, the townspeople stopped and looked after it and occasionally pointed it out to others. We must have been an unusual sight in this sleepy community.

When we got to the baths, we had our first hot showers in eight months. It was wonderful. I could have stood there forever letting the hot water splash over me. Returning to the camp after what I had seen outside gave me the feeling of being slowly strangled to death. Its filth and stench were now absolutely intolerable.

It was not long before the transfer of all the prisoners got under way. The front was moving up, and the sound of the booming cannons was more distinct. The Germans began evacuating us in small groups. Bronka was sent out with one of the earlier groups, and the rest of our fivesome worried that we would never see her again.

When our turn came, we were driven once more through Mittelstein and the town of Glatz to another town by the name of Grafenort—meaning "a place for noblemen." Although the town was, indeed, full of beautiful mansions, these were not residences of noblemen but guest houses and hotels, judging from the Gothic inscriptions stretching across the fronts of the buildings.

Our truck pulled up in front of one such mansion, much larger than the others and situated somewhat apart from them. This building had been turned into a prison. Its windows were boarded up, and a watchtower with the muzzle of a machine gun sticking out was placed at the entrance to its large courtyard, which was enclosed by a high barbed-wire fence. Our sleeping quarters were in a huge hall far too small to accommodate the hundreds of prisoners crammed into it. The bunks were placed next to one another without any space in between. Tumult and chaos reigned everywhere.

When evening came, a group of prisoners who had arrived in the town earlier entered the hall, and we were overjoyed to see Bronka among them. Exhausted and filthy, she ran to meet us and told us of the hard work she had been doing. We soon found out about it ourselves.

The next morning, the Great Whistle sounded, rousing us for a day's work, but there were no roll calls here. As soon as we were up, we formed ranks of five and were marched off to the familiar rhythm of *"Links! Zwei! Drei! Vier!"* After a lengthy march, we reached a forest that was separated from the fields alongside it by deep trenches, evidently meant to serve as a barrier against the advancing Red Army. A bulldozer was digging the trenches, and our job was to follow along behind it, walking in the trenches, and to clear out the loose soil with shovels. We were guarded by *Aufseherins* and countless armed troopers, who kept us working at a murderous pace. If we lagged too far behind the bulldozer, a hail of blows landed on our heads.

I looked up for a moment. Here we were at long last working outside in the fresh air, with the sweet-smelling pine trees on one side and broad fields on the other. But one thing was clear in my mind: we would never survive this. The work was far beyond our capacity. We were nothing but living skeletons, unable to lift the shovelfuls of heavy soil above our heads, let alone work at the speed demanded of us. Luckily, it began to rain the first day and we were ordered to stop work.

Soaked to the skin and utterly exhausted, we reached our new prison and dropped down on our bunks fully clothed and still wearing our mud-caked boots, too weary even to line up for our daily bread ration. We seemed barely to have fallen asleep before the whistle sounded, and we began the long trek to the trenches all over again, amid the screaming and the snarling orders of the *Aufseherins*.

The muffled sounds of the artillery barrages could be heard in the distance, but they had ceased to fill us with hope. We would not survive to the end of this war. The work was grinding us down to nothing. All we prayed for now was rain—it was our only hope. But instead we had days of continuous sunshine. The sun now turned into our greatest enemy, beating down upon us relentlessly.

As the booming came closer, our guards became fidgety and exchanged frequent looks of alarm. But they did not let up, driving us harder and harder until our most ardent desire was for eternal black night to descend and release us from this inferno.

Silent Morning

After a whole week had passed, the long, shrill whistle sounded one morning earlier than usual. Hustling us outside, the *Aufseherins* were in feverish haste to get us into marching order of five abreast. It was not for work we had been roused so early but for the beginning of a long march intended to move us away from the approaching front line.

The *Kommandoführerin* herself turned out early and launched into her usual tirade, which was, however, unusually brief. After the familiar invectives, she told us that we would each receive a whole loaf of bread and that this was the only food we would get on our march of several days' duration. She warned us against any attempt to slow down the pace and promised that all stragglers would be shot.

It was obvious that the Russians were already very close, but their nearness might not do us any good. I remembered from my geography lessons that Germany was a huge country. If we were driven further and further west by forced marches of this kind, none of us stood the least chance of survival. We'd fall by the wayside in droves, merely hours before the war was about to end!

We set out in pitch darkness; it was May 8, 1945. Carrying our loaves of bread and black blankets and escorted by armed guards, we marched off to the hateful rhythm set by the *Aufseherins*. The *Kommandoführerin* herself was traveling with us. Soon the darkness dispersed and the first rays of the hated sun began beating down on our heads. As it got warmer, the sweat streamed down our faces. The blankets and the heavy coats we were wearing became an intolerable burden, and before long we were racked by thirst. Our legs began to buckle beneath us, as we stumbled ahead to the maddening refrain of *"Links!*

Zwei! Drei! Vier!" The occasional crack of a shotgun was a reminder of what was in store for anyone reaching the limits of her endurance.

We were marching along a broad highway when a familiar sight came into view ahead of us. It was an endless line of people in flight, men carrying children on their shoulders, old people almost doubled up beneath huge bundles, others trundling pushcarts loaded to the breaking point. This time, however, the refugees were not Jews being driven from their homes but Germans bereft of all arrogance and self-assurance—the "Master Race" itself, frightened and bewildered, in headlong flight from the Russians. What a sight this was! We praised the Lord for granting the sweet revenge of seeing our loathed enemies in this moment of humiliation, uprooted and fleeing for their lives.

Our joy was short-lived, for we hadn't the strength left to indulge in it. At noon we were allowed a ten-minute respite and the first bite from our loaf of bread. I broke off a piece but was incapable of swallowing it. The bread was hard and dry. What I needed desperately now was water, only some water!

As we sat by the road, we saw an unending stream of refugees lugging their belongings, but they were now going in the opposite direction to us. The *Kommandoführerin* spoke with some of them, and they all pointed fearfully in the direction they had come from. We couldn't make out what was going on. Racked by thirst and utterly exhausted, we were incapable of thinking or comprehending anything. When our short break was up, we could hardly rise to our feet and had to pull each other back up. We shouldn't have sat down at all. Our legs now scarcely obeyed us as we staggered ahead when the marching order was sounded.

Enough! I can't keep it up any longer! I don't care what happens to me. Death would be a welcome deliverance, even more welcome after having seen the terror-stricken faces of those German refugees.

But the march continued. A little while later, the *Kommandoführerin* and the *Aufseherins* approached some other refugees who, likewise, indicated an invisible point in the distance. We were now told to halt. After a brief consultation with her subordinates and the soldiers guarding us, the *Kommandoführerin* issued the order to turn around and march back to the prison in Grafenort.

We immediately felt revived strength surging up in us at the mere mention of returning to our bunks at the camp, where we'd be able to put down our tortured bodies and sleep and sleep and sleep . . . Had we been driven ahead to cover the same distance that lay between us and the camp, almost all of us would have fallen in exhaustion, to be finished off by a bullet. But now we marched as we had never done before. By mustering the last remaining drop of our strength, we reached the prison in the late afternoon. We collapsed onto our bunks, unable to eat any bread or reach the water faucets to slake the thirst that had tormented us throughout the long trek there and back.

When I woke up, I found myself lying on my bunk, with blinding sunlight shining in my eyes. Why hadn't I heard the usual whistle, the shouting, the barking of dogs? Why were we still in our bunks? What was this eerie silence?

I raised my head and looked about me. I saw others looking around in like bewilderment and then lying back again. Something was wrong; it must be a trap set for us by the Germans. The silence was terrifying. We lay in our bunks speechless and paralyzed with fear. An hour passed and another hour, but no *Aufseherins* appeared in the hall. I started nibbling at my bread and saw others doing the same. Then some women got down from their bunks to peep into the courtyard. Within seconds the message raced from mouth to mouth—"The watchtower's abandoned! All the soldiers at the gate are gone!"

We were very frightened. It was undoubtedly a ruse to lure us outside so we could be finished off wholesale. The tension mounted. Our patience was wearing thin, and the uncanny silence about us threatened to snap our already badly jangled nerves. Like frightened mice, we peeped outside. Finally some ventured a little further in the direction of the barred iron gate. It was unlocked! A few of the bolder women opened it and stepped outside into the street. We watched them with bated breath. They were back within a moment, announcing excitedly that there wasn't a soul in sight and that they had decided to risk an escape. I also wanted to take the risk, but Faiga and Surtcha talked me out of it.

When another hour passed and nothing happened, I couldn't stand waiting any longer. Bronka and Blumka decided to join me. Advancing cautiously into the street, we kept casting furtive glances in all directions. This was the first time in six years that we found ourselves moving about on the other side of a barbed-wire fence without a yellow patch and without any armed guards. We moved forward gingerly. The streets were deserted, and a ghostly stillness reigned everywhere.

At the end of the road, we found an isolated cottage with smoke rising from its chimney. The pungent smell of food filled the air, and we became conscious of sharp hunger pangs. We stopped in front of the cottage irresolutely, staring at one another with fear in our eyes. Then the door opened, and a bulky woman stood on the threshold smiling broadly at us. "Welcome, dearies! Come on in! Come on in!"

Though taken aback at her sudden appearance and still unable to conquer our fear, we accepted her offer and stepped across the threshold into a real house. There was a table surrounded by chairs and covered with a beautiful tablecloth, with a vase of flowers in its very center. Good God! Was I dreaming all this? I was afraid to test myself by biting my lips or pinching my flesh. If it was a dream, I'd do nothing to blot it out. Let it last for as long as possible.

The woman urged us to sit down at the table. Then she left the room and reappeared with a big tureen full of savory soup. She ladled it into deep porcelain bowls, which she placed in front of us, along with a basket heaped with slices of fragrant bread. The woman told us to help ourselves to the bread and to eat the soup before it cooled off. While we ate, she kept up a nonstop monologue, as if reeling off a prepared text. At first she launched into a lament at the sight of our emaciated looks. She admitted having heard something about the awful treatment, the beatings and tortures we had been subjected to, but almost in the same breath she exclaimed, "What! You were imprisoned in Grafenort? Right under my nose, at my very doorstep? And none of us had the slightest inkling of what was going on!"

All during the woman's speech, we were gobbling up the soup and the fresh bread that she kept putting in the basket. The wholesome food filled our starved bellies, creating a feeling impossible to describe.

The woman droned on. She told us not to lose heart. From now on, everything would turn out all right for us. The war was over, Hitler was dead, and soon the Russians would be here. Russia and her Anglo-American allies had brought Germany to her knees. They had already signed a document for Germany's unconditional surrender. We'd be able to return home now and be reunited with our families.

"Go on, dearies," she urged us, "help yourselves to more soup. Poor things—nothing but skin and bone. And look at the tattered rags and battered boots you're wearing. Wait! I'll be back in a jiffy."

She went into an adjacent room and returned shortly with a pair of shoes in her hand.

"Here you are, poor child," she said to Blumka. "Try these on and see if they fit you." She turned to the rest of us, opening her hands in a gesture of regret. "I'm so sorry. I haven't any others to give away.

Then the woman addressed us all directly. "I'd like you to do me a favor, girls. When the Russians come, tell them how I took you in, fed you, did all in my power to help you. Tell them that I had no notion of what was going on in that place over there and that I have always been sorry for the Jews."

What a dream this was! The forced march, the fleeing refugees, the return to the prison, the abandoned watchtower, the disappearance of the guards, the unlocked gate. And now this German woman virtually groveling before us, begging protection from us, so recently considered *verfluchte Judinnen* (cursed Jews), against the wrath of the oncoming Russians! I pinched myself until it hurt. I bit my lips and felt the pain. No! It wasn't a dream. The war was really over, and I had survived!

I jumped up and fled the woman's house, with Blumka and Bronka rushing after me. Filled with incredible vigor, lightfooted as if carried on wings, we raced back to the camp, burst into the hall, and embraced our friends, laughing and crying alternately.

"Surtcha! Faiga!" we shouted. "The war's over! Hitler's dead and we're alive! Alive! We're free to go home! Free to rejoin our families!"

But when the first flush of our excitement wore off, we looked at one another with fearful eyes. Each of us thinking about her loved ones. Would we see them again? Had they managed to survive, as we had done? We tried not to dwell on these somber thoughts for long. Everything would be all right, we told ourselves. It had to be all right. All that mattered at this moment was that the war was over and that we were free and alive.

The First Day of Freedom

Around noon on the day of our deliverance, we began to hear a strange rumbling sound in the distance. Several inmates of our camp burst into the hall in breathless excitement, shouting that the Russians were coming. Beside myself with joy, I rushed along with everyone else to the large square in front of the town hall to watch the victorious entry of the Red Army into Grafenort. The rumbling sound became louder and louder until finally the troops came into view, led by a large contingent of soldiers on motorcycles.

Once again, as on that day in Liberty Square more than five years ago, I was a witness to a parade of soldiers from an alien army. But how different this occasion was! When I watched the Germans' triumphant entry into Lodz, I was quivering with fear at the sight of the huge forest of swastika banners and the immobile faces of the jackbooted soldiers. I did not know what was in store for me, but I was conscious of an overwhelming sense of terror. Today I was watching the entry of an army of liberation, of battle-weary soldiers in mud-caked uniforms, their faces radiating cheerful smiles. I stood there with my four friends, all of us throwing kisses, clapping hands, and shouting until we were hoarse. The tears I wept were tears of indescribable joy.

As soon as the parade was over, the Russian soldiers began ransacking the business section of the town. They urged us to join them as they smashed display windows and broke into stores. "We know what you've been through," they said, "so don't be shy. It's all yours. Take anything you want."

Following in the wake of some window-smashing soldiers, Bronka and I entered a wineshop lined with shelves that were stacked with bottles of all shapes and sizes. We longed to have a taste of good wine, but when we tried to open one of the bottles, we discovered that their corks were all sealed with lacquer. Then Bronka found an unsealed, partially filled bottle, which she offered to me. "You take a drink, and I'll take one after you."

I grabbed the bottle, pulled out the cork, and took a big swallow of the liquid inside. Suddenly I felt a choking sensation. I gasped for air and realized that my tongue, teeth, and gums were coated with some kind of thin, filmy substance. Bronka, who was watching me uncomprehendingly, burst out laughing at the face I made and held out her hand for the bottle.

"Let me have some too," she begged. I couldn't get a word out of my sticky throat, but I cautioned her by shaking my head vigorously.

"What's wrong, Salusia?" she cried in alarm. "Is it poison?"

Several minutes passed before I managed to recover my speech. Eventually we discovered that the bottle had contained some of the lacquer used to seal the corked wine bottles. It took me hours to peel the pieces of dried lacquer from my gums and teeth.

As we left the wineshop after this strange experience, we saw a slight figure staggering past almost doubled over beneath the weight of a huge piece of raw meat. To our astonishment, we recognized Blumka. She had meant to surprise us with a feast when we got back to the camp, but the meat she had found turned out to be much too heavy for her to carry alone. It took all three of us to haul it back. When we got there, Faiga produced a large pot into which we put the meat, along with water and some salt. We lit a fire in a pit we had dug in the prison courtyard and set the pot over it. Faiga went foraging and came back carrying a bagful of potatoes, which we added to the meat. Soon we sat down to a truly majestic meal.

All over the courtyard, groups of women were gathered around cooking fires like ours. Everyone had gone on a binge of gluttony, gobbling down whatever seemed edible and drinking themselves into a stupor, as if to make up in one night for all their years of semistarvation. This wolfing of food had disastrous effects on many of the exprisoners. They became violently ill with vomiting and diarrhea, but they went on stuffing themselves. Later we heard of numerous deaths caused by this frantic overeating.

After we had finished our feasts in the courtyard, some of the soldiers from the Red Army came to visit the camp. They were a jolly lot and entertained us with music and songs that expressed a deep longing for their motherland. Watching the Russians singing and dancing for our benefit, I was aware of a pervasive feeling of well being, of once again living in a world where we Jews were no longer persecuted. This feeling brought me close to tears, and I began thinking of Salek. How right he had been in his belief that the world was bound to change for the better after the war. Hitler's theory of the Master Race now lay in shambles, never to rise again. The sight of those kindhearted Russian soldiers filled me with the conviction that Salek's vision would come true.

In return for their kindness, the soldiers had only one request: they wanted us to have sex with them. They couldn't understand why many of us refused what seemed to them the most natural thing in the world. The Russians kept reminding us that, as our liberators, the least they deserved was a demonstration of our gratitude. Our persistent refusal of their pleas was a bitter disappointment for them, but they did nothing to force themselves upon us. They left our camp very late that night to continue their conquest of the German Reich.

The first day of our liberation was now drawing to a close—the first day in many years during which we had not suffered from humiliating treatment or from the pangs of terrible hunger. The future seemed bright, and we were confident of being reunited with our loved ones, whose experiences could scarcely have been worse than ours. All of us in the camp sank into a deep, exhausted sleep, knowing that we would not be roused by the shrill of a whistle or the fierce barking of dogs. Never again . . .

The Way Home

Although my friends and I rejoiced in every moment of our new freedom, we all longed for just one thing: to go home to Poland. But how were we to accomplish it? Transportation in Germany was at a standstill, and covering the great distance on foot was out of the question. The day following our liberation, the five of us were sitting on the curb in front of the prison discussing our problem when a young man approached us. Speaking in fluent Polish, he asked us where we were from. On hearing us exclaim "Lodz" almost with one voice, he asked if we were ready to leave for home immediately. We were too astonished to reply.

The young man introduced himself. "My name is Alexander, but you may call me Alush." He told us that he was a native of Cracow and had been drafted into the Polish army at the beginning of the war. With the fall of Poland, he had been put into a German prison camp, where he had spent the entire war.

"Now," Alush concluded, "I'm returning to Poland and to my family. I have a horse and wagon, and there's room for you girls, if you want to come with me."

We could scarcely believe our ears. Alush seemed like an angel of deliverance, an apparition with his ruddy checks and neat clothing. We eagerly accepted his offer and agreed to meet him in an hour's time, after we had collected our personal belongings. Alush cautioned us not to let anyone else know about our journey; he didn't want any more passengers to tire out the horse on the long trip back to Poland.

It did not take us long to return to the camp and retrieve our possessions, which consisted only of our black blankets from Mittelstein and the food left over from yesterday's meal. Although we tried not to attract any attention, one of our fellow exprisoners, a woman named Luba, noticed our activities and insisted on joining us even though we told her about Alush's orders. The six of us went to the meeting place and waited there with pounding hearts until we finally heard the clickety-clack of hooves on stone and saw Alush and his wagon coming toward us. In the wagon were two pale, thin boys whom Alush introduced to us as Russian prisoners of war. They would accompany us on the journey and lend a hand if any emergencies arose. Alush looked scornfully at our meager possessions, but he did not object when he saw Luba climbing into the wagon along with the rest of us. We were ready to start the long trip home.

In the days that followed, our travels took us away from the horrors of the war and into the splendor of a European spring. It was the month of May, and everything around us had burst into bloom. The air was full of fragrant smells and caressing breezes. As we moved along, I lay on the hay in the bottom of the wagon and watched puffs of clouds floating across the blue sky. I felt as if we were traveling through a Garden of Eden where everything was beautiful and life free from all care.

Each night we took shelter in farmhouses along the way that had been abandoned by their owners. Their cellars were packed with all kinds of provisions—sausages, potatoes, turnips, sacks of flour, jars of preserves, bottles of wine—and we always had plenty to eat. There were chickens on some of the farms, and on one, we found a cow that Alush milked, giving each of us a cupful of warm, foaming milk. With the benefit of this wholesome diet, our sunken cheeks began to fill out and lose their sickly pallor.

During the journey, Alush took complete charge of our welfare, seeing to it that we got plenty of food and rest. He looked after us like a devoted father. Our little group of nine—one Pole, two Russians, and six Jews—traveled together in peaceful accord, just like a close-knit family. Salek's vision of equality and brotherhood seemed to have come to life in us.

But after we had been traveling for about a week, our paradise began dissolving bit by bit. The war had not touched that part of Germany we had been crossing, but the further east we moved, the more evidence we saw of its terrible devastation. The burned ruins of buildings were everywhere, and the earth was scorched for miles around. From the fields we passed, there rose the stench of decomposing bodies. Once we drove by a minefield, and we were all petrified with fear that we would be blown to pieces then and there.

On the eighth day of our journey, things got even worse. Dusk had started to fall, and there was still no sign of a house where we could put up for the night. Just after Alush lit the lantern, two Russian soldiers popped up out of the darkness. One of them caught hold of the horse's reins, and the other, a medal-bedecked officer, demanded to know who we were and where we were going. Alush, obviously alarmed, barely managed to stammer out that we were ex-POWs returning to Poland. When they heard this, the Russians relaxed a little and climbed up onto the wagon, instructing Alush to turn it around and drive in the direction they indicated. Directing friendly smiles at us girls, they told us that we had nothing to fear; they were merely helping us to find suitable sleeping quarters for the night. The officer, who was sitting close to me, asked my name. He didn't take his eyes off me for a moment, and his staring made me very uncomfortable.

Before long, we reached a building guarded by two sentries, who admitted us into a large courtyard. After we got down and Alush had tied the horse to a tree, the officer pointed to an abandoned carpentry shop where we could put up for the night. He himself vanished but was back almost immediately holding up a lighted gas lamp. Addressing me by name, he seized my hand and told me to come with him. He handed the gas lamp to Blumka so that she could light the way ahead of us. Bronka, Surtcha and Faiga followed close behind her. Then suddenly the lamp went out. One of the girls had blown it out, and they all broke into a mad scramble for the carpentry shop, urging me to follow. I tried to disengage my hand from the officer's grip, but he held on tightly.

"Let me go!" I begged, but he refused. Laughing loudly, he said, "Don't be scared of me, my chick!" A whiff of alcohol hit my face.

Dragging me after him easily in spite of my desperate resistance, the Russian officer mounted some stairs and entered a room in the main building. I was scared out of my wits and trembling all over when I saw him lock the door behind us. He tried to calm me, repeating that he meant no harm and that I needn't be so scared of him. He merely wanted to have sex with me.

"Please, sir, let me go!" I pleaded. "Don't do that to me! Don't make me unhappy for the rest of my life now that I have come this far! I'm Jewish, and if you touch me, I'll kill myself!"

His face flushing angrily, the officer raised his voice. "This far, you say! And who have you got to thank for it? Us Russians! We liberated you! And you Jewish girls can't even show your gratitude!"

He brought his face very close to mine, and the reek of alcohol almost overpowered me. I felt like throwing up. Then the officer changed his tactics. He lowered his voice and began stroking my cheeks and throat. "Salusia," he crooned, "I won't harm you. Why won't you let me make love to you? Wait! I have an idea. I'll get some vodka for you. That will make you feel good."

He went into the adjacent room, and I was left standing by the open window. I had no time to remember how many steps we had mounted or what floor the room was on. Within a second, I had climbed onto the window sill and leaped out into the darkness. I fell onto soft ground. The distance couldn't have been very great, for I got up unhurt and made a headlong dash for the carpentry shop. Banging on its wooden door, I shouted frantically, "Surtcha! Blumka! Open up! Let me in quickly!" The heavy door swung open, and I fell weeping hysterically into the arms of my friends.

"Are you all right, Salusia? Are you hurt?"

Surtcha, Blumka, and Alush managed to drop the heavy iron bolt across the door just before the officer reached it. He began hammering at it with his fists, raising a spine-chilling racket. "Salusia! Salusia! I want Salusia! Let me have my Salusia!" he bawled, swearing and charging against the door in an attempt to break it down. Other voices were heard outside, and many fists were now banging against the door. We girls huddled together in a corner of the room, terrified that they would succeed in breaking down the door. But the heayy bolt didn't give way.

The commotion hadn't bothered the two Russian lads, who scarcely looked up from the lice hunt they were engaged in. Only Alush was alarmed by it. He cast a strange look in our direction and blurted out, "Why can't Salusia go out to him? What harm would there be in it?" I saw him moving toward the door and shuddered. I expected him to open it, but no . . . Instead he approached us in our corner and looked at me from top to toe. The door remained shut. Eventually the knocking and shouting subsided and then ceased altogether.

Early the next morning, before dawn, Alush harnessed the horse to the wagon. All of us girls lay down on the floor of the wagon, and Alush, with the help of the two Russians, covered us with hay. Looking out between the slats of the wagon bed, I caught sight of the Russian officer. My heart missed a beat as I saw him approach the wagon, but he made no sign of recognizing Alush or the two Russian boys. Either he had been too drunk last night to recall anything or he meant to dismiss the whole episode from his mind. With a slight nod of his head, he ordered the sentries to raise the barrier and allow us to proceed on our journey.

Alush

On the same day of our escape from the Russian officer, we met the first other Jews we had seen since our journey began. While passing through a small country town, we noticed four men whose appearance set them apart from everyone else. They were frightfully thin, almost skeletal, and their clothes were in tatters. The most curious thing about them was the way their hair was cut; it was of normal length except for a strip shaved off from the nape of the neck to the forehead. We learned that this strange haircut had been given to all Jewish males in the labor camps so that they could easily be identified if they tried to escape. The prisoners joked about their unique hair style, calling it the *lausenstrasse* (louse path). It did indeed give the men a comical look, at the same time that it recalled the tragic circumstances of their imprisonment.

After greeting the four men eagerly, we asked them if they remembered any of our male relatives from their camp. They told us that they had known most of their fellow prisoners by number only, and of course, we had to give the same answer to their inquiries about their wives, mothers, sisters, daughters. It was from these four Jews that we learned for the first time the extent of the atrocities committed by the Nazis. They told us about death camps, gas chambers, the burning of hundreds of thousands of people, most of them Jews. Auschwitz, they said, was a death camp.

"Auschwitz! But we were there ourselves!" we exclaimed. We had witnessed brutal separations of families and merciless floggings, but not mass murders. It was too fantastic to believe. But they reminded us of the tall smokestacks with the dense smoke rising from them day and night—of the curious smell that pervaded the air. They asked us what we thought had happened to the invalids, the aged, the unemployed, the children taken from the ghettos.

Although we refused to believe their horrifying accounts, I was seized by an awful foreboding. I consoled myself with the thought that we would soon reach Lodz, where we were sure to meet with old acquaintances who would tell us the truth. As for now, I mustn't lose hope. Things simply had to turn out for the best!

Before we left the four men, they cautioned us against the Russian soldiers that we would meet in this part of Germany. The advance guard of the Red Army had been generally well behaved, but the troops following them were altogether different. They were plundering and pillaging the countryside, and no one was safe from their attacks. From that time on, we girls traveled hidden beneath the hay in the wagon, with the two Russians seated on top and Alush, our guardian angel, in the driver's seat.

On the twelfth day of our journey, we finally reached the Polish border and discovered that soldiers in Polish uniforms were back in control of their homeland. Three of the soldiers advanced toward our wagon and, after a cursory glance at us, instructed Alush to drive into the inner courtyard of the border control building. The border guards showed no interest in us girls or in the Russian boys. All their attention was centered on Alush, whose face seemed drained of all blood. Not satisfied with Alush's responses to their questions, they ordered him to accompany them into the office. He followed without a word of protest or a look back at us.

An hour passed and then another, and Alush failed to come back. The long wait was getting on our nerves. Why didn't he come out? What was keeping him? After more than two hours, the three soldiers came outside and asked us politely to climb down from the wagon, which, they said, had been requisitioned by the Polish army. They pointed out a nearby train station, telling us that the train would take us to our destination much faster than the wagon could have and that we could also get something to eat at the station. The Russians leaped down at once, gathered up their few belongings, said goodbye to us, and set out in the direction indicated. We girls climbed down as well, but we refused to leave. We told the soldiers that we were determined to wait for Alush, even if it meant sitting there throughout the night. We couldn't possibly go away without taking leave of our kindly protector.

The soldiers measured us with scorn in their eyes. Finally one of them, a sergeant, said, "Sorry, but you'll never see that Alush of yours again. He's been arrested and sent to prison."

"To prison!" we all shouted. "What for? Alush hasn't done any harm!"

The sergeant told us that we needn't feel sorry for Alush. He was not a former prisoner of war, as he had claimed, but a dangerous Nazi who was on the list of wanted war criminals.

"But sir!" we exclaimed. "That couldn't possibly be true. You must be making an awful mistake. He's the kindest person in the world, a virtual angel!"

The soldiers burst out laughing. "An angel indeed! How dumb you girls are!"

One of them went back into the building and returned with a huge album, which the sergeant took and began to leaf through. When he found the page he wanted, he showed it to us. "Here. Take a good look. Do you by any chance recognize the person in this photograph?"

We blanched on seeing Alush looking out at us from the

picture not with the laughing, kindly face we knew but with the stony, arrogant, and cruel expression so characteristic of all Nazi officers. Yes, there was no doubt about it. It was Alush wearing a smart S.S. uniform with the officer's insignia on his shoulders, a swastika on his cap, and a whip in one of his gloved hands.

The sergeant told us that Alush had been born in Cracow, as he said, but he was actually of German descent. At the outbreak of the war, he had been drafted into the Polish army and used his position to pass military secrets on to the Germans. When the Germans entered Poland, he joined them and was appointed commander of an extermination camp, where he caused the deaths of hundreds, if not thousands, of Jews. Alush's offer to bring us home and his seemingly selfless concern for our welfare were apparently part of a plan that would enable him to slip back into Poland unnoticed and pick up his life again as a respectable Polish citizen.

"He almost pulled it off," the sergeant concluded. "But I happened to look through this album of war criminals this morning, and I knew who he was the moment I set eyes on him. This Alush of yours has a lizard-shaped scar above his left eye. That's what gave him away."

With trembling legs, we left the courtyard and made our way to the train station in silence, the same thought pounding in all our heads: How could we have been so wrong about Alush?

Journey's End

When we got to the train station, we found it crowded with refugees, the platform thronged with people talking and shouting in a welter of languages—Polish, Russian, Czech, Dutch, German. Some woman wearing white aprons and Red Cross bands on their sleeves stood behind long tables, distributing soup and bread to everyone. Looking at the women's polite, smiling faces, I began to feel less disturbed about our experience with Alush. I told myself that the world was changing, after all. Food was in plentiful supply, no one was going hungry, and the trains were transporting everyone free of charge.

The first train that arrived at the station was so crowded that we were unable to get on, so we were forced to spend the night on the station platform. Once during the long hours of waiting, Bronka saw a man passing near us and let out a shriek. "Daddy! Daddy!" The man stopped, turned a blank look on her, and then went on. It wasn't her father. Shaken, Bronka clung to me, sobbing bitterly.

The next morning, we managed to squeeze on a train heading east and found places to stand in the corridor next to the windows. We had to change three times in order to get to Lodz, and each train was more crowded than the last. On one leg of our journey, we were forced to ride on the train's roof. We lay flat on our stomachs and held on tightly to each other, not daring even to look up.

Finally, the terrible journey was over, and the six of us stood on the platform of Lodz's central train station. I tried to recall when I had last been there. Of course. It had been just before the "great flood" had washed over all of us. I was going with Uncle Abraham to his home in Kalisz, and Mother and Aunt Hanushka had accompanied us to the station. My uncle and I stood at the train window waving to them—Mother was dabbing her eyes. As the train gathered speed, Mother and Aunt Hanushka grew smaller and smaller until they disappeared from my view. And then I had passed through the station one more time during my hasty return from Kalisz, my vacation ended abruptly because of rumors of an imminent war with Germany . . .

And now, after all those years, I was back in Lodz, frightened and forlorn, not knowing where to turn or what to expect. As my friends and I stood in the midst of the crowd on the platform, we heard a voice saying, "A hearty welcome to all of you!" and turned to see two strangers, a man and a woman, approaching us. They introduced themselves as representatives of the Jewish Committee for the Relief of Jews Returning to Lodz. This committee, they told us, consisted of ghetto inhabitants who had somehow managed to escape the final deportation.

"Then some people did stay behind in the ghetto!" I exclaimed.

"Just a handful," they replied.

Only 900 Jews had eluded the last transport. They had hidden for many days among the graves in Marisin, but the Germans finally caught up with them. Since it wasn't worth their while to transport a mere 900, the soldiers decided to finish them off on the spot. The captives were ordered to dig nine graves in the cemetery, each grave big enough to hold 100 bodies. But the Red Army tanks arrived before the digging was completed. All the Germans fled or were captured, and the 900 Jews were saved.

"If you go to the Marisin cemetery," the woman told us, "you can still see the nine pits."

The representatives of the Relief Committee gave us a slip of paper with the address of their office on it and some money for our streetcar fare there. Encouraged by this warm welcome and the chance of meeting other survivors of the ghetto, we set off. Lodz had changed very little; I felt as if I had been gone for only a few days. The shop windows sparkled, and the streets were full of activity: a chimney sweep carrying his small black ladder, children with satchels hurrying to school, women pushing baby buggies or doing their shopping. Only one thing was different—there was no trace of the quarter-million Jews who had lived in the city before the war.

When we reached the Relief Committee office, we were welcomed joyfully and shown a typed sheet listing the names of all those who had survived in the ghetto itself. My heart would not stop thumping as I scanned the list, but there was no mention of Genia or Rishia. Then I looked at the list of returnees. None of the names on it was familiar to me or to any of my friends. The members of the committee told us not to give up hope: the war had only just ended, and very few survivors had managed to return so far. Many thousands must still be on the roads trying to get back. We must have patience—someone was sure to turn up eventually.

Our names were added to the list of returnees, and we were given the keys to an empty apartment where we could stay for a while. We were also given money for our daily expenses. On our way out of the office building, we noticed all the names scratched on the walls of the hallway; they were the names of survivors and people who had returned to Lodz. I picked up a nail from the floor and scratched my name in large block letters on the wall near the staircase. When my relatives came back, they would see my name—a sign of life—even before they looked at the list of survivors.

Survivors

Early on the morning after our arrival in Lodz, my friends and I were waiting in the courtyard of the Relief Committee office. When a new group of returnees arrived from the train station, we rushed forward to scan their faces, but no one we knew was among them. In dejection we dragged ourselves back to the apartment, only to return several hours later in the vain hope that another train had come in and our relatives had been on it. This became our daily routine, changed only when each of us began to go to the office alone, as if we wished to hide from one another our impatience and our despondency when each day brought another thwarted hope.

As I kept my vigil at the committee office, I saw returnees arriving daily, most of them young people between the ages of twenty and thirty. I occasionally witnessed moving scenes of reunion: a sudden outcry, and two people would fall into each other's arms, weeping without restraint. Those of us who were looking on wept with them.

Each returnee brought new revelations of hair-raising horror. We now learned that none of the people deported from the ghetto in 1941 had survived. They were the first victims of a German experiment in methods of mass extermination by poisoning. The trucks they had been packed into were hermetically sealed and filled with poison gas while rolling toward their destination. On arrival the corpses were unloaded and immediately burned in the crematoria. When I heard this dreadful story, my heart ached for Aunt Tsesia and Uncle Shimshon, who had adopted me as one of their own after Mother's death; for my five cousins, with whom I had grown up.

More harrowing details came to light with the arrival of other returnees. We found out that the stories about gas chambers and crematoria at Auschwitz, which we had heard for the first time on our return journey, were the unadulterated truth. A grisly detail about life in the ghetto was revealed as well. The green soap that had been so plentiful and had smelled so unpleasantly—the soap imprinted with the initials R.J.F.—had been processed from the bodies of cremated Jews! The initials stood for *Reines Juden Fett* (pure Jew fat). Our stomachs turned at this incredible piece of information.

The days of futile anticipation that my friends and I spent at the committee office were painful, but the nights at our apartment were no less hard on us. I often lay awake for hours listening to Bronka weeping or to Surtcha, Faiga, and Blumka groaning and sighing in their sleep. Not a single survivor of their families had turned up so far. Luba, the woman who had come back to Poland with us, had found a cousin and was now living with her. The number of relatives I was waiting for shrank with every day that passed. Now I hung my hopes on the return of Uncle Abraham, Aunt Faiga, and Salek. I lulled my apprehensions by withdrawing inside a web of fantasies in which I imagined that at least Salek had survived and was on his way back.

When I couldn't sleep, I would fasten my thought on Salek's return. I'd imagine our reunion, our joy at seeing each other again, and would make plans for our future together. Then my mind would leap back into our childhood, and I would see myself and some other girls chasing Salek. On catching up with him, I would cover his eyes with my hands, but he'd always guess that it was me by the ring on my finger. Only now my ring was gone . . . Hovering between dream and reality, I often caught myself talking and even squabbling with Salek, accusing him of having abandoned me for such a long time. As soon as the new day dawned, I could barely wait to return to the committee office, telling myself that today Salek was sure to come. But the day passed and many others after that.

There were fewer and fewer returnees, and there was no sign of Salek.

Then one day I was standing in the courtyard of the office when a small group of newcomers arrived. Although I didn't know any of them, I followed them into the reception hall and leaned against the wall, watching the process of their registration. A young man entering the hall recognized one of the group and rushed into his arms. There was great excitement as they launched into a crossfire of the invariable questions: "Have you found a relative?" "Whom have you seen?" "Who was with you in the camp?" I was on the point of leaving when the name of Surtcha's brother caught my ear.

"There were five of us together at Auschwitz," the newcomer was saying. "Fulek Zelver, two of his brothers, and Salek Biderman."

I caught my breath.

"You know the one I mean. That activist from the ghetto with the iron will. Even in Auschwitz, he didn't give up. He was flogged murderously after trying to tell a *Kapo* why he shouldn't beat up his fellow Jews."

The rest of the story reached me as if filtered through a thick mist.

"There was a selection lineup," the young man went on. "We filed naked past Dr. Mengele, who stood there with that monocle in his eye. One of Fulek's brothers and Salek Biderman were sent to the left, the side of the gas chamber . . ."

I didn't hear anything more. Darkness enveloped me, and I felt the ground giving way. Then a splash of cold water on my face brought me back to my senses. On opening my eyes, I found myself sitting on a chair supported by two men. One of the committee women stood beside me.

"What's the matter, girl?" she asked solicitously. "You probably haven't eaten all day and passed out from sheer weakness."

"No, I'm not hungry at all," I heard myself say mechanically as I rose to go.

I stumbled out of the room, and on my way down the stairs, I had to hold on firmly to the bannister. I felt like a torn sack losing its contents bit by bit. At the bottom of the stairs, I caught sight of my name scratched on the

wall. Now it was of no use to anybody. No one would be
coming back to look for me. They had all perished; not
one had survived.

After leaving the committee offices, I roamed the streets
for a long time and eventually found myself walking about
inside the ghetto. Less than nine months ago, the area had
been swarming with people, but now it was completely
deserted, a haunted ghost town. All the buildings had broken doors and windows, and the ground was littered with
scraps of the holy scriptures and torn photographs that
fluttered with every puff of the wind. I climbed the stairs
to Uncle Abraham's apartment, my last home in the ghetto.
The door that he had locked behind him when we left was
gone; the place had been ransacked and stripped bare. All
that was left were the jackets of two of Salek's books lying
on the floor and a snapshot in a corner of the room. It
was a picture of Aunt Tsesia and Uncle Shimshon taken
before they had gone to Palestine. I picked it up and left
the apartment.

As I wandered through the ghetto that day, I saw many
of the places that had been part of my life there. I passed
Genia's house but I didn't go in. Rishia's face flashed into
my mind, and I broke into a run, coming to a halt in front
of the building that had been the ghetto hospital. The
gaping holes where its windows once were looked like the
empty eye sockets in a skull. From the hospital, I made
my way to the field of Marisin, past the ramshackled
house where my father and I had hidden during the
Shpera. I stopped to stare at the spot on the edge of the
ghetto where I had courted the bullets of the German sentries after hearing of my father's death. If I had died then,
how much I would have been spared!

In the cemetery, I stopped at Moniek's grave, with its
monument of a tree with the branches cut off. Then I
went to my mother's grave and stood for a long time engaged in a silent dialogue with her. I told her about her
sisters and her beloved brother, all of whose lives had
ended in the gas chamber and the crematorium. The
nameplate that I had placed on my father's grave so many
years ago was rusty, but the inscription—Anschel Kalman
Plager—was still legible. As I stared down at it, I recalled
his last days at home and the terrible hunger pains he had
suffered. I knew now that there were ordeals worse than

death from hunger. I was happy for my father's sake that
he had been spared them.

In the days that followed, I spent my time wandering
restlessly through the streets of Lodz. I didn't go near the
house on Glovna Street where I had been born. The Polish
neighbors there knew my whole family, and I was
ashamed to tell them what had happened. I couldn't bear
to repeat over and over, "Yes, all of them, everyone is
dead. I'm the only survivor." But I decided to go back to
the house on Novomiska Street where I had spent my
childhood and had lived until the outbreak of the war. I
took the route along sunny Piotrkovska Street and across
Liberty Square, still bare without the Kosciusko monument, but crowded and humming with activity. Peasant
women were squatting beside their buckets of flowers exactly as they had on the day that I had bought lilacs for
my mother. When I crossed the square, no one bothered to
look twice at me now that I no longer wore the yellow
patch.

On Novomiska Street, I slipped quickly into the courtyard of the building and looked up at the windows of our
former apartment. I caught my breath. Yellow curtains—
our yellow curtains—were drawn across them! As I slowly
mounted the familiar stairs, I found myself imagining once
again that all my awful experiences had happened only in
a long nightmare. If I rang the bell of our apartment, it
would be answered by Daddy, who would welcome me
with his usual refrain, "Look who's here! What a visitor!"
And Mother would hurry into the hall to ask in unfeigned
surprise, "Anschel, who is it?"

The door to the apartment was fastened with a large
lock, and the nameplate bore a typically Polish name. I
peeped through the keyhole. The door into the kitchen at
the far end of the corridor was open, and the sun coming
in the large window lit up an orange kitchen dresser. Our
dresser!

When I heard the steps of someone slowly climbing the
staircase, I moved away from the door. A dumpy woman
carrying a basket full of goods lumbered up toward me.
She gazed at me with suspicion and hostility and asked in
a gruff voice, "Who are you looking for?" I almost cried
out that I wasn't looking for anyone, that everything here
belonged to me and to my parents. But instead I heard

myself mumble in a voice that scarcely seemed like mine, "Sorry, I must have gotten the wrong building."

I bolted down the stairs, and at the bottom landing, I ran into a girl. She was about twelve years old and had thick blond braids. On her head was a beret with a school insignia on it, and under her arm she carried a schoolbag. For an instant I stood rooted to the spot. This was what I was like before the war! This could be me coming home from school! The startled girl gave me an inquisitive but not unfriendly look. I pulled myself together and darted out of the building, with only one thought in my mind—to get away from this place where my past was buried.

A Song for the Future

In the ghetto, in the labor camp, on my way back to Poland, I had harbored the illusion that after the war was over, the world would take revenge on our behalf and would put all the German war criminals into prison camps. I longed sorely for revenge and was even ready to serve as a *Kapo* in such a camp. What, after all, was left for me but to exact terrible retribution for what had been done to me and mine. But it didn't take long for me to realize that I would never have my retribution. Most of my enemies would go unpunished—the world would let them get away with their crimes.

During my wandering through the streets of Lodz after news of Salek's death, I often thought of the two *Kommandoführerins* of my camp and all the *Aufseherins* who had persecuted us. I hadn't seen a single photograph of any of them in the album of wanted war criminals. I was sure that they had disguised their real identities, had transformed themselves into respectable members of society. All these monsters in human form would go on living, get married, have children, perhaps become good mothers. That *Kommandoführerin* will never breathe a word about having flogged starving Jewish girls to death. If a child of hers happened to bring home stories about the extermination of Jews, about the concentration camps, the gas chambers, and the crematoria, she would shrug them off as horror tales concocted by Germany's foes.

It's not those people who will be punished for their horrible crimes, but we Jews—we who were the victims! We are being punished daily by the Poles around us who don't even bother to conceal their hatred and resentment. My friends and I had experienced this hatred at first hand when we went into a shop soon after our arrival in Lodz. A Polish woman saw us and said to her companion, "Imagine! There are still some dirty Jews left alive here! And they told us that Hitler had finished them all off!" Those of us left alive were the walking tombstones of the six million who had perished. Bronka, Blumka, Faiga, Surtcha, and I were living reminders to a world that wanted to ignore the outrageous crimes committed against our people.

My four friends and I no longer made the daily trip to the Relief Committee offices, for we had all given up hope of seeing any of our relatives again. We lived aimlessly from day to day, each absorbed by her own concerns and sorrows. Then one day something happened. I was returning to our apartment after one of my spells of wandering when I noticed a young woman following close behind me. She inquired if I knew someone living here named Zelver. I took her into the apartment, and she introduced herself to Surtcha as Sara Stern. The name meant nothing to me.

Leaving Surtcha with her visitor, I went into the next room and sat down on my bed. Bronka was lying on her own bed with eyes red and swollen from recent weeping. I now recalled that she had gone that day to visit the place where she and her family had lived before the war. Blumka and Faiga were also at home. Despite all of us being together, it was very quiet in the apartment. We exchanged few words, for there was nothing we had to say to each other. In the stillness, the voice of the woman talking to Surtcha could be heard distinctly.

"You're wrong," Sara Stern said loudly. "Each one of you is wrong. There's nothing worse than giving in to your despondency. Can't you see that you are just finishing the job for Hitler? You've got to go on living, to reconstruct your lives."

"What's there left for us to do in this world?" I heard Surtcha ask.

"Left for you to do!" exclaimed the woman in a high-pitched voice. "What you have to do is draw the line under your past. It will never return. You have no choice but to stop this wallowing in your sorrow. The dead can never be revived. We can only perpetuate their memory by carrying on with our own lives and by looking into the future. We've got to get out of here, to leave this place where we are unwanted, and begin a new life somewhere else."

"Leave Poland? And go where? No one wants us anywhere else!" I heard Surtcha protest.

"To our own country, to *Eretz Israel*," Sara Stern replied in a confident tone.

"There's no place for us there either," Surtcha argued. "The English are keeping everyone out. No Jews are allowed to enter."

"You're mistaken!" The woman was virtually shouting at Surtcha. "The Land of Israel is the only place where people are crying out for us. They need us desperately. Over there someone's fighting for your sakes. Every night, boat loads of refugees reach secret landings on the shores of *Eretz Israel*. True, many have been intercepted and some refugees have been killed in the process. But there are always others who will carry on the struggle to bring us all to the safest place in the world for us. The time has come for us Jews to have a country of our own. Even if the world thinks otherwise, we have no choice but to fight for what we believe to be our right."

Sara Stern's impassioned speech had attracted the attention of the four of us in the next room. We were all listening when she went on to say that although the Land of Israel was small, it was large enough to absorb all the Jews who wanted to live there. She didn't deny that the Arabs violently opposed our return to the tiny area they called Palestine, in spite of the fact that they themselves inhabited enormous stretches of land in the Middle East and in Africa. But this time we would not give up the fight for our homeland, no matter what the cost. That's why, she concluded, it was our duty to help those who were sacrificing their own lives so that we refugees could find a new home in the land of our forefathers.

"I have already recruited hundreds of refugees," she said. "We've set up a kind of kibbutz here in Lodz where we are waiting for the signal from our brothers and sisters in Israel. When it comes, we will be ready to join them. Here's the address of the kibbutz. Think about what I've told you."

After Sara Stern left the apartment, I sat in silence for a long time, listening to the pounding of my heart. Had I heard rightly? Was there, after all, a land that belonged to us? Were there people crying out for our help, fighting and sacrificing their lives on our behalf? Salek, why couldn't you have heard all this with your own ears?

It was getting dark outside, but the street lamps had not been lighted yet. In the deepening dusk, five figures could be seen walking slowly along the street. My four friends and I were going to the address that Sara Stern had given us, each carrying her black blankets from the Mittelstein labor camp under her arm. As we approached the house where the kibbutz was located, the sound of singing voices reached our ears. The melody struck a deep note within me. I had heard it somewhere else a long time ago. I strained hard to recall where and when it had been, and then I remembered.

Many years before the war, Mother and I had spent part of a summer vacation on Uncle Abraham's country estate. One day, Daddy joined us there, together with Aunt Tsesia, Uncle Shimshon, and their children. At sunset, we were all gathered together at the edge of the forest. I was sitting on the ground along with Moniek, Salek, and Aunt Tsesia's children. Everyone was singing or humming the song I was hearing now, and above their voices rose Daddy's tenor, clear and beautiful: *"Od lo avedah tikvatenu . . ."*

Surtcha called us all to a halt. "Let's stand at attention," she said. "It's our national anthem. The anthem of the People of Israel."

> *Od lo avedah tikvatenu*
> *Ha-tikvah bat shenot alpayim*
> *Lihyot am hofshi be-arzenu*
> *Erez Ziyyon vi-Yrushalayim.*

Our hope is not yet lost,
The hope of two thousand years,
To be a free people in our land,
The land of Zion and Jerusalem.

With tears streaming down my face, I listened to the familiar words and knew that some day soon I would understand their true meaning.

Epilogue

The Final Journey

Sara Plager eventually reached *Eretz Israel*, but her journey was a long and arduous one. During the months following the war, the borders of many European countries were closed against the large numbers of refugees who were seeking new homes. Aided by a Jewish relief group called Escape, Sara and other members of the Lodz kibbutz got out of Poland by using forged identity papers. After their escape, they wandered through Europe for two years, sneaking across national borders under cover of darkness. Finally Sara and her friends reached Palestine on May 15, 1947. Because of British restrictions on Jewish emigration, they were forced to enter the country illegally.

Sara's dream of reaching *Eretz Israel* had been realized, and soon she was able to fulfill another dream when she was sent to a kibbutz to continue her education. But her studies were interrupted in May 1948 when Israel, after declaring its independence, was attacked by neighboring Arab states. Along with thousands of other young people, twenty-year-old Sara joined the Israeli Army of Defense. By the end of the year, the Arab forces had been defeated, but the underlying causes of the bitter conflict remained unresolved.

In December 1948, during the last month of the war, Sara Plager married Eliezer Zyskind, a fellow soldier and old friend from Poland. Sara had met Eliezer in the Lodz kibbutz, but she had first heard his story at the Mittelstein labor camp when Surtcha told her about the young man's courageous efforts to save his family. Eliezer's family, like Sara's, did not survive the war, and the two young people had been drawn together by their mutual tragedy. Sara and Eliezer had made the hazardous journey to Israel together, and now they were beginning a new life pledged to each other and to their new land.

Today Sara and Eliezer Zyskind make their home in Tel Aviv. Two of their children—Miriam and Yossi—are grown and have children of their own; their daughter Shlomith is a student. Sara has maintained her ties with her four sisters from Auschwitz: Bronka, who lives in the United States, and Faiga, Surtcha, and Blumka, who, like Sara, traveled the long road that led from Poland to the Land of Israel.

ABOUT THE AUTHOR

Sara Plager Zyskind's life has taken many turns since the end of the Second World War, when she was finally free once again. Today Mrs. Zyskind lives and works in Tel Aviv with her husband, Eliezer, who is also a Holocaust survivor. They have three children.